Killing Enmity

Killing Enmity

VIOLENCE AND THE NEW TESTAMENT

THOMAS R. YODER NEUFELD

Baker Academic
a division of Baker Publishing Group
Grand Rapids, Michigan

Published in 2011 by Baker Academic
a division of Baker Publishing Group
P.O. Box 6287, Grand Rapids, MI 49516-6287
www.bakeracademic.com

Originally published in the United Kingdom in 2011 by Society for Promoting Christian Knowledge as *Jesus and the Subversion of Violence: Wrestling with the New Testament Evidence*

Printed in the United States of America

Library of Congress Cataloging-in-Publication Data
Neufeld, Thomas R.
    Killing enmity : violence and the New Testament / Thomas R. Yoder
Neufeld.
        p.   cm.
    Includes bibliographical references (p.   ) and indexes.
    ISBN 978-0-8010-3901-0 (pbk.)
    1. Violence—Biblical teaching. 2. Bible. N.T.—Criticism, interpretation,
etc. I. Title.
BS2545.V55N48 2011
225.8′3036—dc23   2011029435

Scripture quotations are either the author's own translation or are taken from the New Revised Standard Version of the Bible, Anglicized Edition, copyright © 1989, 1995 by the Division of Christian Education of the National Council of the Churches of Christ in the USA. Used by permission. All rights reserved.

Cover image: *Metamorphosis* (2004), by Paraguayan sculptor Hermann Guggiari, b. 1925, who fashioned it out of *shiv* (improvised weapons), given to Pastor Jonathan Beachy by prisoners of Tacumbú Prison in Asunción as a sign of 'being conquered by divine love'. Property of Prof. Alfred Neufeld, Evangelical University of Paraguay.

For Hedy, Esther, Mary and Peter
Faithful and courageous followers of the Lamb

₁₁ Remember, then, that at one time you Gentiles in flesh, called 'the uncircumcision' by 'the circumcision' made in the flesh by human hands, ₁₂ were at that time without Christ, alienated from the commonwealth of Israel and strangers to the covenants of promise, having no hope and without God in the world.

₁₃ But now in Christ Jesus you who once were far off have been brought near through the blood of Christ.

> ₁₄ For he is our peace,
> who made both into one
> and has broken down the dividing
> wall – the enmity – in his flesh.
> ₁₅ He has abolished the law in its
> rules and regulations,
> so that he might create the two into
> one new human in himself, thereby
> making peace,
> ₁₆ and might reconcile both to God in
> one body through the cross, thereby
> killing the enmity.

₁₇ And he came proclaiming the good news of peace to you who were far off and peace to those who were near; ₁₈ for through him we both have access in one Spirit to the Father.

₁₉ So then you are no longer strangers and outsiders, but you are citizens together with the saints and members of God's household, ₂₀ built on the foundation of the apostles and prophets, with Christ Jesus himself the cornerstone. ₂₁ In him the whole structure is joined together and grows into a holy temple in the Lord; ₂₂ in whom you also are together built into a dwelling for God in Spirit.

Translation by Thomas R. Yoder Neufeld

Contents

Preface

At the very centre of the first half of the letter to the Ephesians is arguably the greatest peace text in the Bible.[1] In chiastic fashion Ephesians 2.11–22 celebrates the mending of the human family – enemies, strangers, Jews and non-Jews – as the most immediately experienced dimension of God's grand healing of all rifts, partings and partitions in a cosmic 'gathering up' of all things in and through the Messiah (Eph. 1.10). The core of this text, verses 14–16, constitutes an act of worship, a hymn celebrating Jesus as 'our peace'.

We should not be surprised to find in such peaceable poetry the image of the birth of a 'new human' made up of erstwhile enemies (v. 15). But we might be surprised to encounter violence at the very centre of the creation of peace. There is the shattering of walls that define and protect identities, but that also reinforce enmities between people and between them and God (v. 14). There is blood (v. 13), terse shorthand for Jesus' own death on the cross (v. 16). We should remember that there was not yet a shred of romance around that instrument of lethal torture and imperial state terrorism. Perhaps most surprising is that Jesus' violent death is the instrument by which he himself committed murder. In and through his own death Jesus 'killed enmity', he 'murdered hostility'.

We are put before a question we will face again and again throughout this investigation: do we see in this remarkable poetry a way in which the vocabulary, images and metaphors of violence create a space for violence, validating, even enshrining, violence at the core of the message? Or does the presence of such language intend to subvert and finally 'murder' violence? This is the challenge we take up in this book.

It is not a straightforward matter to meet such a challenge. Where some see courageous suffering of violence, others see passivity and

---

[1] See epigraph. For a full discussion of Eph. 2.11–22, see Thomas R. Yoder Neufeld, *Ephesians* (BCBC; Scottdale, PA/Waterloo, ON: Herald, 2002), 106–37; Yoder Neufeld, '"For he is our peace": Ephesians 2:11–22', in *Beautiful upon the Mountains: Biblical Essays on Mission, Peace, and the Reign of God* (ed. Mary H. Schertz and Ivan Friesen; Elkhart, IN: Institute of Mennonite Studies/Scottdale, PA/Waterloo, ON: Herald Press, 2003), 215–33.

the willing acceptance of victimization; where some see the urgent rhetoric of a prophet, others see violent threats and ultimate sanctions; where some see a bracing call to resolute discipleship in a violent world, others see an exclusionary and for that very reason violent religious imagination; where some see a loving saviour, others see an abject victim of divine parental abuse. Some might thus be tempted to dismiss the stories and teachings in the New Testament precisely because they deem them violent. Others might be tempted to quarantine troublesome texts rather than wrestle with their implications, or simply to explain the violence away, trivialize its offence and silence those who object to its presence.

This book was from its inception to be an exploration of how the New Testament relates to the issue of violence, with attention to the variety of approaches interpreters bring to the subject. I have thus attempted to resist each of these temptations. I have undertaken, nevertheless, to wrestle with how such 'texts of trouble' might, ironically, have the potential to subvert the very violence that troubles us in them. I invite readers attuned to the urgent issue of violence to engage the New Testament with an ear to hear – afresh.

Acknowledgements

I wish first of all to thank Philip Law of SPCK and James Ernest of Baker Academic and their respective staff for their remarkable patience and encouragement in the writing of this book, as well as Bruce Longenecker and Rebecca Mulhearn, who first invited me to undertake the task. I was able to begin the work on this book during a brief sabbatical leave, enjoying the kind hospitality of Fuller Seminary in Pasadena, in particular, old friends in administration and faculty, Howard Loewen, Alvin Dueck, Glen Stassen and the now sadly departed David Scholer. I also wish to thank Conrad Grebel University College at the University of Waterloo, my academic home, for the encouragement and generous assistance in making it possible for me to complete the book. Words fail to convey my gratitude for the many expressions of encouragement from friends and family alike, most especially my wife, Rebecca, and our children, Miriam, David and Gina.

Abbreviations

ABD	*Anchor Bible Dictionary*
BCBC	Believers Church Bible Commentary
BECNT	Baker Exegetical Commentary on the New Testament
BTB	*Biblical Theology Bulletin*
CBQ	*Catholic Biblical Quarterly*
ESCJ	Electronic Sixteenth Century Journal
ICC	International Critical Commentary
IDBSup	*Interpreter's Dictionary of the Bible: Supplementary Volume*
JAAR	*Journal of the American Academy of Religion*
JBL	*Journal of Biblical Literature*
JR	*Journal of Religion*
JSNT	*Journal for the Study of the New Testament*
JSOTSup	Journal for the Study of the New Testament: Supplement Series
MQR	*Mennonite Quarterly Review*
NTS	*New Testament Studies*
SNTSMS	Society for New Testament Studies Monograph Series
TDNT	*Theological Dictionary of the New Testament*
TLZ	*Theologische Literaturzeitung*
WBC	Word Biblical Commentary
WUNT	Wissenschaftliche Untersuchungen zum Neuen Testament
ZECNT	Zondervan Exegetical Commentary on the New Testament

1

'Violence' and 'New Testament'

We begin our investigation with an exploration of what we mean with 'violence' and 'New Testament'. It may seem obvious what these terms mean, but in actual fact there is a wide range of meanings persons give to these two concepts, and to the approaches taken to them. Given the brevity of this study, the limited number of texts and the limited attention we will be able to give them, this chapter will serve not only as an introduction to the theme but point the way to resources that can help further investigation.

'Violence'

Reflecting dictionaries generally, the first meaning of 'violence' in the *Oxford English Dictionary* is as follows:

> The exercise of physical force so as to inflict injury on, or cause damage to, persons or property; action or conduct characterized by this; treatment or usage tending to cause bodily injury or forcibly interfering with personal freedom.

Violence is intentional physical harm and injury. We think of crimes of violence such as battery or murder, or of war, in which massive harm is done to others, whether by soldiers or civilians. To state the obvious, 'violence', 'violent' and 'to violate' have unambiguously negative implications. Even when such violence is deemed necessary in certain circumstances, it is viewed as highly regrettable. Synonyms of violence are force, coercion, abuse, aggression, fighting, hostility, brutality, cruelty, carnage, ferocity, vehemence and many more. The dictionaries point out that sometimes 'violence' can denote vehemence of feelings that come to expression in gestures or words, even if they are not accompanied by physical harm, and that 'violence' can be used to designate someone's use of language in improper ways, or even wilful distortion of the words of others, including texts. But intended physical harm is the primary lexical meaning.

Were violence as 'intent to injure' the sole way it is understood in our culture, this book would probably not have been written. More than once I have had to respond to the question, 'You mean "Old Testament", right?' The common assumption is that the New Testament is generally against violence. Jesus' teaching on non-retaliation in the Sermon on the Mount comes most quickly to mind. However, what counts as 'violence' has widened dramatically, with significant implications for how the New Testament relates to violence.

To illustrate, Johan Galtung coined the by now deeply entrenched terms 'structural' and 'cultural violence', showing that there is violence other than 'direct' violence engaged in and suffered by individuals.[1] Political and economic ways in which society is 'ordered' can violate whole peoples and classes. Robert McAfee Brown likewise expands the notion of violence:

> Whatever 'violates' another, in the sense of infringing upon or disregard-ing or abusing or denying that other, whether physical harm is involved or not, can be understood as an act of violence. The basic overall definition of violence would then become violation of personhood.[2]

Such 'an act that depersonalizes would be an act of violence' and might not be obvious 'except to the victim'.[3] Importantly, in such a case the determination of what constitutes violence has shifted from the intent of the perpetrator to the one who experiences it. Brown cites Brazil's Dom Helder Camara's notion of a 'spiral of violence', where 'direct' violence is often already a response to 'structural' (economic, racial, class) violence, a notion Richard Horsley has taken up on his *Jesus and the Spiral of Violence*.[4] Similarly, the late

---

[1] Johan Galtung, 'Violence, Peace and Peace Research', *Journal of Peace Research* 6/3 (1969), 167–91; Galtung, 'Cultural Violence', *Journal of Peace Research* 27/3 (1990), 291–305. Philip L. Tite would like to add 'sociological violence' to this insight, which he sees as less static, in *Conceiving Peace and Violence: A New Testament Legacy* (Dallas, TX/New York/Oxford: University Press of America, 2004), 37; see also Warren Carter, 'Constructions of Violence and Identities in Matthew's Gospel', in *Violence in the New Testament* (ed. Shelley Matthews and E. Leigh Gibson; New York/London: T&T Clark, 2005), 81–108 (90–2).

[2] Robert MacAfee Brown, *Religion and Violence* (2nd edn; Philadelphia, PA: Westminster, [1973] 1987), 7.

[3] Brown, *Religion and Violence*, 7.

[4] Richard A. Horsley, *Jesus and the Spiral of Violence: Popular Jewish Resistance in Roman Palestine* (San Francisco, CA: Harper & Row, 1987), 22–6.

French sociologist and theologian Jacques Ellul identifies the conflict between economic classes as 'violent competition'.

> The violence done by the superior may be physical (the most common kind, and it provokes hostile moral reaction), or it may be psychological or spiritual, as when the superior makes use of morality and even of Christianity to inculcate submission and a servile attitude; and this is the most heinous of all forms of violence.[5]

These perspectives reflect the issues surrounding violence particularly during the 60s and 70s of the last century, when the threat of nuclear annihilation, revolution and the war in Vietnam established the context for a consideration of the relationship of violence and the New Testament. Was the 'historical' Jesus a 'Zealot'? Did he harbour sympathies for resistance and revolutionary movements? Or was he resolutely anti-violent in his teachings on non-retaliation and love of enemies?[6] Do Paul's famous words in Romans 13.1–7 regarding being subordinate to the authorities imply he was anti-revolutionary, thus supportive of state violence ('sword')? Or does 'Romans 13' furnish the grounds for resistance to an unjust and thus ultimately illegitimate regime? Is John's Apocalypse a blistering prophetic critique against a violent Roman Empire? Or is it a fevered apocalyptic vision of divinely initiated end-time violence, providing theological cover for those dreaming of nuclear Armageddon?

The Vietnam War ended; the Cold War came to an end of sorts; revolutionary rhetoric disappeared from common discourse in the global North. The focus of 'violence' has since shifted to terrorism, especially when religiously motivated. More, 'violence' has come to be identified not only as deliberate physical harm or injury but also harm done to the environment, through economic inequalities, persistent gender inequalities, racial, sexual and class discrimination, and marginalization and intolerance in general, whether buttressed by state power, culture or religion and, more specifically, sacred texts. Not just 'fundamentalism', but religion more generally, has come

---

[5] Jacques Ellul, *Violence: Reflections from a Christian Perspective* (trans. Cecelia Gaul Kings; New York: Seabury, 1969), 87.

[6] E.g. S. G. F. Brandon, *Jesus and the Zealots: A Study of the Political Factor in Primitive Christianity* (New York: Charles Scribner's Sons; Manchester: Manchester University Press, 1967). In opposition, see George R. Edwards, *Jesus and the Politics of Violence* (New York and London: Harper & Row, 1972).

under intense scrutiny on whether it is a resource against violence or whether it might not be an incubator for it. There is heightened sensitivity to the potential of religion not only to countenance violence but also to nurture and to incite it. Needless to say, this has brought also the New Testament to the attention of critics.

To complicate matters yet more, there is growing awareness of the role of power, social location and vested interests at work in human discourse. This has undermined confidence in interpreting texts as having a particular meaning and, at the same time, increased alertness to the way texts are themselves involved in the exercise and maintenance of power, often masking the violence at work in them. In a postmodern context, the very notion of authority, of revelation and the claim to universal validity fall under the suspicion of purveying violence, broadly conceived.

If the meaning of texts does not reside simply in the author's intentions, which may or may not be accessible to the reader or interpreter in any case, but rather in the interaction between readers and the text, then a text becomes violent if the interpreter or the reader experiences or employs it as such. This is one aspect of the way in which the shift in determining whether some action or word is violent moves from actor to victim. Clearly texts can themselves fall victim to the use interpreters put them to. We speak frequently of 'doing violence to a text.' We might then also ask whether a text ceases to be 'violent' if readers do not 'take it' that way, or use it that way. For example, scholars might determine a text to be violent in its implications, but not taken that way by a believing community. Should one blame the community for not being faithful to the text's violence?

Not surprisingly, this way of construing violence as very broad has had a significant impact on the question of the relationship between violence and the New Testament. It has widened the texts that 'count' in such an investigation, but it has also opened the door to much greater and more radical critique. As Jonathan Klawans points out, 'the broader the definition [of violence], the easier it is to indict biblical texts and those who, guilty by association, deem them to be sacred.'[7] In *Violence in the New Testament*, for example, various authors

---

[7] Jonathan Klawans, 'Introduction: Religion, Violence, and the Bible', in *Religion and Violence: The Biblical Heritage* (ed. David A. Bernat and Jonathan Klawans; Sheffield: Sheffield Phoenix, 2007), 1–15 (7).

explore ways in which the documents of the New Testament are implicated in the violence of 'empire', even as these writings attempt to varying degrees to escape or critique it.[8] The massive four-volume *The Destructive Power of Religion*,[9] which contains many articles focused on the New Testament, adds psychology to the mix of criticism, exploring, among other things, the personality (disorders) of Jesus and Paul, the destructive effects of the intolerance in pronouncements of judgement and the violence deemed to be inherent in claims of revelatory truth.

Feminists have drawn attention not only to what they see as the implicit violence in the suppression of memory of the role women played in the early decades of the Church[10] but also to what they consider to be dimensions of the religion reflected in the New Testament as 'dangerous to [women's] health'.[11] In particular they have focused on texts requiring subordination of women to men, on what is deemed to be the valorization of suffering and, closely related, on the role of the death of Jesus in atonement and salvation. Some see it as a kind of 'divine child abuse',[12] viewing the violence of the cross as anything but 'redemptive'.

This is by no means a concern only of feminists. Walter Wink has made the critique of 'redemptive violence' central to his work on the New Testament,[13] as has the French anthropologist and literary

---

[8] Matthews and Gibson, *Violence in the New Testament*; see also, e.g., the collection of articles in Ra'anan S. Boustan, Alex Jassen and Calvin J. Roetzel, eds, *Violence, Scripture, and Textual Practices in Early Judaism and Christianity*, *Biblical Interpretation* XVII/1–2 (2009).

[9] J. Harold Ellens, ed., *The Destructive Power of Religion: Violence in Judaism, Christianity, and Islam* (Westport, CT/London: Praeger, 2004): *Vol. 1, Sacred Scriptures, Ideology, and Violence*; *Vol. 2, Religion, Psychology, and Violence*; *Vol. 3, Models and Cases of Violence in Religion*; *Vol. 4, Contemporary Views on Spirituality and Violence*.

[10] E.g. most famously Elisabeth Schüssler Fiorenza, *In Memory of Her: A Feminist Theological Reconstruction of Christian Origins* (New York: Crossroad, 1983), and the many studies that followed it.

[11] Letty M. Russell, 'Authority and the Challenge of Feminist Interpretation', in *Feminist Interpretation of the Bible* (ed. Letty M. Russell; Philadelphia, PA: Westminster, 1985), 137–46 (141).

[12] E.g. Joanne Carlson Brown and Rebecca Parker, 'For God so Loved the World?', in *Christianity, Patriarchy, and Abuse: A Feminist Critique* (ed. Joanne Carlson Brown and Carole R. Bohn; New York: Pilgrim, 1989), 1–30.

[13] Walter Wink, particularly the last volume in his trilogy on the 'powers', *Engaging the Powers: Discernment and Resistance in a World of Domination* (Philadelphia, PA: Fortress Press, 1992).

critic, René Girard, whose attention has focused on the sacrificial dimensions of religion, in particular of atonement theories in Christian theology, viewing sacrifice as participation in deep-seated violence endemic to human culture.[14]

If one enquires about the origin of violence, the explanations are again diverse. René Girard sees it as emerging from 'mimetic rivalry',[15] in effect from wanting what the other wants. This leads ultimately to murder and then to the various mechanisms to mask that murder and to contain the resulting cycle of violence, including scapegoating and sacrifice. In short, violence adheres to the very core of religion, particularly in the sacrificial and scapegoating mechanisms he sees as central to religion.

Hector Avalos has suggested, rather, that violence emerges from scarce resources and the deliberate restricting of access.[16] With respect to the New Testament, the restriction of salvation only to the elect, or only to believers, thus renders it violent at its very core.

Others propose that human beings are 'hard-wired' by nature for competition and rivalry for what it takes to live, and are thus predisposed to violence. Nature is 'red in tooth and claw', in Alfred Lord Tennyson's words.[17]

Jacques Ellul sees violence as reflective of nature, yes, but of a fallen and corrupted nature, an inextricable aspect of the bleak 'order of necessity'. Violence is not only sin but also rooted in primordial sin that pervades the way things are. With characteristic decisiveness, Ellul sees violence as therefore 'absolutely' prohibited for a Christian, as is any justification of violence, precisely because the Christian is 'free' from the necessity of the fallen order.

> [Christians] must struggle against violence precisely *because*, apart from Christ, violence is the form that human relations *normally* and *necessarily* take . . . If we are free in Jesus Christ, we shall reject violence precisely because violence is necessary! . . . And mind, this means all

[14] René Girard, *Violence and the Sacred* (trans. Patrick Gregory; Baltimore: Johns Hopkins University Press, 1977); Girard, *The Scapegoat* (trans. Yvonne Freccero; Baltimore: Johns Hopkins University Press, 1986).

[15] René Girard, *Things Hidden since the Foundation of the World* (trans. Stephen Bann and Michael Metteer; Stanford, CA: Stanford University Press, 1987).

[16] Hector Avalos, *Fighting Words: The Origins of Religious Violence* (Amherst, NY: Prometheus Books, 2005).

[17] Alfred Lord Tennyson, 'In Memoriam A.H.H.', Canto 56.

kinds and ways of violence: psychological manipulation, doctrinal terrorism, economic imperialism, the venomous warfare of free competition, as well as torture, guerrilla movements, police action.[18]

(emphasis added)

Some have pushed back against such a wide construal of violence. Glen Stassen, for example, wishes to establish a thoroughgoing peaceable ethic based on the Sermon on the Mount, while recognizing the need for constraints and even a modicum of force in the interests of protection.[19] Without wishing to downplay the variety of ways persons can mistreat and abuse each other, putting a mugging and a forceful pulling of a person out of danger into the same category is seen as undercutting meaningful ethical discernment and debate.

Our brief survey on the meaning of 'violence' suggests that no one definition is by itself operative in public discourse. While there is general agreement that Jesus and the writers of the New Testament for the most part prohibit *physical* violence, the pervasive presence of warnings of judgement for those who do not live in accordance with the will of God, or who do not confess Jesus as Lord and Messiah, are seen to constitute not just the threat of violence in the future but a form of verbal violence in the present. The clear delineation between believers and unbelievers, between good and bad, are seen to create a mindset predisposed to violence. The prominence of the theme of suffering is under suspicion as valorizing violence, even if the violence is suffered rather than meted out. In the eyes of many the New Testament is androcentric and misogynistic, and thereby violent. Jonneke Bekkenkamp and Yvonne Sherwood insist that pervading the New Testament is a kind of '*domestic* violence', that is, 'violence not only as violation/abuse of essentially good material' but violence taking place 'at the very heart' of the New Testament.[20]

---

[18] Ellul, *Violence*, 127, 130.

[19] Glen Stassen, *Living the Sermon on the Mount: A Practical Hope for Grace and Deliverance* (San Francisco, CA: Jossey-Bass, 2006); Glen Stassen with Michael Westmoreland White, 'Defining Violence and Nonviolence', in *Teaching Peace: Nonviolence and the Liberal Arts* (ed. J. Denny Weaver and Gerald Biesecker-Mast; Lanham, ML: Rowman and Littlefield, 2003), 17–37.

[20] Yvonne Sherwood and Jonneke Bekkenkamp, 'Introduction: The Thin Blade of Difference between Real Swords and Words about "Sharp-Edged Iron Things" – Reflections on How People Use the Word', in *Sanctified Aggression: Legacies of Biblical and Post-Biblical Vocabularies of Violence* (ed. Yvonne Sherwood and Jonneke Bekkenkamp; London/New York: T&T Clark, 2003), 1–9 (2).

These are deeply vexing matters, partly because the meaning of 'violence' is not possible to delineate carefully, and most especially because the meaning of texts and their effect is not thought to reside so much in the intentions of the authors as in the interplay between readers and texts located in various contexts.[21] In his *Peace and Violence in the New Testament*, Michel Desjardins puts it quite simply: 'Non-physical types of peace and violence cannot be delimited with precision.'[22] However regrettable, to work with a wide definition of violence 'means giving up the possibility of arriving at a specific understanding of violence that is shared by all'.[23]

'New Testament'

If 'violence' is a complex reality so is 'New Testament', and if the New Testament is complex so are the communities invested in it, and the interpreters serving those communities, whether within the Church or in the academy.

As is well known, 'New Testament' refers to the 27 diverse documents making up the latter part of the Christian Bible. While now the second part of a 'book,' it is a composite of diverse narratives of Jesus' life, ministry, teaching, death, and resurrection, of letters written by emissaries ('apostles') and others unknown to us and addressed to diverse groups of adherents throughout the eastern half of the Roman Empire, as well as an apocalypse, penned by a prisoner languishing on an island in the Aegean. Written over roughly a century, from mid-first to mid-second century, these documents reflect an astonishing period of change: from a Jewish renewal movement, more

---

[21] Sherwood and Bekkenkamp, 'Introduction', 3: '[B]iblical, Jewish and Christian vocabularies are not sealed off in hermetic worlds unto themselves, answerable only to themselves, but . . . biblical, Jewish and Christian words, figures, scripts and themes are recycled, appealed to, exploited, banalized, as they circulate as part of ongoing vocabularies.'

[22] Michel Desjardins, *Peace, Violence, and the New Testament* (Sheffield: Sheffield Academic Press, 1997), 12.

[23] Desjardins, *Peace, Violence, and the New Testament*; see the study of diverse conceptions of violence by Desjardins's student, Philip Tite, *Conceiving Peace and Violence*, 1–42; cf. Jonathan Klawans, 'Introduction'; John Howard Yoder, 'A Theological Critique of Violence', *in The War of the Lamb: The Ethics of Nonviolence and Peacemaking* (ed. Glen Stassen, Mark Thiessen Nation and Matt Hamsher; Grand Rapids, MI: Brazos, 2009), 27–41.

or less on the radical edges of Jewish society, to increasingly non-Jewish (Gentile) Hellenistic circles of devotees of this Jewish messiah; from rural and small village life to cosmopolitan urban diversity; from the creativity and 'holy chaos' of an intensely future-oriented and expectant movement to increasingly routinized and institution-alized life more suited to a 'long haul'.[24]

We should thus expect to find diverse dimensions of what counts as 'violence' reflected on the pages of the New Testament. It is not an exaggeration to say that violence pervaded the world of Jesus and his followers. Herodian and Roman imperial rule, sparking sporadic resistance, and culminating in the catastrophic war against Rome in 66–70 CE, created an ambience of pervasive violence.[25] In addition to the political and military brutalities, the growing disparities between rich and poor, landowners and landless, form a vivid background to Jesus' parables, for example. The conflict between the rural poor and the temple state centred in Jerusalem is reflected in the final days of Jesus' life. If what counts as violence is marginalization on the basis of religion and sex, the pages of the Gospels reflect the per-vasiveness of such violence as well. The presence in the narratives of Jesus' life of lepers, prostitutes, tax collectors, haemorrhaging women, and Samaritans testifies to what can fairly be called 'structural,' 'cultural' and 'religious violence'. Equally, the landowners, slaveholders, centurions, suspicious and judgemental religious leaders, local kings and Roman overlords populating the narratives of Jesus' life and his parables represent those in charge of maintaining an order soaked in violence. Violence is seldom if ever beyond the horizon in the Gospels.

When we move beyond Palestine into the wider Mediterranean world, and view that world from the vantage point of believers in Jesus, we see that it too is marked by pervasive violence. Even when the Jesus movement benefited from the order and 'peace' the security state brought them, making possible the rapid spread of the movement,

---

[24] These issues are surveyed and discussed at length in countless 'introductions' to the New Testament and in encyclopedias.

[25] See, e.g., Richard A. Horsley's numerous writings, including *Jesus and the Spiral of Violence*; see also: Ched Myers, *Binding the Strong Man: A Political Reading of Mark's Story of Jesus* (2nd edn; Maryknoll, NY: Orbis Books, 2008); and William R. Herzog II, *Parables as Subversive Speech: Jesus as Pedagogue of the Oppressed* (Louisville, KY: John Knox, 1994).

the violence of that system was never far out of sight. Apart from the hostility and even physical violence early Jesus-believers experienced at the hands of their fellow Jews, Roman authorities also frequently responded to them as a threat to civic order and peace.

To take seriously the way Jesus' followers viewed reality means that we recognize the violence of the spiritual realm as well. The 'air' was filled with violence (e.g. Eph. 2.1–3). Jews and non-Jews alike saw their world to be a battle ground of invisible forces impinging in both positive and malevolent ways on the lives of people. These 'powers' were understood both as demonic and satanic and to be fully enmeshed with the visible forces of governors, armies, nations and empires. Just as a division between 'religious' and 'secular' does not fit the world of the New Testament, neither does a division between 'spiritual' and 'material' or 'physical'. What helped shape such a view was the strong eschatological or apocalyptic orientation of New Testament writers: dualistic, intensely conflictive and deeply imbued with a sense of temporal urgency. Put simply, much of the New Testament reflects a sense of living in a time of war that was about to culminate in the final and ultimate overcoming of resistance to God's reign, and with it the demise of sin and death. That the language of violent confrontation should mark these writings should thus not come as a surprise.

There is yet one more dimension of violence. As stated earlier, the literature we call the New Testament was not written as Scripture. These documents emerged out of the early history of a movement that already had Scriptures, namely, those shared with the syna-gogue – the Law, the Prophets and the Writings. Those Scriptures narrate the often violent history of Israel. They also contain frequent prophetic warnings of violent divine judgement, specifically also depictions of God as a fierce warrior, sometimes as liberator, other times as punisher. While some of this tradition undergoes radical recasting in the New Testament, as we shall see, there is no sense of estrangement from scriptural moorings in any of the New Testament writings.

Reading the New Testament as Scripture

It matters greatly how the New Testament is read, also with respect to the issue of violence. It matters whether one is a tenured university professor in the Global North addressing the issue of violence from the safety of a secure job and an ample office, or whether the New Testament, including its texts of violence and anger, is read by those suffering poverty and oppression. It matters whether such violence emerges from a world hostile to the Bible, or whether it emerges from within a 'Christian' religious culture. And it matters greatly whether 'New Testament' is simply the label given to a collection of ancient documents or whether they together as 'New Testament' constitute *Scripture* – authoritative, revelatory, 'word of God'.

Many scholars, regardless of their own beliefs, approach the New Testament as a collection of historical documents. With respect to the issue of violence, those writings are then placed into their historical context and analysed with respect to how they both reflect and challenge the prevailing cultural and political context in which they were written. Such study of New Testament texts is common today, even among those who study it as Scripture.

When the New Testament is read as *Scripture*, however, additional and quite different questions are asked. What kinds of views and behaviours does the New Testament reflect, and therefore warrant or demand of the faithful? Are the actions and teachings of Jesus and Paul, for example, violent? If so, are they to be imitated by those who read the New Testament as Scripture? Philip Tite is thus right to ask whether the New Testament 'promotes violence',[26] even if that too depends very much on who is reading it, from where, for what and with what disposition.

According to Michel Desjardins, 'the authority given to the New Testament by Christians complicates matters considerably'.[27] He has drawn attention to what he sees as selective or even distorted reading of the New Testament by those who see it as normative or revelatory. Violent aspects of the New Testament are typically muted in favour of the non-violent and peaceful.[28] No doubt that is sometimes true. The argument is often made, however, that the New Testament is indeed violent, and that this constitutes a problem because people accord it normative force. In his 2002 presidential address to the Society of Biblical Literature, John J. Collins stated

---

[26] Tite, *Conceiving Peace and Violence*, 33.
[27] Desjardins, *Peace, Violence and the New Testament*, 120.
[28] Desjardins, *Peace, Violence and the New Testament*, 14.

that the appeal to the Bible because of its 'presumed divine authority' gives it an 'aura of certitude' that represents

> the most basic connection between the Bible and violence, more basic than any command or teaching it contains ... The Bible has contributed to violence in the world precisely because it has been taken to confer a degree of certitude that transcends human discussion and argumentation. Perhaps the most constructive thing a biblical critic can do toward lessening the contribution of the Bible to violence in the world, is to show that that certitude is an illusion.[29]

True, people do use the Bible, including the New Testament, in ways that are deeply injurious to themselves and others. In some respects this book is intended to be a contribution to lessening the hold of certain kinds of certitude, most especially when in the service of violence. We are particularly sensitive about that in our day when those who intentionally frighten the community do so from a position of moral and spiritual certitude. At the same time, there are traditions such as the Anabaptist and Quaker traditions that understand the New Testament to summon followers of Jesus unambiguously to costly forgiveness, defencelessness and love of enemies – a stance resolutely opposed to violence. In this case a normative and revelatory reading of the New Testament delegitim-izes prevailing assumptions about violence as the solution to violence. The breathtaking act of forgiveness on the part of the Amish of Nickel Mines, PA, when their children were murdered in their school house on 2 October 2006, will surely stand as an example of persons who acted as they did because of the revela-tory and normative hold the New Testament had on them. As the Amish would see it, it is not the revelatory authority of the New Testament that is the problem; it is the unwillingness of most Christians to heed that authority with respect to violence that is the problem.[30]

---

[29] John J. Collins, 'The Zeal of Phinehas, the Bible, and the Legitimation of Violence', in *The Destructive Power of Religion: Violence in Judaism, Christianity, and Islam*; Vol. 1, *Sacred Scriptures, Ideology, and Violence* (ed. J. Harold Ellens; Westport, CT/London: Praeger, 2004), 11–33 (25–6), reprinted from *JBL* 122 (2003), 3–21; published as *Does the Bible Justify Violence?* (Facets; Augsburg: Fortress Press, 2004).

[30] See Donald B. Kraybill, Steven M. Nolt and David Weaver-Zercher, *Amish Grace: How Forgiveness Transcended Tragedy* (San Francisco, CA: Jossey-Bass, 2007).

Readers of the New Testament as Scripture clearly do bring to bear on it a particular kind of 'complication', to use Desjardins's word. They will always read it within a highly charged force field of needing to know what the text says and warrants, and what the situation they are in calls for and thus demands of them. They will be often torn between wishing the text did not say 'that' and knowing they need in some sense to submit to its authority.

For some, Scripture functions more or less as command. The challenge then will be which words to obey. It is often not Scriptures themselves but prevailing social and political mores that nudge one or another text to the forefront. For others, Scripture represents a kind of orienting shared memory, part of the tradition that goes with being a part of this or that community. The specificity of words once read as commands gives way to a kind of general gist, which, one suspects, is vulnerable to being given impetus more by prevailing political and social values than by the Scriptures themselves. The normativity of the New Testament as Scripture is thus more arms-length, and questions of violence settled at greater distance from the text. Whereas the first group will argue over what the words demand, the second will argue over whether they ought to be allowed a say at all when they run counter to what is generally held to be true. In short, 'proof-texting' is not the province only of a 'biblicistic' or 'literalistic' reading of the New Testament.

The role of the New Testament in relation to violence is thus truly 'complicated', and not only by belief. No one comes to the reading of the New Testament without an agenda. Those who do not see the New Testament as Scripture, but for whom violence is an urgent concern, will be sensitive to the New Testament's role in the culture, shaping imagination and providing either brakes on or warrants for attitudes and behaviour. That does not answer the question as to whether the New Testament will be seen either as an ally or as an impediment in that struggle.

That said, for the New Testament to function as Scripture also implies that *it*, and not just the malleable intersection between reader and text, has normative priority. That is what gives weight and urgency to engagement with the texts. That is what gives considerable resonance to the arguments over whether this or that text is violent, or whether this or that way of interpreting the text is violent.

My approach to the New Testament

In the interests of allowing readers to assess my own point of departure in this study, I wish to identify my own location and orientation. I am a former pastor and prison and hospital chaplain, and for the past three decades a university professor of New Testament. My commitment to active non-violence spans my adult life, a commitment honed within a church tradition that has made peacemaking a centrepiece of Christian faith and practice. This predisposes me not so much to read the New Testament in a certain way as to struggle with certain texts and historical interpretations, or to feel the pinch, as it were, of certain aspects of the New Testament in ways others might not.

I read the New Testament as Scripture, and thus as revelatory and normative. I take this to mean not that it is a string of oracles, nor that it is a simple matter of taking it 'literally' but that, in the mystery of reading, interpreting and interacting with other readers also listening for the word of God, the 'word' can become 'flesh', in the sense that it finds an audience among blood-and-flesh human beings intent on responding with their lives to what they hear. Such an 'incarnational' understanding of revelation also makes it mandatory, in my view, to know as much as we can of the historical embeddedness of 'the word' in the time the New Testament was written. This does not settle one way or another the question of violence in the New Testament nor whether it combats or promotes violence. Nor does it prevent attention to the experiences of those whose way of approaching the text might be very different and whose experiences might predispose them to hear it quite differently.

I read the New Testament as good news – 'gospel'. To say that is not to reduce the New Testament to a set of predictable doctrines or convictions, nor do I wish to mute the diversity of voices emerging from that volatile century in the pages of the New Testament. It does mean that I have experienced the New Testament as a source of *good* news. That does not prevent me from listening to those who hear the opposite, and wrestle with what emerges in their hearing and reading – and to learn from them. It is often in the encounter with others whose experience and perspective is very different that one encounters the familiar in unfamiliar ways, and vice versa. That can bring with it the upheaval of estrangement and disorientation, but finally of a fuller grasp of truth.

Does that bias me? Probably. More than those on the lookout for discreditable signs of violence? Probably not. Does this bias provide blinkers against the presence of violence in the New Testament? Perhaps. But might it also be a means by which to sort out the vexatious issue of violence, even if not in any final sense? Perhaps too. I offer the following studies of specific topics and texts as examples of honest searching and listening, as well as offerings intended to aid in the careful reading of the New Testament by those for whom violence is profoundly troubling. It is impossible within the confines of this book to be exhaustive. I have thus chosen a few texts for their representative character as a set of probes or soundings into the relationship of the New Testament and violence.

Much is at stake in approaching the New Testament with the question of violence. The question is legitimate because it is one with which our time is wrestling with the utmost urgency. It is an open question, however, whether it represents the best way into the New Testament. Would we achieve a better reading of the core concern of the New Testament writers were we to have come with the question of peace, as Willard Swartley contends?[31] I believe Swartley is correct at a fundamental level. Even so, sometimes entering through the back door lets you see things that coming through the front door might not have shown you. That can be very revealing, but also troubling.

---

[31] Willard M. Swartley, *Covenant of Peace: The Missing Peace in New Testament Theology and Ethics* (Grand Rapids, MI: Eerdmans, 2006), 1–10; see also Horsley, *Jesus and the Spiral of Violence*, 150.

2

Turn the cheek and love your enemies!

As pointed out in Chapter 1, the relationship between Jesus and violence is complex. The narratives describing his life in Galilee and Judaea are suffused with violence: born to a young mother forced to endure the hardship of a journey from Nazareth to the ancestral village of Bethlehem by edict of Roman emperor Augustus, born during the brutal reign of Herod the Great, fleeing the slaughter of the infants in Bethlehem, enduring the virtually constant hostility of the authorities during his brief ministry, Jesus dies the death the empire meted out to troublemakers – a slow death by torture we know as crucifixion.

If we employ a broad definition of violence, we encounter a Jesus who calls for radical repentance in view of the coming reign of God, who warns of judgement on those who do not repent, has fiercely condemning things to say about religious leaders, and acts in ways that seem to invite both ridicule and outright hostility.

However much violence or the threat of it laces the story of Jesus, he is most often associated with the opposite. He is for many an example of non-judgementalism and inclusiveness, eating and drinking with those rejected by proper society. Best known are his teachings regarding forgiveness, 'turning the cheek', and loving enemies. Count Leo Tolstoy, Mahatma Gandhi, Martin Luther King, Jr., Dorothy Day and Thomas Merton, to name only a few of the recent figures associated with non-violence and peacemaking, have all drawn inspiration from Jesus. History is replete with many more examples, including movements and groups such as Waldensians, Czech Brethren, Anabaptists and Quakers. Many renewal movements within the Church today no longer identified with pacifism were at the time of their beginnings 'pacifist', given their desire to be biblically uncompromising in following Jesus.[1] Even those not sharing

---

[1] See Theron F. Schlabach and Richard T. Hughes, *Proclaim Peace: Christian Pacifism from Unexpected Quarters* (Urbana, IL: University of Illinois, 1997).

16

a commitment to non-violence or pacifism agree that Jesus taught something like what those words imply, whether or not it is realistic to emulate him in actual life.[2]

As Chapter 1 suggested, one of the realities of assessing Jesus' attitude to violence is that his teachings and way of life are known to us via the recollections and creative narratives of the evangelists, notably Matthew, Mark, Luke and John, and to a lesser extent via the writings of the great emissaries such as the Apostle Paul, who were themselves dependent on eyewitnesses and second-hand oral tradition. This means that we have access to Jesus as remembered or recalled by those who came to believe in him.[3] This has permitted scholars to second-guess the memories and recollections of those early witnesses with respect to Jesus and violence. Words or actions attributed to Jesus that seem to strike a discordantly violent note are then sometimes ascribed to the tradition or the evangelists rather than to Jesus himself. Matthew is seen as particularly vengeful, Luke as an apologist of the Roman Empire, and John as dangerously dualistic and anti-Semitic, for example. Others are quite prepared to see Jesus himself as violent in both action (the temple action discussed in Chapter 4) and spirit (e.g. Matthew 10.35).

In the next chapters we will take some select soundings in a few texts that have either played a significant role with respect to Jesus and violence or that can serve as representative of the kind of teachings associated with Jesus in the Gospels. It is impossible, given the wealth of biblical literature, the intensity of scholarly debate and the wideness of the definitions of violence, to do more than scrape the surface of the issue. Hopefully these few core samples will spark the reader's own investigation into the issue of violence and the New Testament. The vexing issue of anti-Judaism as it pertains to the Gospels' depiction of Jesus and his adversarial relationship with his contemporaries cannot, regrettably, be given the full attention

---

[2] As pointed out most recently by A. James Reimer, *Christians and War: A Brief History of the Church's Teaching and Practices* (Minneapolis: Fortress Press, 2010).

[3] The titles of two recent books on Jesus remind us of that 'remembered' quality explicitly, even if it is a mainstay of Jesus scholarship: James D. G. Dunn, *Jesus Remembered* (Christianity in the Making, Vol. 1; Grand Rapids, MI/Cambridge: Eerdmans, 2003); Allen Verhey, *Remembering Jesus: Christian Community, Scripture, and the Moral Life* (Rapids, MI/Cambridge: Eerdmans, 2002). For what follows see also my *Recovering Jesus: The Witness of the New Testament* (Grand Rapids, MI: Brazos; London: SPCK, 2007).

it deserves. Readers are directed to a recent exploration of precisely that phenomenon as it relates to the New Testament by Terence Donaldson.[4]

In this chapter we will take up the famous texts regarding non-retaliation and the love of enemies, and in subsequent chapters Jesus' parable of the Unforgiving Slave, and his prophetic demonstration in the temple, before completing the focus on Jesus with an exploration of the significance of his death for the question of violence.

Turn the cheek and love your enemies!

The familiar injunctions to turn the cheek and to love enemies are found in two places in the Gospels. The shorter and lesser known of the two, often called the 'Sermon on the Plain', is found in Luke 6.20–49. The longer is Matthew's justly famous Sermon on the Mount (Matt. 5—7). Both are compilations of some of Jesus' instructions on how to live in light of the reign of God, quite possibly drawn from a shared written source that predates both Matthew and Luke.[5]

Luke presents the commands not to retaliate, to be generous and to love enemies as one integrated injunction (6.27–36). The command to 'love enemies' serves as a heading for a variety of expressions of such love: doing good to haters, blessing cursers, praying for abusers, turning the other cheek to the violent, and withholding nothing from robbers and beggars. Luke's Jesus sums this up with the so-called 'Golden Rule': 'As you wish that others would do to you, do so to them' (6.31). Reciprocated love is 'normal'. 'Even sinners love those who love them' (6.32). Love of enemies is the exact opposite of a quid pro quo approach to love. Even so, a great reward awaits those who act in such a loving way: they will be 'sons of the Most High' (6.35). Such behaviour is nothing less than the imitation of a kind and merciful divine 'Father' (6.36).

---

[4] Terence L. Donaldson, *Jews and Anti-Judaism in the New Testament: Decision Points and Divergent Interpretations* (Waco, TX: Baylor University Press; London: SPCK, 2010).

[5] For a recent and thorough discussion, see John P. Meier, *A Marginal Jew: Rethinking the Historical Jesus; Vol. 4, Law and Love* (New Haven/London: Yale University Press, 2009), 528–31. Note particularly the excellent bibliography of scholarly studies of this tradition at 576–80. In addition there is a large number of commentaries on both Luke and Matthew, as well as on the Sermon on the Mount, that furnish scholarly background to this discussion.

This is sometimes interpreted as the non-violence of those who have no alternative, given their victim status.[6] We should not miss, though, that such behaviour is demanded of those who thereby achieve the status accorded kings and emperors. Turning the cheek, lending without control over repayment and, most especially, loving enemies is sovereign behaviour, befitting being 'sons' of the Most High God.[7]

To resist or not to resist?

These notes are echoed by Matthew's Jesus as well. In Matthew's 'sermon', however, the matter of retaliation is separated out from that of love of enemies. Both injunctions appear as the last in a series of so-called 'antitheses': 'You have heard it said . . . but I say to you . . .' While as in Luke these instructions follow the beatitudes, Matthew wedges between them and the antitheses Jesus' insistence on his Torah fidelity and the demand that his followers outdo the Pharisees in 'righteousness', that is, in conformity to the will of God (Matt. 5.17–20). Matthew stresses thereby that Jesus' instructions on non-retaliation and love of enemies are not an alternative to Torah, or a superseding of law, but an 'intensification' of Torah, driving to the very heart or spirit of God's law, even if it ends up contradicting the inherited traditions of interpretation that have grown up around it.

Why raise this point in a discussion of violence? On the one hand, we might see this as rather unseemly competitiveness at Torah fidelity. But for those tempted or taught, then as now, to place Jesus over against his own Jewish roots, including Torah, not least with respect to violence, Matthew is making a critically important point. In his view, Jesus' stance on violence is *not* discontinuous with Torah, as

---

[6] Luise Schottroff, 'Nonviolence and the Love of One's Enemies', in *Essays on the Love Commandment* (ed. Reginald H. Fuller; Philadelphia, PA: Fortress Press, 1978), 9–39. As many point out, the circumstances reflected in the 'case studies' suggest a social location of powerlessness. But the behaviour, disposition and status as 'sons' attributes great status and freedom to them.

[7] I retain here the literal translation of *huioi* as 'sons' precisely because it allows us to see the status implications in the attribution. Better to expand that to 'sons and daughters' than to replace it with 'children'.

Marcion[8] would insist a half century later, and as many Christians still do today. Matthew is more than willing to show Jesus' teachings as discontinuous with the traditions of the elders ('You have heard it said . . .'). That is, after all, why he shapes them into antitheses in this 'sermon' (compare with Luke 6). However, in the way he presents Jesus' teachings, Matthew wishes to locate non-retaliation and love of enemies at the very heart of Torah.

This 'intensification' is there already in Jesus' teaching on murder (5.21–26). Taking up the explicit command not to kill or murder from Exodus 20.13, Jesus suggests that disparagement of the 'brother' is much like murder and subject to the same ultimate sanction. This is surely as sharp an intensification of the command not to kill as one might imagine, deeply anti-violent in its implications for human relationships, almost unhuman in its demand. It certainly reflects a widening of what constitutes violence in the way it extends the meaning of 'lethal' to include the breaking of relationships through disrespect and disdain.

We observe the same radicalism in the antithesis regarding adultery (Matt. 5.27–30). Jesus makes lust itself the equivalent of adultery, going far beyond our own day in the critique of the objectification of women. Jesus rejects lust as the violation of others and their covenants, even if it is only 'in one's heart' (5.28). A broad interpretation of violence, as discussed in the previous chapter, brings this under the umbrella of radical anti-violence, probably deemed by most today at least as unrealistic as the earlier injunction against 'murder' by disdain.

Coexisting with this thoroughgoing anti-violence is, however, Jesus' intensification, at least at the rhetorical level, of the consequences of not heeding his intensified Torah. What awaits those who disparage and mistreat their kin is the 'Gehenna of fire', a metaphor familiar to those living in the environs of Jerusalem as it referred to the ever burning garbage dump outside the city (5.22). And with respect to adultery, better to rip off the offending body part than to have one's whole body thrown into Gehenna (5.30; see also Matt. 18.8, 9; Mark 9). Respect for the brother and sister and

---

[8] Marcion of Sinope was a mid-second-century influential Church figure who proposed in vain abandoning the Scriptures shared with the synagogue in favour of a heavily edited Gospel of Luke and letters of Paul as the new Scriptures of the Church.

their spouses is to be lived out against the backdrop of divine accounting and judgement.

Should we see this violent language as metaphorical hyperbole? Does this go back to Jesus, or should we 'blame' Matthew for this threat? Even if we might credit Matthew with some of the hyperbole surrounding judgement,[9] certainty of judgement at the hands of a sovereign and just God is simply an unquestioned backdrop to all human action, for Jesus no less than for Matthew or any of their contemporaries. We will revisit this question repeatedly throughout coming chapters.

In the fifth antithesis (5.38–42), Jesus addresses the principle of payback or the law of *talion* (*jus talionis*), deeply rooted in common sense, in the laws of many nations, ancient and modern, and in Torah: 'life for life, eye for eye, tooth for tooth, hand for hand, foot for foot, burn for burn, wound for wound, stripe for stripe', to quote Exodus 21.23–25 (cf. Lev. 24.20; Deut. 19.21).[10] Ched Myers and Elaine Enns state provocatively the hold the *jus talionis* has on us: 'It is a pillar of Mother Culture, and formed our hearts and minds through the relentless catechism of family socialization, playground protocol, the popular media, and politics as usual.'[11] The notion of re*tali*ation reflects a deeply held conviction that wrongs incur debts that must be repaid in order for the wrong to be set right, informing a wide range of practices in the justice systems of nations, then as today, from compensation, restitution, to the death penalty, depending on the offence or crime.[12] It is reflected also in the Lord's prayer, where some versions have 'debts' rather than 'trespasses' (compare Matt. 6.12; Luke 11.4).

---

[9] See, e.g., David J. Neville, 'Toward a Teleology of Peace: Contesting Matthew's Violent Eschatology', *JSNT* 30/2 (2007), 131–61; Barbara E. Reid, OP, 'Violent Endings in Matthew's Parables and Christian Nonviolence', *CBQ* 66 (2004), 237–55, esp. 249.

[10] It has been noted that Jesus does not include the 'life for life' in his recitation (e.g. Hans Dieter Betz, *The Sermon on the Mount* (Hermeneia; Minneapolis, MN: Fortress Press, 1995), 278. In my view, we should see the 'list' as representative and not limiting.

[11] Ched Myers and Elaine Enns, *Ambassadors of Reconciliation: Vol. 1, New Testament Reflections on Restorative Justice and Peacemaking* (Maryknoll, NY: Orbis Books, 2009), 55.

[12] Restorative justice rightly distinguishes itself from 'retributive justice' but nevertheless retains an important place for restitution, which witnesses to the principle of *talion* in its own way.

The antithesis to this principle of payback can be translated variously:

- 'Do not resist (*anthistēmi*) evil!'
- 'Do not resist the evil one!'
- 'Do not *violently* resist the evil one!'
- 'Do not resist by means of evil!'

Each of these translations of '*mē antistēnai tō ponērō*' lends a different nuance to the phrase. Is Jesus prohibiting resistance to evil and evil persons? Many read the text this way, and derive the ethic of 'non-resistance' from it. Or is he not prohibiting resistance at all, but rather rejecting *violent* resistance or the vengeful payback, as in 'resist evil, but not by evil means!' Those rejecting the former rendering as supporting a kind of passivity in the face of violence clearly prefer this reading. We leave the question unanswered for now, since the parable-like illustrations Jesus now gives might help with the answer.

As illustrations of what it means either not to resist or not to resist by means of evil, Matthew's Jesus offers a set of 'mini-parables':

- If anyone strikes you on the right cheek, turn the other also.
- If anyone wants to sue you and take your shirt, give your coat as well.
- If anyone forces you to go one mile, go also the second mile.
- Give to everyone who begs from you, and do not refuse anyone who wants to borrow from you.

To refer to these vignettes as parable-like is to point to their evocative and riddle-like character. But what is it that we are intended to 'get?' Given that Matthew has organized this into a larger set of antitheses, does he view Jesus as driving the law to its core also in this instance, suggesting an alternative form of retaliation? Or is Jesus subverting the law of equivalency, in effect undermining the broadly held notion of fairness, to say nothing of good common sense? Is he thus departing not only from the letter but also from the spirit of Torah?

The answer might depend on whether we see at the heart of the principle of *talion* in the Torah a *requirement* of equivalency, or whether its 'spirit' is to *limit* retaliation to *no more than* equivalency. If it is the latter, then Jesus can be seen as once again 'intensifying'

Torah in the direction it was already pointing, namely, to break an otherwise endless cycle of retaliatory violence.[13]

But we should be cautious. While the *talion* commands in Exodus 21.24 and Leviticus 24.20 might lend themselves to such a 'limiting' interpretation, Deuteronomy makes that somewhat more difficult. In Deuteronomy the law of *talion* is preceded by the phrase 'show no pity' (19.21) in the act of 'purging evil' (19.13).[14] Avenging a wrong thus has a kind of purgative function for which any amelioration is to leave the impurity in place.

It remains the case that in a culture of the blood feud the principle of *talion* or equivalency, while not non-violent, serves to break the spiral of violence by limiting the violence to a measure of equivalency. Perhaps, then, Jesus' injunctions to turn the cheek, to give the last bit of clothing, and to walk the second mile do represent a creative intensification of Torah rather than an abrogation of it. These mini-parables become then examples of subversive responses or 'transforming initiatives' to violence rather than acquiescence to it.[15]

In numerous publications Walter Wink has drawn attention to the possibility that each of these parable-like scenes reflects a seizing of initiative by victims, by those ostensibly powerless within recognizable and specific contexts of violence and oppression.[16] Wink proposes that with these initiatives, or what Robert Tannehill calls

---

[13] E.g. Richard B. Hays, *The Moral Vision of the New Testament: A Contemporary Introduction to New Testament Ethics* (San Francisco, CA: HarperSanFrancisco, 1996), 324; Reid, 'Violent Endings', 242.

[14] For a study of the relationship between Deut. 19 and Matt. 5, see Dorothy Jean Weaver, 'Transforming Nonresistance: From *Lex Talionis* to "Do Not Resist the Evil One"', in *The Love of Enemy and Nonretaliation in the New Testament* (ed. Willard M. Swartley; Studies of Peace and Scripture, Institute of Mennonite Studies; Louisville, KY: Westminster/ John Knox, 1992), 38–47. Weaver sees Matt. 5.38–42 as continuous with Deut. 19 precisely because they are both concerned to eliminate the evil from the community, albeit by radically different means.

[15] Glen H. Stassen, *Just Peacemaking: Transforming Initiatives for Justice and Peace* (Louisville, KY: Westminster/John Knox, 1992), 53–88; Stassen, *Living the Sermon on the Mount: A Practical Hope for Grace and Deliverance* (San Francisco, CA: Jossey-Bass, 2006), 89–105.

[16] E.g. Walter Wink, *Engaging the Powers: Discernment and Resistance in a World of Domination* (Minneapolis, MN: Fortress Press, 1992), 175–93; Wink, 'Neither Passivity nor Violence: Jesus' Third Way (Matt. 5.38–42 par.)', in *Love of Enemy* (ed. Swartley), 102–25. Wink has been highly influential on, e.g., Myers and Enns, *Ambassadors*, 53–4; Stassen, *Just Peacemaking*, 63–70; and countless others.

'focal instances',[17] Jesus points to a 'third way' between acquiescence and passivity on the one hand, and violent resistance and retaliation on the other.

The first example envisions a person being struck on the *right* cheek, which implies a backhanded strike clearly intended to denigrate and humiliate. The second example conjures up a setting like a debtor's court, where one with already next to nothing is sued for one of his two pieces of clothing. The third example is one recognizable as typical of Roman imperial humiliation of subject peoples, where a soldier could command a hapless passerby to carry his pack for a mile.

When we recognize the settings (and Jesus' audience as well as Matthew's would have immediately), the response to violence or abuse in each of these is precisely *not* passive suffering, as 'turning the cheek' has come to symbolize, but a creative, even risky, response. To turn the left cheek toward a right-handed insulter is to assert one's dignity by challenging the victimizer to an act of aggression that treats the victim as an equal. One needs only to imagine a context of bullying to see that this is everything but a passive response. When you have only two pieces of clothing, and the one has already been taken, offering the remaining clothing to the one bringing suit becomes a bit of burlesque clearly embarrassing to the one bringing suit. Moreover, in a Jewish context in which looking on nakedness was an offence, such an act would have left the onlooker in the position of being the offender.[18] Finally, since Roman soldiers were only allowed to press a local into service for one mile of pack carrying, for such a person to offer to carry the soldier's bag for two miles would more than likely have thrown the soldier off balance. We should likely see in this a clear assertion of dignity and essential freedom. There can be little doubt that the one offering to carry the pack would have courted danger every step of the way, whether from the soldier or from those suspecting the one carrying the pack of collaboration, as anyone knows who lives under occupation today. In each of these 'mini-parables' victims do not behave as victims. Nor do they perform a predictable script of rebellion, retaliation or acquiescence. These

---

[17] Robert C. Tannehill, 'The "Focal Instance" as a Form of New Testament Speech: A Study of Matthew 5.39–42', *JR* 50 (1970), 372–85; cf. Hays, *Moral Vision*, 329; Reid, 'Violent Endings', 244.

[18] Wink, *Engaging the Powers*, 178; Reid, 'Violent Endings', 244.

are clearly ways in which the 'spiral of violence' is disrupted if not broken.

Today we call such behaviour 'creative non-violence', or even 'non-violent resistance'. Wink captures it perfectly with 'defiant vulnerability'.[19] The characters in these vignettes are 'vulnerable' in that they are clearly victims abused by someone who has power over them, but vulnerable also in that by the nature of their response they are deliberately opening the door to further abuse or violence against themselves.[20] They are 'defiant' in that in doing so they are seizing the initiative, one that has a chance of undoing the predictable scripts of violence and counterviolence. Along with many, Wink considers *anthistēmi* to refer to *violent* resistance in particular, and thus not to the kind of resistance represented by the examples given.[21]

We might then translate verse 39 as, 'Resist, but not in an evil way!' While grammatically somewhat clumsy, it is possible, since the dative *tō ponērō* can either refer to whom or what one is not to resist ('Do not resist evil, or the evil one!'), or it can refer to the means by which one is not to resist ('Do not resist *by means of* evil!').[22] The problem then is not resistance per se but what *kind* of resistance is to be offered. We are reminded of Paul in Romans 12.17, 21:

> [17] Do not repay anyone evil for evil . . . [21] Do not be *overcome* by evil, but *overcome* evil with good.   (emphasis added)

Notice Paul's stress on 'overcoming' or 'being victorious over' (*nikaō*) evil. To view our text through this lens has Jesus calling not for *non-*resistance to evil but to a form of non-violent resistance. Importantly,

---

[19] Wink, 'Neither Passivity nor Violence', 115.

[20] William Klassen, *Love of Enemies: The Way to Peace* (Overtures to Biblical Theology 15; Philadelphia, PA: Fortress Press, 1984), 86.

[21] Wink, *Engaging the Powers*, 185.

[22] The great pacifist and integrationist founder of the Koinonia community in Georgia, USA, Clarence Jordan (PhD in New Testament), renders it freely but consistent with this understanding: 'But I'm telling you, never respond *with evil*' (*Cotton Patch Version*; emphasis added). He suggests that the phrase should be carefully translated as 'not to retaliate revengefully by evil means' (*The Substance of Faith and Other Cotton Patch Sermons* (New York: Association Press, 1972), 69). While Jordan has influenced count-less peacemakers and activists, his reading is reflected also in recent scholarship: see, e.g., Pinchas Lapide, *Sermon on the Mount* (Maryknoll, NY: Orbis, 1986); Willard M. Swartley, 'War and Peace in the New Testament', *Aufstieg und Niedergang der Römischen Welt*, 2.26.3, 2338.

Wink formulated this very influential interpretation of Matthew
5.38–42 in relation to the struggle against apartheid in South Africa,
attempting to see how Jesus' teachings might relate to a setting in
which the struggle is between those with power and those ostensibly
without.[23]

The relationship of these responses to violence is more complex,
however, than might first appear. It does not require a particularly
vivid imagination to see that these actions as Wink has characterized
them can easily become a means of goading to greater violence. In
fact, non-retaliation can emerge from hatred for the victimizer. When
joining the covenanters at Qumran at the Dead Sea, for example, the
following pledge would be given:

> I shall not repay anyone with an evil reward; with goodness I shall
> pursue the man. For to God belongs the judgement of every living
> being, and it is he who pays man his wages. I shall not be involved
> at all in any dispute of the men of the pit until the day of vengeance.
> *However, I shall not remove my anger from wicked men nor shall I be
> appeased until God carries out his judgement.*
>
> (1QS 10.19–21; emphasis added)

There is no hint that kindness motivates such refusing to pay back.
Deferred gratification might be a more fitting characterization. Might
such defiant vulnerability even be a form of entrapment, wishing
thereby to have judgement fall all the harder on the victimizer?[24] Paul's
words in Romans 12 have sometimes been read in this light:[25]

> [19] Beloved, never avenge yourselves, but leave room for the wrath [of
> God]; for it is written, 'Vengeance is mine, I will repay, says the Lord.'
> [20] No, 'if your enemies are hungry, feed them; if they are thirsty, give
> them something to drink; for by doing this you will heap burning
> coals on their heads.'

By themselves, then, these examples of ingenuity in the face of violence
may be little more than the tactics of victims with little power. They

---

[23] Wink holds Matthew responsible for preparing the ground for identifying Jesus with
passivity in the face of violence by, unlike Luke, explicitly connecting Jesus' words with
the issue of *talion* ('Neither Passivity nor Violence', 117).

[24] One can see this in the 'martyr theology' in, e.g., 2 Macc. 7; 4 Macc.

[25] There is in my view no *Schadenfreude* in Paul's words, only a recognition that the 'heavy
lifting' of judgement is to be left to God. More in Chapter 7 below.

may be a creative way of taking the initiative, of asserting dignity and of subverting the ostensible power relationships. That is of considerable significance, but it is not yet all Jesus was asking of his followers, as both Luke and Matthew remember it in their 'sermons'.[26]

Love your enemies!

In Luke 6 the examples of responses to violence are framed by the command to love enemies (6.27, 35). There is no room for vindictive non-retaliation in the way Luke has shaped Jesus' 'sermon'. That is true for Matthew as well, only he has separated out the instructions on retaliation and love of enemies into two antitheses, 5.38–42 on non-retaliation and 5.43–48 on love for enemies. Left by itself, the antithesis regarding retaliation might, as we have seen, be (mis)read as an invitation to another form of enmity – non-violent in the moment, maybe, but not necessarily in spirit, nor in relation to coming judgement. For that reason alone, Matthew no doubt never intended that antithesis to be read apart from the final one:

> [43] You have heard that it was said, 'You shall love your neighbour and hate your enemy.' [44] But I say to you, Love your enemies and pray for those who persecute you, [45] so that you may be children ('sons') of your Father in heaven; for he makes his sun rise on the evil and on the good, and sends rain on the righteous and on the unrighteous.
>
> (Matt. 5.43–45)

The 'thesis' contains two parts: love your neighbour; hate your enemy. Along with the primary obligation to love God, love of neighbour was in Jewish tradition the summation of Torah, as reflected also in the New Testament.[27] What is *not* found in Torah is any explicit injunction to hate the enemy. Since the previous antitheses all take up a Torah command only to 'intensify' it, this antithesis is jarring. Is Jesus (or Matthew) maligning or deliberately mischaracterizing Torah, in the process doing violence to the tradition of neighbour love?

---

[26] Meier, *Marginal Jew*, 4, 529, 616, nn. 179, 180.
[27] Lev. 19.18; cf. in the New Testament, e.g., Matt. 22.37–40//Mark 12.29–34; Rom. 13.8–10; 1 Cor. 13; Gal. 5.14; James 2.8; 1 John 4.

The background to this stark antithesis between love and hatred lies not in anti-Judaism but in drawing out the implications of covenantal solidarity.[28] We recall that at Qumran covenanters promised not to allow their anger at the 'men of the pit' to subside until God's judgement would deal with them. Those 'of the pit' were decidedly not 'neighbours' to be loved. Whereas to leave them to the imminent eschatological judgement of God is in keeping with God's prerogative, to *love* them would be to break solidarity with God. To pledge unremitting hatred to God's enemies was thus a pledge of loyalty and fidelity to God. Psalm 139 captures this perfectly, pronouncing what amounts to a curse on God's enemies, precisely as evidence of the integrity of the psalmist's loyalty to God:

> O that you would kill the wicked, O God,
> and that the bloodthirsty would depart from me—
> those who speak of you maliciously,
> and lift themselves up against you for evil!
>
> *Do I not hate those who hate you, O LORD?*
> *And do I not loathe those who rise up against you?*
> *I hate them with perfect hatred;*
> *I count them my enemies.*
>
> Search me, O God, and know my heart;
> test me and know my thoughts.
> See if there is any wicked way in me,
> and lead me in the way everlasting. (Ps. 139.19–24; emphasis
>   added)

The pairing of neighbour love with enemy hatred is thus not calumny against inherited tradition but a succinct characterization of the reverse side of the coin of neighbourly love. In effect, your enemies are my enemies; you can count on me! 'Neighbour', as understood in Leviticus 19, means 'fellow member of the covenant community' – one of 'us'. Enemies are those who threaten that community of solidarity,

---

[28] See, e.g., Meier, *Marginal Jew*, 4, 532–9. How dissimilar Jesus' terse command to 'love enemies' is to the wisdom of his age, whether within or outside the Jewish community, is debated. Meier insists on its uniqueness, whereas others parse such love as kind treatment and non-retaliation, and thus find many parallels. See, e.g., Klassen, *Love of Enemies*; Pheme Perkins, *Love Commands in the New Testament* (New York: Paulist, 1982), 28–38.

whoever they are.[29] It is unlikely that such a pairing of love and hatred would have shocked Jesus' or Matthew's contemporaries. What might well have shocked them is Jesus' call to love not just neighbours but enemies, those who threaten the very bonds 'neighbour' signifies.

Matthew's Jesus compounds the shock by stating that such strange love is required of all those who would be 'sons of [their] father in heaven' (5.45).[30] The Wisdom tradition of Israel is close at hand. The just or the righteous (Heb. *tzaddik*; Gk *dikaios*)[31] are true to the covenant with God, obey the will of God, most especially as expressed in Torah. They keep their distance from injustice or unrighteousness, and thus also from the unjust. In doing so, they show themselves to be 'sons of God' (e.g. Wisd. 2.18).[32] Covenant loyalty, living in keeping with God's will, Jesus insists surprisingly, requires the imitation of a God who loves enemies. This is thus nothing less than 'love turned inside out', covenant solidarity directed toward enemies.

The wisdom character of this teaching is also shown in the way in which creation is drawn into this love. God *makes* the sun to rise and the rain to fall on both the just and the unjust (Matt. 5.45). The fact that on any given day that which makes life possible is lavishly bestowed on those who threaten that very life with violence and oppression is nothing other than divine love for God's rebellious and often violent creatures. The dawn of each new day is, in the light of the pervasiveness of injustice, oppression and violence, nothing less than a love that risks being mistaken for impunity on the part of the violent or callousness on the part of their victims. But it is a way of deliberately keeping the future open for turning from violence

---

[29] Richard Horsley parses 'enemy' as the hostile member of the local community ('Ethics and Exegesis: "Love Your enemies" and the Doctrine of Non-violence', *JAAR* LIV/1 (1986), 3–32 (22–4)); Weaver identifies enemies as hostile fellow Jews ('Transforming Nonresistance', 52). I agree with Barbara Reid ('Violent Endings', 245–6), etc., that the plural is to be taken as inclusive rather than limiting. 'Enemies' might be the neighbourhood bully, hostile and persecuting religious authorities, but also imperial overlords and their enforcers.

[30] Recall that in the beatitudes it is peacemakers who are called 'sons of God' (Matt. 5.9).

[31] See especially the figure of the 'just' in Wisd. 2—5 and the Servant in Isa. 53 on which it is based. See also Gottlob Schrenk, 'δίκη, κτλ.', *TDNT* 2.182–91.

[32] Interestingly, the *dikaios* is identified in the Wisdom of Solomon as 'son of God' (2.18), an identification that is reflected in the words of the centurion when looking on the suffering of Jesus on the cross. Mark has him referring to Jesus as 'a son of God' (Mark 15.39//Matt. 27.54), Luke as a 'just one' (*dikaios*; Luke 23.47).

to love, for true repentance and reconciliation. To love enemies is thus to imitate such a 'father in heaven' as 'sons' (and daughters) of such a scandalously loving God.

This antithesis, and with it the antitheses as a whole, ends with the imperative to 'be perfect (*teleios*) as your heavenly Father is perfect' (5.48). Luke's parallel in 6.36 reads: 'Be merciful (*oiktirmōn*), just as your Father is merciful!' Is Matthew altering mercy into a demand for perfection? No one doubts that it is possible for persons to be merciful. But perfect?

Teleios is typically translated as 'perfect' but would more likely in the Aramaic have had overtones of wholeness or completeness.[33] But even that does not fully mitigate the shock. Wisdom of Solomon 11 and 12, a relatively contemporaneous Jewish wisdom writing, provides a glimpse at the close relationship between mercy and perfection.

> 11.23 *But you are merciful* (eleeis) *to all, for you can do all things,*
> and you overlook people's sins, so that they may repent.
> 24 For you love all things that exist,
> and detest none of the things that you have made,
> for you would not have made anything if you had hated it.
> . . .
> 26 You spare all things, for they are yours, O Lord, you who love the living.
> . . .
> 12.16 For your strength is the source of righteousness,
> and *your sovereignty over all causes you to spare all.*
> 17 For you *show your strength when people doubt the completeness* (or 'perfection' *teleiotēs*)[34] *of your power,* and you rebuke any insolence among those who know it.
> 18 Although you are sovereign in strength, you judge with mildness,
> and with great forbearance (*pheidō*) you govern us;[35] for you have power to act whenever you choose.
> 19 Through such works you have taught your people
> that the righteous [or the just] must be kind,

---

[33] Deut. 18.13 demands that the people entering the land be *teleios*, thus having overtones of 'holy' (Hays, *Moral Vision*, 328).

[34] Compare '*teleios*' in Matt. 5.48.

[35] A more slavish translation of the Greek reflects the relationship of sovereignty to mildness and patience more clearly: 'But/and controlling things (*despozō*) with power, you judge with clemency (*epieikeia*), and with all restraint (*pheidō*) you rule us, for you do whatever you wish.'

and you have filled your children (lit. 'sons') with good hope,
because you give repentance for sins.

(Wisd. 11.21–26; 12.16–19; emphasis added)

Enemy love is 'perfection', in that it seeks repentance and restoration of creation; it is 'mercy', in that it creates the space for repentance.[36] Moreover, by linking enemy love to 'sonship', Matthew makes it clear that it is the exercise not of victimhood but of sovereignty and power, however much, as in the case of the Messiah Jesus, it looks like power-lessness vis-à-vis violence.

We return briefly to the previous antithesis in Matthew 5.38–42. Along with Wink and many others we earlier viewed the parable-like examples of responses to violence as 'focal instances' of 'defiant vulnerability', creative strategies intended to take the initiative away from victimizers, and thus break the cycles and spirals of violence. Such a reading comports well with an activist understanding of peace-making. But when read in close connection to the command to love enemies in 5.43–48, it becomes apparent that *by itself* such a reading is not complete.

First, love is not the same as strategy or tactic, as much as they might serve as love's devices. Non-retaliation, even non-violence, is not the same thing as love, as much as love might well demand such. True, love is not primarily an emotion or 'feeling' but it is creativity driven by a deep and persistent desire to see good for the other, including the enemy, regardless of whether it is reciprocated.

Second, such love is not only characterized by what it *does* but also by what it might *not* do, that is, by its patience, its forbearance, by keeping the future open in a way that looks maddeningly passive vis-à-vis violence, and might in fact be taken as abject weakness by the violent. Enemy love does surely have an objective or goal, namely, repentance and then reconciliation, and thus a transformation of the relationship.[37] Such patient love is both hopeful and scandalously

---

[36] For a fuller discussion of the close relationship between Wisdom and Solomon and our present text, see Thomas R. Yoder Neufeld, 'Power, Love, and Creation: The Mercy of the Divine Warrior in the Wisdom of Solomon', in *Peace and Justice Shall Embrace: Power and Theopolitics in the Bible* (ed. Ted Grimsrud and Loren L. Johns; Millard Lind Festschrift; Telford, PA: Pandora Press US, 1999), 174–91.

[37] E.g. Schottroff, 'Non-violence', 14, 23. Meier and others disagree that there is any quid pro quo to this love (*Marginal Jew*, 4, 530 and literature cited there).

non-coercive, however, as is implied in the use of sun and rain as metaphors for enemy love (Matt. 5.45). It is risky in the extreme, in that it opens up a space violence might fill. Hence the frequent charge of moral irresponsibility. Interestingly, whereas today it is the violence of judgement and the imagery of a forcefully intervening God that causes offence, in the Bible itself it is at least as often the patience and forbearance of God in view of injustice and violence that puzzles and enrages victims. The urgent question of the martyrs under the altar in Revelation 6.10 – 'How long, O Lord?' – echoes a theme that pervades the Scriptures. Matthew 5, as also Wisdom 11 and 12, explain this as the love of a creator for errant creation, providing yet another day for 'turning', for repentance from violence and enmity.[38]

By its very nature, however, patience has its limit, even as that limit remains hidden in the mystery of God's love. Matthew may well stress eschatological judgement with a violence that many scholars do not wish to attribute to Jesus,[39] but at no point is it ever questioned anywhere by anyone in the New Testament, including specifically also in the Sermon on the Mount, as we see in the antitheses on hatred and adultery (5.22, 30), that at the 'end' everyone will face the judge. We will encounter this apparent conundrum again. But it is mercy, fuelled by love, and not non-violence that informs enemy love. And mercy is unintelligible apart from judgement. It is that which gives love of enemies its edge in the Sermons on the Mount and Plain. Love destabilizes any systems or rigid expectations, whether violent or non-violent, anchoring the treatment of the enemy in a much deeper and more resilient and at the same time pliable place. It is love for all, including enemies, that risks all by creating the space (sun and rain) to exercise the creativity (cheek, shirt, second mile and open wallet) with which to 'kill' enmity.

To be sure, there is much teachable wisdom to be garnered in the practice of such creativity. Witness the non-violent liberation movements, conflict transformation initiatives and peace study programmes. While love gives rise and sustains a great deal of this creativity, love of enemies is neither constrained by nor satisfied with the practical wisdom of tactics and strategies, and will persist even when those

---

[38] 2 Pet. 3.8–10 reflects this sovereign patience that can be most trying for those yearning for liberation from violence.

[39] Neville, 'Toward a Teleology of Peace', 131–61.

practices have failed 'this time'. As Paul asserts in 1 Corinthians 13, love is beyond a calculus of success. The love of enemies, as we will see later, is even willing to be defeated by those enemies, to the point of crucifixion, if that is what it takes to reconcile with them, as Paul also makes clear in Romans 5.10 (more on that in Chapter 5). Put bluntly, the love of enemies cannot be separated from suffering and, finally, the cross.

Third, such vulnerability is chosen with full confidence in the vindication of God. As Luke 6.35 reminds readers, a great, if unsought, reward awaits lovers of enemies. This conviction is deeply ingrained in the paradigmatic figure of the 'just' or 'righteous one'. In choosing to remain faithful to God's will, the just person is deliberately vulnerable, 'turning his cheek to the smiter' (Lam. 3.30), like a 'lamb that is led to the slaughter' (Isa. 53.7). It is not difficult to see the degree to which this paradigm provides the lens through which evangelists and apostles view Jesus. However, as Habakkuk 2.4 states: 'The just will live by faith', both by his or her own faithfulness and trust in God, as the Hebrew has it, and by the faithfulness of God, as the LXX has it.[40] The beatitudes in both Luke (6.20–23) and Matthew (5.3–12) reflect this paradigmatic suffering of the just, as they do a God whose faithfulness both provides a model for their chosen vulnerability as well as a promise of a new future without violence.

> ₉ Blessed are the peacemakers, for they will be called children ('sons') of God.
> ₁₀ Blessed are those who are persecuted for righteousness' sake, for theirs is the kingdom of heaven.
> ₁₁ Blessed are you when people revile you and persecute you and utter all kinds of evil against you falsely on my account. ₁₂ Rejoice and be glad, for your reward is great in heaven, for in the same way they persecuted the prophets who were before you.   (Matt. 5.9–12)

Biblically such deliberate vulnerability and willing suffering thus only makes sense in the light of divine vindication, even when that vindication is understood eschatologically as judgement and resurrection. There is hope but no guarantee that turning the cheek, taking off one's last bit of clothing, or walking the forbidden mile will subvert

---

[40] The verse is cited in Rom. 1.17; Gal. 3.11; Heb. 10.38.

and end the cycle of violence. There is hope but no guarantee that loving enemies will kill enmity. To take a vindicating God out of the picture as a relic of violence transforms these parabolic actions from expressions of patient and vulnerable love into tactics that have to 'work', which can and must be abandoned when they do not.

Viewed in this light, the translation 'Do not resist the evil one!' is not a mistake. It is highly regrettable that English cannot retain the ambiguity of the Greek, one that leaves the reader no secure place against either the summons to patient suffering (*non*-resistance) or the call to creative subversion (non-violent resistance).[41] Both alternatives are inadequate by themselves. It is love that keeps such a stance from degenerating into passivity. It is love that gives scandalous elasticity to patience, and charges such patience with hope and the readiness to suffer rather than to inflict suffering. It is love, and not a commitment to the superior practicality of non-violence, that is willing to risk the disappointment represented by the cross, in the knowledge, gained after Good Friday, that even that calamity can serve, in the ingenuity of the divine peacemaker, to bring about salvation for the enemies (Rom. 5; Eph. 2).[42]

Fourth, the instruction to love the enemy is so general as to include all enemies. However, as cheek, shirt, mile and wallet indicate, it is always also so specific as to include all enemies, from neighbourhood and church to empire. There is no enmity in which the sons and daughters of God might find themselves in which love is not to be given full reign. At the same time, the terseness of Jesus' command and the parable-like nature of the 'case studies' make Jesus' teaching ill suited for ethical casuistry. Such casuistry has too often allowed Christians to know ahead of time where to draw lines for when such deliberate vulnerability of love is *not* or *no longer* to be practised.[43]

We ask then, finally, how this tradition of non-retaliation and enemy love relates to violence. Our assessment is ambiguous. It depends on who is doing the reading and interpretation. On the one hand,

---

[41] Thomas R. Yoder Neufeld, 'Resistance and Nonresistance: The Two Legs of a Biblical Peace Stance', *Conrad Grebel Review* 21 (2003), 56–81.

[42] Klassen, *Love of Enemies*, 88.

[43] Richard Hays conveniently summarizes the evasion techniques employed in the Christian tradition to slip out from under Jesus' love of enemies command (*Moral Vision*, 320). The long history of justified violence since at least Augustine finds repeated if sometimes reluctant defenders among Christian ethicists.

when divorced from enemy love, our texts can underwrite forms of shaming or goading to further violence or encourage exposure of the adversary or enemy to the anticipated violence of final judgement. On the other hand, the strategies implied by the parabolic examples can be examples of creative non-violence, and have spawned a great deal of courageous and creative non-violent engagement for peace and justice. They become instances of violence subversion and an invitation to reconciliation when exercised by a love that is deliberately vulnerable and risk-taking in hopes of 'killing enmity'. But that deliberate 'non-resistant' stance is precisely what opens it to the charge of leaving the door open to yet more violence. Perhaps the most famous case illustrating this conundrum is Dietrich Bonhoeffer who, as author of the *Cost of Discipleship*, nevertheless participated in the plot to murder Hitler.

The practical challenges of such enemy love are *necessarily* great, since it is *enemies* who are loved – enemies who are seldom on the lookout for opportunities for reconciliation. It thus remains *necessarily* an open question as to whether enemy love reduces violence or opens space for it. The answer will be different for those experiencing violence at the hands of the powerful and the callous, and for those for whom violence is readily at hand in the exercise of social responsibility.[44] The moment Jesus' teaching went beyond the Galilean neighbourhood and headed for Jerusalem, and then beyond that into the empire, and over time into the palace itself, the summons to love 'our' enemies would need to be heard again and again in relation to new specific contexts of violence. Just so, as 'bizarre' as the mini-parables were in Jesus' and then in Matthew's and Luke's settings, so they must continue to be. Jesus' instructions, regardless of whether one is hearing them as a migrant worker or as a president, will always have about them a maddening mix of a counter-cultural and counter-intuitive ideal and a demand to practise such love in relation to real enemies. It is an ethic that cannot be divorced from confidence in a just and merciful God whose reign will be asserted in the end.

---

[44] For example, even from within the pacifist traditions there are those in the wake of events such as the Rwanda genocide who urge the adoption of the doctrine of the 'Responsibility to Protect' vulnerable populations, or who make room for the paradigm of policing rather than war as a way of exerting limited force in the interests of protection and public order. E.g. Gerald W. Schlabach, ed., *Just Policing, Not War: An Alternative Response to World Violence* (Collegeville, MN: Liturgical Press, 2007).

3

Forgive, or else!

Forgiveness surely stands alongside love of enemies as a prime characteristic of Jesus in popular imagination. The relationship of forgiveness to the issue of violence is obvious, both as a response to violation and, as in the case of love for enemies, as a door left open to it. In this chapter the sounding or core sample we will take is an exploration of another 'sermon', this time a 'Sermon on Living in Community' in Matthew 18, in particular the parable of the Unforgiving Slave in verses 23–35. As in the previous chapter we encounter the clash between grace and violence, only now with a particular focus on forgiveness. What emerges even more prominently this time is the theme of judgement. In the process we will also briefly examine the role and nature of parables, and the context of this immediate parable within the discourse on communal relations in Matthew 18.

The parable of the Unforgiving Slave

In the parable of the Unforgiving Slave Jesus likens the kingdom of heaven to a king who wishes to settle accounts with his slaves. Crossan aptly refers to it as a 'small masterpiece of dramatic choreography' in three 'scenes'.[1] In the first one, a slave owes an absurdly large sum of ten thousand talents.[2] Naturally, the slave is unable to pay,

---

[1] John Dominic Crossan, *In Parables: The Challenge of the Historical Jesus* (New York/London: Harper & Row, 1973), 106. For full commentary and discussion of literature see the numerous commentaries, but also, e.g., Herzog, *Parables as Subversive Speech: Jesus as Pedagogue of the Oppressed* (Louisville, KY: John Knox, 1994), 131–49; Arland J. Hultgren, *The Parables of Jesus: A Commentary* (Grand Rapids, MI/Cambridge: Eerdmans, 2000), 21–33; Klyne R. Snodgrass, *Stories with Intent: A Comprehensive Guide to the Parables of Jesus* (Grand Rapids, MI/Cambridge: Eerdmans, 2008), 61–77.

[2] One talent was the equivalent of 6,000 denarii. One denarius was worth one day's labour. To owe 10,000 talents, or 60 million denarii, would mean that the slave owed 164,000 years of labour. Marvin A. Powell, 'Weights and Measures', *ABD* 6.907–8; Snodgrass, *Stories with Intent*, 66; Ched Myers and Elaine Enns, *Ambassadors of Reconciliation:*

and so the king orders him, his family and all his possessions sold as compensation. The slave prostrates himself, pleading for patience, assuring the king that he will repay all. The master is moved with pity (*splanchnizomai*)[3] and not only releases him but also cancels his entire 'loan'.

In the scene that now follows, that very same slave, upon meeting a fellow slave who owes him the comparatively small amount of one hundred denarii,[4] violently demands payment in full. When that slave pleads for mercy exactly as the first slave had earlier (cf. vv. 26 and 28), he has him thrown into prison.

In the final scene, upon learning of this from other slaves, the lord accuses the slave of not acting mercifully (*eleeō*) as he himself had, and hands him over to the torturers until the entire debt is repaid (we are surely meant to recall that the debt is unpayable). As if that were not enough of a jolt, the parable ends with a pointed warning that should Jesus' disciples not forgive 'from [their] hearts', the 'heavenly father' will do to them as the king did to the unforgiving slave (18.35).

While the parable may seem like a straightforward tale with an unambiguous lesson about the importance of forgiveness, it has become a 'theological briar patch',[5] not least because of the violence that permeates the parable. The king is both severe and magnanimous in extremes. Slaves grovel, knowing their fate, should there be no mercy. The threat of torture serves as a motivation for forgiveness. What is perhaps most striking is that this tale is placed in immediate proximity with Jesus' summons to boundless grace. In order to analyse our 'core sample', we will briefly examine the nature of parables, as well as the immediate context in which Matthew has placed this parable. We are again guided in our investigation by the question of violence.

Vol 1, New Testament Reflections on Restorative Justice and Peacemaking (Maryknoll, NY: Orbis Books, 2009), 76. So even if we imagine a royal court, the amounts are no doubt deliberately exaggerated.

[3] A term most often associated with Jesus' own compassion for those who suffer (e.g. Mark 6.34//Matt. 9.36; Mark 8.2//Matt. 15.32), but also of the Samaritan and the 'prodigal' father (Luke 10.33; 15.20).

[4] One denarius was the equivalent to one day's labour.

[5] Snodgrass, *Stories with Intent*, 61.

Parables

Parables figure prominently in the teaching of Jesus, as depicted in the Synoptic Gospels as well as in popular imagination. No doubt with some exaggeration Mark and Matthew claim that Jesus never taught other than in parables (Mark 4.34–35; Matt. 13.34–35).[6] Sometimes short and pithy sayings, at other times stories,[7] parables were his favourite means of alerting his hearers to both the present and impending 'kingdom of God' or 'heaven'. 'The kingdom of God (or of heaven) is like . . .' introduces many of his parables.

'Kingdom' translates *basileia*, variously translated also as 'reign', 'dominion' or even as 'imperial rule'.[8] The term has deep roots in the ancient traditions of Israel in which God is conceived of as cosmic sovereign, whose power and glory is likened to that of an earthly monarch. God is 'king' as creator, liberator, warrior, lawgiver and judge. As metaphor the '*basileia* of God' or 'of heaven' (Matthew's euphemism for 'God') thus draws on prevailing notions of authority, power and control. But when Jesus employs it, those associations are as often as not employed for the purpose of challenging those notions.

There is thus an enigmatic character to the parables. On the one hand, they are highly accessible forms of communication. Jesus' parables do not presuppose learning or great intelligence. They are hospitable to anyone 'with ears to hear'. They are easily retold. They typically fuse the familiar with the element of surprise, with a twist. Like a good joke, they leave it to the hearer to 'get it'. In that sense they are deeply respectful of listeners and (re)tellers, inviting their participation in determining the parable's import.

On the other, that also makes them highly discriminatory. Just as jokes sift those with a sense of humour from dullards who need the joke explained, so parables sift those 'with ears' open to the *basileia*

---

[6] Surprisingly, the Gospel of John contains none of the parables we know from the Synoptics and never uses the term 'parable'. Instead, John uses the term *paroimia*, often translated as 'figure of speech', in relation to the sheep, shepherd and sheepfold sayings in 10.6 and in the farewell discourse in 16.25.

[7] It is apparent then why it might be difficult if not impossible to find one definition that encompasses all of the parables. See most recently Snodgrass, *Stories with Intent*, 7–22. See also my discussion in *Recovering Jesus: The Witness of the New Testament* (Grand Rapids, MI: Brazos; London: SPCK, 2007), 159–82.

[8] The choice of the Jesus Seminar's Scholars Version.

of God from those closed to it and its demands.[9] In that sense the parables participate in the judgement of God, not only by warning of it but also through their function of 'sifting' the audience for those 'with ears'. A very wide understanding of violence might thus raise questions both about the metaphor of kingdom and the 'judgement' dimension of parables, most especially when heightened with the ambience of eschatological urgency.

Parables are very different from each other, both in style and content. Some express breathtaking love and generosity, such as the familiar Lukan parables, the Good Samaritan (10.25–37) and the Prodigal Son (15.11–32). Others evoke scenes all too familiar to an audience without means and social standing, such as the destitute but stubbornly persistent widow who pesters a callous judge into doing right by her (Luke 18.1–8), or day labourers still having no work at the end of the day (Matt. 20.1–16). By shining a light on such commonly experienced injustices, Jesus lays bare the world of abuse and violence his audience knows well. Remarkably, in the hands of the evangelists these very same parables become 'lessons' in persistent prayer and unearned grace. Is it possible that such parables are both exposé and lesson, requiring interpreters to be extraordinarily nimble?

Many parables freely employ the vocabulary of violence. Most often it serves to warn of judgement. The phrase 'weeping and gnashing of teeth', even though unique to Matthew, captures well the character of such parables of warning or threat.[10] Luke 12 is a virtual storehouse of warnings of judgement, including the parable of the slave who in his master's absence callously abuses his fellow slaves (12.42–46// Matt. 24.45–51). Upon being discovered, he is 'cut into pieces' by his angry master (Luke 12.46). Jesus then utters the frightful words: 'I came to bring fire to the earth, and how I wish it were already kindled! . . . Do you think that I have come to bring peace to the

---

[9] For example, Isa. 6.9, 10, in which the prophet is given words to speak that will stop the ears and close the eyes of the people, is quoted in immediate relation to the parables in Matt. 13.10–17; Mark 4.10–12; and Luke 8.9, 10, indicating an awareness of the role of parables in divine judgement; cf. the way John uses that same passage to show the 'sifting' mechanism of the 'signs' that serve much like enacted parables (John 12.40).

[10] For a thorough examination of the issue of violence in Matthew and an evaluation of scholarly attempts to wrestle with it, see David J. Neville, 'Toward a Teleology of Peace: Contesting Matthew's Violent Eschatology', *JSNT* 30/2 (2007), 131–61.

earth? No, I tell you, but rather division!' (Luke 12.49, 51; 'sword', says Matthew's Jesus in 10.35). The evangelists do not depict Jesus as shy about using the language of violence to describe his mission and its effect. Conflict, division and terrifying judgement are not anomalies in the parables of Jesus or in his teaching as a whole.[11] In a real sense, parables are by their very nature a way of bringing 'division'.

Some parables, such as the familiar parable of the Great Banquet (Matt. 22.2–14//Luke 14.16–24), place generosity, grace and judgement in immediate proximity to each other. The parable has become well known for its theme of generosity toward those otherwise never invited to a banquet. The VIPs have all found a reason to refuse the invitation and, in Matthew's version, have violently attacked the king's servants issuing the invitation. Luke's banquet giver, angry at the VIPs' excuses, has his slave collect folks from the margins of society, vowing never to let the initially invited guests taste the food. In Matthew, the king's anger turns into a massacre by his troops (22.7), and only then into an invitation to all and sundry. Matthew then attaches to this what appears to be a once freestanding parable of a man who is discovered not to have proper wedding attire. He concludes with the cryptic saying: 'Many are called, few are chosen' (22.14). Baffling hospitality stands next to equally shocking discrimination. Do we hear in this parable the voice of Jesus? Or is Matthew retelling the parable with a particularly violent twist at odds with the otherwise generous hospitality of Jesus?

Matthew 18: a 'sermon' on relationships within the community

Questions such as this appear with particular vividness in the parable of the Unforgiving Slave in Matthew 18.23–35. But before engaging with that parable directly we need to attend to the immediate setting into which Matthew has placed the parable. Regrettably there is not the space to give the whole of Matthew 18 full attention, since it is

---

[11] Marius Reiser, *Jesus and Judgment: The Eschatological Proclamation in Its Jewish Context* (trans. Linda M. Maloney; Minneapolis, MN: Fortress Press, 1997); Stephen H. Travis, *Christ and the Judgement of God: The Limits of Divine Retribution in New Testament Thought* (Peabody, MA: Hendrickson/Milton Keynes: Paternoster, 2008).

so rich in relation to our question of violence.[12] I will thus do little more than identify some of the features so as to set the context for a closer reading of the parable.

Matthew 18 is the fourth of Matthew's five major discourses.[13] As in the first discourse, the Sermon on the Mount (Matt. 5—7), Jesus' teachings are directed to his students. In this discourse, however, they are not being instructed in how to relate to those outside their circle but rather largely to relationships within the *ekklēsia*.[14] The discourse comprises the whole of Matthew 18, in which, as in the Sermon on the Mount, Matthew collates and organizes Jesus' teachings on status, conflict, sin, confrontation, restoration and forgiveness.

Matthew 18 begins with the disciples' question: 'Who is the greatest in the kingdom of heaven'? Matthew uses that question to group a set of Jesus' sayings into a discourse around the themes of power, vulnerability, patience, discipline and forgiveness within the *ekklēsia*. Jesus responds to the disciples' question by placing a child (*paidion*) before his status-oriented and competitive students. It is the child, the embodiment of insignificance and vulnerability, who is at the same time the very epitome of greatness in the *basileia* of God (vv. 3, 4).[15] As if that were not enough to overturn the applecart, Jesus then identifies himself with these inconsequential members of the community: 'Whoever receives one such child in my name receives me' (v. 5).[16]

---

[12] Craig S. Keener, *A Commentary on the Gospel of Matthew* (Grand Rapids, MI/Cambridge: Eerdmans, 1999), 447–61, and scholarship cited there.

[13] The Sermon on the Mount in chapters 5—7, the Missionary Discourse in chapter 10, the parables of the Kingdom in chapter 13, the Community Relations in chapter 18, and Apocalypse in chapters 24—25.

[14] I leave the term untranslated, since 'church' is anachronistic. *Ekklēsia* means 'assembly of those called out', and at the time of Jesus or of Matthew had no uniquely 'Christian' meaning as 'church' does. If it goes back to Jesus, it would refer either to Jews in community or to the community of his followers and disciples; in the case of Matthew, it refers to the post-Easter cells of believers in Jesus, made up of both Jews and Gentiles.

[15] The contrast is heightened by the fact that *paidion* is the diminutive of *pais*, which can mean 'child' and also 'young slave', reflecting the social standing of children in Jesus' time. See Keener, *Commentary*, 447–8, and extensive secondary literature cited there.

[16] See also the parable of the Sheep and the Goats in Matt. 25.31–46, especially vv. 40 and 45.

This radical subversion of status is matched by the rage directed at those who exploit (lit. 'scandalize' as in 'cause to stumble')[17] the vulnerability of the 'little ones' (*mikroi*). Matthew takes up a tradition of very harsh words preserved earlier in Mark 9.42–48, and found in terse form in Luke 17.1–2. A millstone should be hung around the necks of abusers and they should be drowned (v. 6)! Then, recalling the Sermon on the Mount (5.27–30), Jesus warns that it is better to amputate one's own offending limb or organ than to have to face the 'Gehenna of fire' (vv. 8, 9). The rage of Jesus, indeed God's, is violent in the extreme, but ironically a measure of the gravity of violence, most especially against 'little ones'. Small wonder that in Luke the disciples are left pleading: 'Increase our faith!' (17.5).

The violence of this imagery, reflective of a mix of extreme care for the vulnerable and white-hot rage at violence and abuse, is no doubt meant to serve as a measure of the gravity of abuse, and at the same time as a warning of the reckoning to come for those who persist in such violence and abuse ('Woe!' in v. 7).[18] After all, these 'little ones' may seem like an easy mark, but they all have representatives 'before the face of God', just to emphasize the divine attentiveness to violence against the vulnerable (v. 11). Whereas the 'world' (*kosmos*) is singled out as the source of stumbling, Matthew's setting allows us to see the 'scandalizers' as not simply outsiders but also members of the community who abuse their positions of power.[19]

The focus shifts now from warnings of judgement to rescue. With the parable of the lost sheep (vv. 10–14; cf. Luke 15.4–7) Jesus makes clear that should even one of these 'little ones' stumble and get lost, falling prey to the corrupting influence of those more powerful, no effort is to be spared to rescue them. The parable highlights the value of the least and most vulnerable in the eyes of God, and serves to urge the same care on the part of Jesus' disciples.

---

[17] Lev. 19.14 commands against putting up a stumbling block (LXX *skandalon*) before the blind. Here that prohibition is extended to all who are vulnerable to 'falling'.

[18] The Scholar's Version: 'Damn the world for the snares it sets!'

[19] In Luke 17.1–2 the words or warning are explicitly addressed to the disciples.

Matthew now appends a tradition often called the 'Rule of Christ' (vv. 15–20).[20] Matthew intends this well-worn nugget[21] on communal discipline and restoration to serve as an example of how the *ekklēsia* can bring such 'lost' sheep back into the fold. In the light of the parable at the end of the discourse, in which there are both outrageously huge and relatively small debts, it seems clear that Matthew wishes both the lost 'little ones' and those who have led them astray to be included in the 'brother or sister' in 18.15.

Those who are erring are to be confronted and their wrongful actions laid bare (*elenchō*) to them, with the intention of 'gaining' them back. Such 'exposing' or 'reproving' is nothing other than love of neighbour at work, as Leviticus 19.17–18 indicates.[22]

> 17 You shall not hate in your heart anyone of your kin; you shall reprove (LXX *elenchō*) your neighbour, or you will incur guilt yourself. 18 You shall not take vengeance or bear a grudge against any of your people, but you shall love your neighbour as yourself: I am the LORD.

Note that such love is exercised in Leviticus against the backdrop of judgement. Not to engage the sister or the brother over errant behaviour is to incur guilt oneself, not least by exposing the sister or brother to the judgement of God. Nothing guarantees that this will work, as anyone knows who has ever followed even the most enlightened alternative dispute resolution procedures. Should the brother or sister resist repeated and intensified efforts at setting things right, the offender is to be treated like a 'Gentile and a tax collector' (v. 17).

---

[20] For both commentary and history of interpretation and application, see John Howard Yoder, 'Practicing the Rule of Christ', in *Virtues and Practices in the Christian Tradition: Christian Ethics after MacIntyre* (ed. Nancey Murphy, Brad J. Kallenberg and Mark Thiessen Nation; Harrisburg, PA: Trinity Press International, 1997), 132–60.

[21] Notice the 'legal' structure of the saying: 'If . . . then'. There is some textual ambiguity as to whether the brother or sister sins 'against you' or whether one is to act simply when observing the transgression of a fellow member of the covenant community. The usually most reliable manuscripts do not contain 'against you'.

[22] Recall the importance of Lev. 19.17 in the New Testament: e.g. Matt. 22.37–40//Mark 12.29–34; Rom. 13.8–10; 1 Cor. 13; Gal. 5.14; James 2.8; 1 John 4. Of importance here is that love of neighbour or fellow member of the covenant community is linked most immediately to the 'laying bare' (LXX *elenchō*) of the other's transgression. This is echoed in Eph. 4.25–27; see Thomas R. Yoder Neufeld, *Ephesians* (BCBC; Scottdale, PA/Waterloo, ON: Herald, 2002), 209–13, 219–222, and literature cited there.

That sounds very much like a reversion to stereotype and prejudice, and quickly brings to mind the kind of expulsion and shunning we view in our own day as a form of violence.[23] However, there is good reason not to view this reference to Gentiles and tax collectors as grace having run out. We should remember that Jesus is remembered throughout the Gospels, including Matthew, as consorting scandalously with tax collectors and 'sinners' (see, e.g., Matt. 11.19). We recall too that in Matthew 5.43–48 God's sun and rain are bestowed by an enemy-loving God on both just and the unjust. And surely Matthew and his readers knew well that the *ekklēsia* to whom this gospel was addressed included precisely 'Gentiles'. It should not elude us that the tradition assigned this Gospel to the tax collector Matthew himself (Matt. 10.3). In no way can this be taken to call for closure. On the contrary, it means that the persistent sinner is to be pursued with even more persistent love.[24]

Even so, in our day the 'Rule of Christ' is often viewed as a form of communal coercion, of community violating the sanctity of the individual's freedom to choose. Indeed, most churches today have long since given up on such communal discipline. What is missed is the astonishing respect shown for the gathered community in this tradition. Even two or three can count on the presence of the (risen) Messiah as they exercise the responsibility to 'bind and loose', to decide what is normally left to God (v. 18). Whether the 'two or three' represents a kind of quorum of 'witnesses', à la Deuteronomy 17.6–7, or whether this is simply a way of stressing how small an instance of community can be and still 'make it stick' in heaven, does not change the fact that together with Jesus they do represent a quorum. It is the gathered community, and not only authorized individuals, whether priests or prophets, that exercises this task of seeking and correcting lost and errant members of the community. And with them is the Shekinah, Jesus as 'God with us'.[25]

Some sheep keep getting lost, trying the patience of the community to breaking point. Peter's question regarding how often one

---

[23] One of the first people with whom I discussed this present book asked me whether I would be addressing the issue of shunning. I have not forgotten that that was the very first issue raised, and that for that reason alone a 'broad' definition of violence would need to be operative in this investigation (see Chapter 1).

[24] So also Myers and Enns, *Ambassadors*, 68.

[25] Keener, *Commentary*, 455–6.

is to forgive is intended to illustrate the strain of such communal patience. 'Is seven times enough?' (18.21). Given that biblically the number seven already symbolizes fullness or completion, Jesus' answer here is rather surprising: 'Seventy times seven!'[26] In short, enough is never enough. Forgiveness, as Jesus conceives it, thus participates not only in the patient suffering but also in the radical if vulnerable hope we identified in the last chapter with love for enemies.

It is to this command that Matthew now appends the parable of the Unforgiving Slave, which thus serves as a climax to the discourse as a whole. Unlike some of the previous elements of this discourse, the parable is unique to Matthew.

Interpreting the parable of the Unforgiving Slave

A traditional interpretation of the parable reads it as a straightforward lesson on the importance of forgiveness, reinforcing the words of Jesus to Peter in 18.21–22. God forgives a debt greater than anyone could possibly ever repay. Recipients of such mercy are to do likewise, or they will face the severe judgement of God. This quid pro quo is familiar to us in a different form in the Lord's Prayer: 'Forgive us, as we have forgiven!' (Matt. 6.12, 14–15; Luke 11.4; Mark 11.25).[27]

Forgiveness is a non-negotiable 'must' for those wishing to participate in the kingdom of God. In that sense the parable is resolutely anti-retaliatory, and in that sense non-violent. But given the warning of judgement, most especially via its linkage to the king who throws the unforgiving slave to the torturers, it is also seen as using violence as a means of enforcing such non-violence.

Some questions arise upon closer reading, however. First, unlike the advice Jesus gives about repeated forgiveness in verse 22, the king forgives a virtually immeasurable amount, but only once. After that it's 'To the torturers!' The parable thus does not flow easily from the

---

[26] It matters little whether the answer is seventy times seven or seventy, as some variants have it. They suggest with equal force that keeping count is precisely *not* the point. Luke 17.4 simply has Jesus saying that the disciple is obligated to forgive the sinning brother, even if he repents seven times. It is quite evident that in Luke 'seven' already stands for an equivalent to 'as many times as needed'.

[27] There is a remarkable resonance between this reading of the parable and Ecclus. 27.30—28.7.

patience demanded in the preceding verses, despite the 'therefore' or 'for this reason' (*dia touto*) in verse 23.

Second, many readers are troubled by the stark contrast between the breathtaking mercy of the king, on the one hand, and both his initial ordering the slave and all he has to be sold into slavery and the final act of having him thrown to the torturers, on the other. That is difficult enough. But it is when this parable is said to provide an analogy for the kingdom of heaven (18.23),[28] and for the way God responds to lack of forgiveness, as verse 35 states unequivocally, that the questions take on great urgency, not least for those concerned about violence. How is this story 'like' the 'kingdom of heaven'? And how is this 'human king' like God? Is the God who magnanimously offers forgiveness the same God who 'promises them hellfire'?[29] Is God's grace conditional on being imitated? Does this parable inscribe violence into the very heart of how Jesus' message is recalled and depicted? In short, does this parable represent God in a light that is theologically difficult, if not unacceptable?[30] Answers to this will vary depending on the theological traditions from which this issue is engaged.

Scholars thus wonder whether this parable fits its present context and whether it goes back to Jesus at all. It is quite possible that the parable was placed by Matthew at the conclusion of the discourse in chapter 18 because of its theme of forgiveness. 'Therefore' (*dia touto*) in verse 23 may thus be little more than a device for stitching the parable to what has preceded it. As to whether it goes back to Jesus, most do not doubt its authenticity.[31] The fact that the parable does *not* follow easily from the previous passage argues against Matthew creating it for present purposes. But some see not only verse 23 but also verse 35 and perhaps also verse 34 as Matthean additions. In

---

[28] That is the usual meaning of *homoioō* (cf., e.g., Matt. 13.24; 18.23; 22.2; *homoiōthēsetai*, Matt. 25.1).

[29] Keener, *Commentary*, 461.

[30] See here especially Neville, 'Toward a Teleology of Peace', in particular the survey of scholarship on this point. Robert H. Gundry, *Matthew: A Commentary on His Literary and Theological Art* (Grand Rapids, MI: Eerdmans, 1982), 373, proposes not only that Matthew composes the parable but also that he wishes to identify the king with Jesus, which would only sharpen the issue for many.

[31] Exceptions are, e.g., Gundry, *Matthew*, 371–2, who sees it as Matthew's adaptation of the brief parable of two debtors in Luke 7.41–42; also Reiser, *Jesus and Judgment*, 273.

other words, the core of the present parable goes back to Jesus, but the highly vindictive tone is ascribed to Matthew.

Recent interpreters like William Herzog II as well as Ched Myers and Elaine Enns, for example, have suggested that Jesus is not opening a window on God at all but, rather like a 'political cartoon', exposing a brutal world of caprice and violence.[32] The 'human king' reflects not God but the tyranny familiar to Jesus' audience in the rule of Roman and Herodian overlords. Slaves are not stand-ins for members of the community but represent the 'retainer' class, high-level functionaries within the royal bureaucracy, running the day-to-day operations of the kingdom, chiefly the raising of extortionate taxes. Judging from the gargantuan amount owed and 'forgiven', both Jesus' and Matthew's audiences would have recognized in the first slave a chief tax officer, or what Myers and Enns aptly call the 'CFO' of the kingdom.[33] The other slaves in this story, including the hapless one who is throttled by the more highly positioned slave, would have been viewed as lower level functionaries within a bureaucracy permeated by cut-throat competition. The 'forgiveness' offered in this tale, which others view as an example of Jubilee generosity and justice,[34] has, according to Myers and Enns, 'little to do with grace, and everything to do with the kings' assessment that he has put a dissident retainer back in his place and/or averted long-term economic disaster through this one-time special amnesty'.[35] Similarly, according to Herzog, the king's 'decision to forgive the debt no less than his final withdrawal of mercy expresses his absolute power and total command'.[36] Apparent benevolence is quite obviously no more than a cynical device to strengthen the patronal ties binding slave to master. There is thus little if any moral distance between the forgiveness offered the slave and his being thrown to the torturers; both are intended equally to shore up tyrannical control.

This interpretation addresses the violence in the parable by distancing it from both the kingdom of heaven, from God and from Jesus'

---

[32] Herzog, *Parables*, 135; Myers and Enns, *Ambassadors*, 76.

[33] Myers and Enns, *Ambassadors*, 77.

[34] Sylvia C. Keesmaat, 'Strange Neighbors and Risky Care (Matt 18:21-35; Luke 14:7-14; Luke 10:25-37)', in *The Challenge of Jesus' Parables* (ed. Richard N. Longenecker; Grand Rapids, MI/Cambridge: Eerdmans, 2000), 263–85 (270); Snodgrass, *Stories with Intent*, 72.

[35] Myers and Enns, *Ambassadors*, 77.

[36] Herzog, *Parables*, 139.

message. The violence in the parable is a picture taken of a society the kingdom of God will *replace*. *Parabolē* means 'to throw one thing alongside another'. In this case Jesus intends stark contrast, not illuminating simile.

While this interpretation clearly illumines the 'story world'[37] of the parable, and certainly functions in this way as a 'warning parable' or 'cautionary tale',[38] it absolves Jesus from viewing God as 'violent' at the price of downloading that view onto the (re)teller of the parable, Matthew. By tying the parable to the theme of forgiveness initiated by Peter, and by identifying the rage of the human king with that of the 'heavenly father', Matthew in effect shows that he does not 'get' the parable he retells. More, he recasts it into the opposite of what Jesus presumably intended, which is not to give an insight into God and the kingdom of God but into the world it will do away with. He takes it to be a warning of God's judgement for those who do not forgive as God does, when he should have taken it as 'laying bare' the brutality of court. While this might 'solve' the problem of violence, many readers of the Scriptures will find pitting Matthew against Jesus a pill too large to swallow.

We should not be forced, however, into a choice we do not need to make, in which this parable is either a searing depiction of a recognizably violent world or a 'lesson' on forgiveness and violent judgement. Barbara Reid reminds us that there is always an 'is' and an 'is not' about parables.[39] Parables as often as not shock, frequently by using reprehensible characters, or offensive contexts, to make a point, as here. The 'story world' of a parable is often one recognizable to Jesus' and the evangelists' audiences, and as often as not a deeply troubling one, as here. That does not prevent such parables from 'teaching', even if the 'lesson' is learned the way one 'gets' a joke or catches irony. Parables are neither easily uncoded allegories nor unambiguous snapshots of a world going to hell. They are sometimes, as in this case, I would argue, deliberately disturbing stories, loaded with reprehensible characters and troubling circumstance, stretching analogies to the limit, all intended to impress themselves on the imagination.[40]

---

[37] Snodgrass, *Stories*, 73.

[38] Myers and Enns, *Ambassadors*, 71–2.

[39] Barbara E. Reid, OP, 'Violent Endings in Matthew's Parables and Christian Nonviolence', *CBQ* 66 (2004), 237–66 (254).

[40] Snodgrass, *Stories*, 28, 71.

Interpreting the parable exclusively as a social and political critique of empire and its system of domination might avoid the old allegorical or spiritualizing interpretations but may run as great a risk of being reductionist and potentially distorting. Whereas today's readers might well need educating on the economics and politics of Jesus' day, that would have been true neither of Jesus' nor of Matthew's audience. They would have had an easier time with the 'is' and 'is not'.

Even if we grant that Matthew has placed this parable into this 'sermon', and that he may well have (over)stressed the lesson in verse 35, is there a way in which we can read this parable as Jesus' teaching on forgiveness? Let me propose some ways. I will focus on particularly those features that raise the issue of violence most sharply.

First, the parable as it presently exists draws a link between the 'human king' and God. 'King' (*melech, basileus*) as symbol for God goes back to the earliest stories of Israel. God is 'king' in being creator, liberator, lawgiver and judge.[41] Jesus made the 'kingdom' or 'reign (*basileia*) of God' the centrepiece of his proclamation in word and deed, most particularly as remembered in the Synoptic Gospels. Even if Matthew had not made the link explicit, both his and Jesus' audience would have, despite ways in which this king is more a troubling analogy than a depiction of God.

Selling into slavery as a means of repayment? Sending to the torturers until all is paid? Here we are again reminded of Reid's 'is' and 'is not.' There is something clearly absurd about the elements of this story, and they were probably meant to be recognized as such. No slave, however highly placed, and however large a family, could fetch a price that would do more than put the tiniest dent in the debt of ten thousand talents. And no one, already unable to pay, would be able to do so from within the torture chamber. But the storyteller knows that. The features of the human king within the 'story world' are indeed those of a tyrant whose magnanimity is matched by his rage. But the absurdities are part of the 'joke' being told, and no more absurd than the number of times Jesus demands that one forgive.

---

[41] E.g. Exod. 15, Pss. 96; 97. See Thomas R. Yoder Neufeld, *Recovering Jesus: The Witness of the New Testament* (Grand Rapids, MI: Brazos; London: SPCK, 2007), 125–38.

Second, can this disturbing 'man-king' serve then as an example of forgiveness? In some ways, yes, in that the character of the sovereign emphasizes that forgiveness is an act of power, granted freely by those who can demand what is theirs. In short, forgiveness is sovereign freedom at work for the benefit of the one who 'owes' and not the one to whom is owed.

Third, the parable also serves to make a link between the king or lord and his slaves. The one whom much was forgiven was expected to emulate his master's treatment of him. While the 'story world' is that of kings and slaves, or of elites and their retainers, Jesus' and Matthew's audience would have been familiar with casting the relationship between the faithful and God as that between lord and servant. While 'slave of God' (*ebed YHWH*) was a position of high honour, for the righteous, for prophets, kings and Messiah, it also indicated with absolute clarity who is 'boss', and who is to be emulated. Given how prominently the violent features of this parable press themselves on us, and given that violence is our focus, we might miss that the central offence in this parable is that the slave who owed much did not emulate his master's breathtaking generosity in forgiveness. As one whom much was forgiven, he should have known that his status as slave of such a master demanded the same sovereign freedom of him.

The image of 'slave' alternates with that of 'son' throughout the Scriptures, also in the New Testament, no doubt reflecting the patriarchal cultural context. Small wonder then that Matthew ends the parable by having Jesus make a connection between not slaves and master but between sons and 'heavenly father' (18.35). Such 'sonship' is not, as we saw with the love of enemies in 5.45, so much a metaphor of dependency as of imitation and participation in the divine sovereignty. It is this lofty status that is presupposed in the 'binding and loosing' of 18.15–20. Forgiveness is nothing less than 'loosing', freeing the debtor from the bondage of the debt. And as the parable suggests, forgiveness is part of the inherent surprise of grace, offered by those 'in charge'. To connect forgiveness to the sovereignty of God, in the mini-drama of this parable disturbingly represented by a tyrannical king, highlights the sovereign freedom inherent in true forgiveness, forgiveness 'from the heart' (v. 35). It is an act of 'lordship' practised by a 'slave', a 'loosing' that not only emulates God but also makes stick in heaven what is enacted on earth.

Fourth, forgiveness is connected in the parable with the request for mercy and the promise of repentance, in this case the resolve to pay it all back (vv. 26, 29). It matters not that the first of the debts is clearly unpayable. The slave makes repayment the premise of his plea. Given the placing of the parable into the context of the discourse of Matthew 18 as a whole, we are invited to see binding and loosing in 18.15–20 as essentially a cajoling to repentance. Luke 17.3 makes repentance virtually a precondition of forgiveness. Just as forgiveness is essential within a 'kingdom' ethic, so is repentance. Repentance is not simply regret, or even acknowledgement of wrongdoing, although both are essential to it. It is rather a turning away from that behaviour (see v. 3).[42]

One might be tempted thus to make forgiveness dependent on repentance, that is, to give it a specific place within the 'system' or order of dealing with sin, injury and debt. Luke's terse formulation in his parallel tradition virtually begs for that: 'If he repents, forgive him' (17.3). We recall that behind this discourse in Matthew 18, particularly verses 15–20, lies the command to love the neighbour (Lev. 19.17). Confronting, repenting and forgiving are not to be separated from each other. But precisely because forgiveness emerges from love of the neighbour who has in some sense become the enemy, forgiveness is neither constrained by nor limited to this stress on repentance, as Luke's Jesus shows on the cross: 'Father, forgive them; they don't know what they are doing.' Forgiveness is a sovereign and free act, a deliberate gesture 'from the heart', as our parable has it. The character of the unconstrained tyrant illustrates that forcefully even if rather disturbingly. Forgiveness is both a commanded response to sincere repentance and, at times, a patient and vulnerable keeping the future open for such 'turning'. Anything more or less empties forgiveness of its role in the relational dynamic of the sovereign and free reign of a merciful God.

Forgiveness is by its very nature something both necessary inside and outside the system, so to speak. It has an essential but not specific place. Without a relationship to repentance it becomes impunity, the very opposite of mercy or grace. At the same time forgiveness is inherently risky behaviour, since the future is opened rather than

---

[42] Greek *metanoia*: second thoughts, change of mind or disposition; Hebrew *teshuvah*: turning around.

controlled by it, most especially when offered as a deliberate invitation to repentance. Its openness to repentance necessarily implies
an openness to disappointment and potentially even violence. Hence
the risk. That too is illustrated within the twisted 'story world' of
this parable. The king forgives a life shattering debt only to have
that mercy squandered by the one to whom so much was forgiven.
Forgiveness thus carries within it the implicit vulnerability of the
love of enemies, observed in Matthew 5 and Luke 6, and at the same
time the implication of power and sovereignty of which such love is
the imitation.

Fifth, forgiveness is offered within the framework of divine account-
ability and reckoning. Those whom grace has called into the community of 'binding and loosing' face the extreme displeasure of
the one who called them to this high task if they do not themselves
practise such grace. Our parable makes that point in a way that is
offensive to many contemporary readers. It is the violence associated
with the consequences of not forgiving that constitutes the *skandalon*
of this passage.[43]

One way to avoid this scandal, as noted above, is to see the parable
as not about God, God's reign, or even forgiveness at all. The parable
is a picture of a truly violent, evil world, and in no sense a positive
'lesson' on God and forgiveness. But even if we could agree to that
interpretation with Herzog, Myers and Enns, et al., and even if we
agreed that Matthew had his hand in depicting Jesus using violent
imagery and making violent threats, there is simply too much evidence
that Jesus shared with those who tell us of him, whether evangelists
or apostles, the conviction that God is judge.[44] Indeed, Matthew
remembers him as anticipating that the 'son of man' will himself
come in judgement, and that the faithful will join him in that activity
(16.27; 19.28).

---

[43] In addition to Herzog and Myers and Enns, see, e.g., Warren Carter, 'Constructions
of Violence and Identities in Matthew's Gospel', in *Violence in the New Testament* (ed.
Shelley Matthews and E. Leigh Gibson; New York/London: T&T Clark, 2005), 81–108;
Reid, 'Violent Endings'; and Neville, 'Toward a Teleology of Peace', and the examples
cited there.

[44] Reiser, *Jesus and Judgment*, and Travis, *Christ and the Judgement of God*. The nature of
that judgement is variously anticipated, as is the certainty of its violence; see, e.g.,
Christopher D. Marshall, *Beyond Retribution: A New Testament Vision for Justice, Crime,
and Punishment* (Grand Rapids, MI: Eerdmans, 2001).

A related way to deal with the offence in this parable, and everywhere else this stone of stumbling appears, is to redefine judgement as largely the inexorable consequences of sin. In short, it is not God who brings the pain of punishment; such pain is the effect of that which *human* decisions cause.[45] This parable, and others like it, thus warns not of *God*'s response but shows what happens when human beings don't forgive. Lack of forgiveness leads to a world of the payback, even torture. Otherwise, Myers and Enns argue, 'the cosmos is retributive', with God bringing down a 'hammer' at the end of the age – the exact opposite of the restorative approach of which the rest of the discourse in Matthew 18 speaks.[46]

As attractive and widely held such a view is in our day, it fits less into the world of the New Testament. In Jesus' day the imagery associated with judgement was influenced by biblical images of the intervention of the divine warrior, heightened to a further level of intensity by the motifs and images of apocalyptic expectation. These motifs are themselves parabolic, and should be treated as such.[47] Even so, they do depict God as intervening in judgement, not simply 'handing over' humanity to the effects of their sin.[48] To leave God out of it, as it were, would have been inconceivable to Jesus and his Jewish contemporaries. If judgement is not in the end God's *doing* – however mysterious and unanticipated its outworking – then the cosmos itself is indeed retributive. If judgement is another word for a causal 'what happens when . . .', then how is grace not also 'what doesn't happen when . . .'? Getting away with it would be impossible to distinguish from grace. 'Binding and loosing' in Matthew 18.15–20 clearly implies participating in divine judgement as *act*, both in the present and in relation to the future. Does this tough neighbourly love not emulate an actively intervening 'binding and loosing' God?

Another 'solution' is to suggest with Willard Swartley that in the Bible the vocabulary of 'violence' per se is not typically carried over

---

[45] Reiser, *Jesus and Judgment*, 281, does call it 'self-chosen judgment', but that does not preclude that God is judge. So also Travis, *Christ and the Judgement of God*, 240.

[46] Myers and Enns, *Ambassadors*, 71, 80.

[47] E.g. Snodgrass, *Stories with Intent*, 72.

[48] While that conception of judgement is surely present (e.g. Rom. 1.29), it is by no means the norm, and by itself hardly solves the problem of violence, in that it really does make the 'cosmos', creation as ordered by God, inherently retributive.

to God, and that to do so is to commit a 'category fallacy'.[49] That case is difficult to make in the specific instance of our parable in which, at least in its present form, the king's consigning of the unforgiving debtor to the 'torturers' (very clearly technical violence vocabulary) is explicitly paralleled with what the 'heavenly father' will do to the unforgiving (*houtōs*, 'so also'; v. 35). It is difficult to make the case more broadly as well, given the wide use in the Scriptures of metaphors of war and physical violence for God's judging. This imagery will both continue to be a *scandalon* and to resist quarantining.

To borrow words from Paul, there is about the divine judge both 'severity and kindness' (Rom. 11.22; cf. Ecclus. 5.4–7). Our parable points to that in a provocative way. As much as mercy and forgiveness emerge from divine love and justice (Rom. 3.21–26), so true is it that by their very nature mercy and grace are always in an important sense 'news', 'gospel'. In fact, mercy, grace and forgiveness only make sense within a conceptual framework in which they come not automatically but always as unearned gift motivated by fathomless love, never to be presumed upon. Whereas there is no place in the Bible, including the Gospels, for the elimination of judgement, or for redefining it as the inexorability of cause and effect, there *is* ample space in the Bible, including in the traditions related to Jesus, for judgement withheld and cancelled (grace and mercy), judgement absorbed (forgiveness) and for love offered in ways that drive the calculators of justice mad (sun and rain, cross and resurrection).

Let me propose that this parable has a limited function. We should allow it to lay bare a brutal world but also to lend weight and urgency to the injunction to forgive. We should not take it to set out a theory of judgement, or even to serve by itself as an adequate analogy of judgement. The 'story world' of this parable should not be allowed to undermine the fundamental conviction pervading the writings of the evangelists that the divine judge is just, loving, merciful and always, from a 'debtor's' perspective, surprisingly so.[50]

Nor should the parable by itself set out a theory of forgiveness.

---

[49] Willard M. Swartley, *Covenant of Peace: The Missing Peace in New Testament Theology and Ethics* (Grand Rapids, MI: Eerdmans, 2006), 393–5.

[50] Mercy *is* the face of God's justice no less, if not more, than judgement, as the earliest of the NT writers puts it in Rom. 3.21–26. Cf. Wisd. 11.21—12.2.

That word carries in our culture a wide diversity of meaning, from the victim's 'letting go', to the acceptance of apology and contrition. Here it is conceived of as 'forgiving' a debt incurred, whether morally or financially. It has to do with forgoing what one is 'owed' and thus, essentially, with carrying the burden of the harm. The drama of this parable still needs to be 'acted out' in relation to myriad harms done and experienced, from the trivial to the horrific.

On 2 October 2006, in the hamlet of Nickel Mines, Pennsylvania, an intruder shot and killed six girls in an Amish school before taking his own life.[51] As the world looked on in horror, the Amish immediately reached out to the family of the killer and assured them of their forgiveness, going so far as to attend the funeral of the shooter. If the murder of the children shook the watching world, the act of forgiveness baffled them no less. When asked to explain themselves, the Amish reached for precisely the text we have been considering. First they mentioned that they pray the Lord's Prayer repeatedly each day, drawing attention in particular to the phrase 'Forgive us as we have forgiven those who sin against us', noting that that is the only part of the prayer to which Jesus gives added emphasis. Then they went on to buttress that with Jesus' words to Peter and the parable in Matthew 18. In short, 'if we do not forgive, how can we expect to be forgiven'?[52] The Amish are not squeamish about the importance of forgiving as a precondition of God's forgiving. That has made it the deeply ingrained cultural reflex that came to such startling expression in the midst of the horror of mass murder.

It is thus not easy to sort out the violence question. For many today, including many scholars, this parable is viewed as an instance of Matthew's penchant for violence, inscribing into the imagination of those who read it as Scripture a propensity for violence. For the Amish, who take this and other texts dealing with forgiveness more 'literally' than the most 'literalistic' readers of the Bible, it has contributed to a culture of non-violence, whose communally ingrained reflex in the face of even the most shocking horror is forgiveness. Who gets the violence question right? Who gets the parable right?

---

[51] Donald B. Kraybill, Steven M. Nolt and David Weaver-Zercher, *Amish Grace: How Forgiveness Transcended Tragedy* (San Francisco, CA: Jossey-Bass, 2007).

[52] Kraybill, Nolt and Weaver-Zercher, *Amish Grace*, 95; see all of 88–98. The intensely hard and fragile work of forgiveness is fully acknowledged by the Amish (119–21).

It is too easy to take offence at the violence in the imagery and in its apparent insinuation that God is violent long before one can fully appreciate the radical care expressed for the most vulnerable, the incomparable authority invested in ordinary folk to do nothing less than the work of God at restoring the errant, and finally the forcefulness (quite literally) with which *measureless* forgiveness – whether in number or amount – is made absolutely mandatory for the community. And just to add a twist at the end: as absolutely mandatory as it is for sons and daughters of the 'father in heaven', it is nothing less than sovereign magnanimity 'from the heart'.

From the very beginning – from its initial telling to its inclusion in Matthew's discourse – this parable has sat alongside the practice of unanticipated forgiveness and baffling inclusion of the usual rejects by both Jesus and his followers. It has sat alongside Jesus' withering criticisms of the arrogance of those who see themselves entitled, whether the rich, or the righteous and pious, to either power or grace. It also sits, notably also in the Gospel of Matthew, alongside the injunction *not* to judge, lest one be judged by the same measure (Matt. 7.1–5//Luke 6.37–42). Matthew's placing of this parable following the 'Rule of Christ' in verses 15–20 has the similar function of puncturing the self-importance of those just granted the role of judges who are called to 'bind and loose'.[53] The members of the *ekklēsia* are, in effect, the 'retainers' of the divine king. They had better know their business, which is to forgive more often than they can count and amounts greater than they can measure.

A God for whom forgiveness means this much is a God into whose hands one might just dare to fall, 'for equal to his majesty is his mercy' (Ecclus. 2.17).

---

[53] Kraybill, Nolt and Weaver-Zercher, *Amish Grace*. When the Amish celebrate the Lord's Supper, typically twice a year, Matt. 18, the whole of it, serves as a test of fidelity to Jesus' teaching.

4

Violence in the temple?

Few episodes in the narratives of Jesus' short life occasion as much attention with respect to violence as his Passover outburst in the temple, conventionally called 'the cleansing of the temple'. In the last chapter we considered Jesus' way of confronting his world and his followers with parables. This episode has rightly been called an 'acted parable'.[1] In this chapter we will consider not so much a prophetic parabolic word as a prophetic parabolic act.

The temple incident

A brief and vivid account of Jesus' temple action is found in all four of the canonical Gospels (Matt. 21.10–17; Mark 11.15–19; Luke 19.45–46; John 2.13–22).[2] The setting for the story is Jesus' visit to Jerusalem during the highly volatile time of the Passover, that greatest of Jewish festivals celebrating God's liberation of the people from enslavement. We should imagine Jerusalem swamped with tens, perhaps hundreds of thousands of pilgrims, intensely focused on the rituals of liberation. Temple activity is at its highest. The mix of hyperactivity and a crush of excited humanity no doubt contributes mightily to the edginess of the authorities, both temple and Roman. Pilate has made sure he is in town. The evangelists do not camouflage the volatility of the moment, even if scholars debate to what extent the evangelists exaggerate the

---

[1] N. T. Wright, *Jesus and the Victory of God* (Christian Origins and the Question of God, Vol. 2; Minneapolis, MN: Fortress Press, 1997), 334, 416.

[2] Readers are again reminded that commentaries on all four Gospels treat this incident thoroughly and with full attention to scholarship. The discussion here is focused in particular on the issue of violence, and citations are intended to serve that limited focus. No attempt has been made fully to plumb the volume of scholarship. Each of the works cited contains further bibliographical riches.

public hubbub surrounding both 'triumphal entry' and temple demonstration.[3]

Following his dramatic entry into Jerusalem we find Jesus creating a disturbance on the temple grounds. Mark, on whose account Matthew and Luke more than likely depend,[4] describes him as 'throwing out' sellers and buyers (of sacrificial animals, we should assume), kicking over seats and tables of currency changers and pigeon sellers, all the while 'teaching' (should we assume quite loud and urgent teaching?) words from the great prophets Isaiah and Jeremiah: 'My house shall be a house of prayer; but you have made it a den of robbers!'[5] Mark asserts that Jesus allows no one to carry anything through the temple (11.16). The Fourth Gospel also mentions sheep and bulls and, of course, the famous whip with which Jesus does the 'throwing out' (John 2.14, 15). John too has Jesus utter prophetic words of judgement, only now from Zechariah 14.21: 'Stop making my Father's house a marketplace!' (lit. 'house of commerce'; 2.16). Seeing it all unfold, Jesus' disciples recall Psalm 69.10: 'Zeal for your house will consume me' (John 2.17). John thereby helps readers connect Jesus' action with that long history of religiously motivated radicalism, even violence, going back to the arch-zealot Phineas (Num. 25.11–13).[6] In John's account the authorities then demand a 'sign' of Jesus' right to act in this way. In response, Jesus raises the tension markedly: 'Destroy this temple, and in three days I will raise it up!' (2.19). What seems to begin in John as a 'cleansing' of the temple ends with an allusion to Jesus' death and resurrection, and along with it a cryptic announcement of the temple's destruction and

---

[3] E.g. E. P. Sanders, *The Historical Figure of Jesus* (New York/London: Penguin, 1995), 253–7; Paula Fredriksen, *Jesus of Nazareth, King of the Jews: A Jewish Life and the Emergence of Christianity* (New York: Vintage, 1999), 230.

[4] Markan priority is not essential to our discussion; what is clear is that the Synoptic Gospels draw from the same tradition. Whether John's account is dependent on the Synoptic tradition, or whether there were multiple 'floating' versions of the story taken up variously by the evangelists Mark and John, is finally neither determinative for our study, nor, for that matter, finally determinable (see, e.g., Fredriksen, *Jesus*, 230).

[5] Isa. 56.7; Jer. 7.11.

[6] Horsley cautions not to make 'zeal' into a 'movement' or even 'idea' of resistance during the time of Jesus (Richard A. Horsley, *Jesus and the Spiral of Violence: Popular Jewish Resistance in Roman Palestine* (San Francisco, CA: Harper & Row, 1987), 121–9). See also William Klassen, 'Jesus and Phineas: A Rejected Role Model', *Society of Biblical Literature Seminar Papers* 25 (1986), 490–500.

replacement. The response to Jesus' action is lethal. In the Synoptic Gospels the incident serves as the immediate trigger bringing about Jesus' death.

These are the essential elements of the story. Conscientious objectors have stood before many a tribunal, forced to defend their refusal to take up arms as fidelity to Jesus in the light of what is viewed as Jesus' own violence in the Jerusalem temple. The Christian tradition has historically used the incident to justify violence. Today it frequently serves to implicate Jesus in violence, and thus to discredit his supposed non-violence.

Our focus is again limited, in that we will do little more than give a careful reading to the accounts, and explore a number of ways in which the issue of violence intersects with this narrative. What do the evangelists claim Jesus did in the temple? Was he physically violent? Did he 'lose it' in a manic outburst, or did he quite sanely perform a kind of prophetic symbolic act? If so, what did he intend to symbolize? 'Cleaning up' his divine father's home? The destruction of the temple? Or was it a means by which Jesus deliberately goaded the authorities into killing him?

Complicating matters in responding to these questions is that the various accounts of the temple incident are not like a video, but rather memories deeply impacted by years of recollection and reflection, in the light both of the death and resurrection of Jesus, and of the catastrophe of the Jewish war against Rome, which resulted in the destruction of the temple. It is difficult to know when we are hearing Jesus directly, or when we hear his followers interpret his words and actions in the light of their growing post-Easter insights and experiences (as is most immediately noticeable in John's account). The majority of scholars trust that memory to recall for us a major episode in Jesus' life. But even were those to be right who question whether it ever happened, the place of this story in the long history of how Jesus is understood in relation to violence makes it necessary to include it in our study.

What did Jesus do?

The accounts all agree that Jesus entered the temple and 'threw out' (*ekballō*) the sellers (Luke) and the buyers (Matthew and Mark), and/ or the sheep and the oxen (John). Was such 'throwing out' violent?

Numerous scholars believe Jesus did nothing physically violent.[7] *Ekballō* need not literally mean to 'throw out', and may on occasion mean no more than 'send away' or 'send out' (e.g. Matt. 9.38).[8] But it is the terminology of choice for exorcism and judgement (e.g. Matt. 12.24–28, etc.). Such use of the term is 'non-violent' only if one does not share a world view in which divine judgement or life-and-death struggles with demons are experiential realities. In keeping with how *ekballō* is most often used, we should take 'throwing out' as carrying an unambiguous implication of forceful expulsion of persons and their business from the temple precincts. Whether that implies physical violence the evangelists leave to the readers' imagination.

According to John, Jesus made a whip (*phragellion*) of cords and with it threw 'all of them' out of the temple (2.15). There are two issues: one is what we imagine the 'whip of cords' was, the other to what or to whom 'all' (*pantas*) refers. It is the answer to the second question that will help shed light on the first.

The Greek construction *te . . . kai* typically means 'both . . . and'. Many commentators and some leading translations (e.g. NIV, NRSV) thus take 'both . . . and' and 'all' in this verse to refer to the sheep and the cattle, and not to the people: 'he drove them all out of the temple, both the sheep and the cattle'. Other commentators and translations prefer, somewhat against normal grammatical usage, 'with the sheep and the oxen', taking 'all' to refer to persons and their animals.[9]

This would be trivial, were it not for the fact that the whip has taken on iconic stature with respect to Jesus and violence. 'Ever since the early Christian centuries, the whip in the temple has been considered the one act in the life of Jesus which could be appealed

---

[7] E.g. John Howard Yoder, *The Politics of Jesus: Vicit Agnus Noster* (2nd edn; Grand Rapids, MI: Eerdmans/Carlisle: Paternoster, 1994), 39–45; David Flusser with R. Steven Notley, *Jesus* (Jerusalem: Hebrew University Magnes Press, 1997), 138–42.

[8] Yoder understates the lexical evidence in claiming that the term 'posits no violence' and that elsewhere it means 'send away' (*Politics*, 43).

[9] The term for 'all' (*pantas*) in John 2.15 is masculine. Scholars differ on whether that implies persons, and then also their animals, or whether it might be masculine, given the male gender of the oxen or bulls. See, e.g., Jennifer A. Glancy, 'Violence as Sign in the Fourth Gospel', *Biblical Interpretation* 17 (2009), 100–17 (109–10). But see Jean Lassere, 'A Tenacious Misinterpretation', in *Occasional Papers of the Council of Mennonite Seminaries and Institute of Mennonite Studies*, No. 1 (ed. Willard M. Swartley; Elkhart, IN, 1981), 35–47.

to as precedent for the Christian's violence'.[10] More recently, rather than using the episode to justify violence, the whip has come to be a favourite means with which to scourge both Jesus and the author of the Fourth Gospel with the charge that they are violent. Careful translation is thus mandatory. It won't stop people from being violent, but it might undermine one of its justifications. Normal Greek grammar suggests that John, the only evangelist to mention the whip, understands Jesus as physically shooing animals out of the temple precincts. Indeed, comparison with the other evangelists indicates that the sole mention of a whip in the Fourth Gospel goes hand in hand with the sole mention of animals. There is thus little reason to think of the whip as much more than a means of shooing animals, made on the spot perhaps with straw lying about. At the same time, 'throwing out' cautions us not to downplay the forcefulness or the disruptiveness of Jesus' actions as depicted by the evangelists.

The evangelists describe Jesus as not only acting but also speaking. He is remembered as 'throwing out' while quoting words from the prophets of Israel. Indeed, Jesus' actions and words anticipate in eerie fashion his near contemporary and namesake, Jesus son of Hananiah, who, according to Josephus, spent more than seven years prior to the Jewish–Roman war warning of Jerusalem's and the temple's demise.[11] Turning the temple from a 'house of prayer' into a 'den of robbers' (Matthew–Mark–Luke) is taken from Isaiah 56.7 and Jeremiah 7.11, the 'house of my Father' into a 'house of commerce' (John 2.16) from Zechariah 14.21. Jesus and his contemporaries would have perceived prophetic words of condemnation as far graver and more fearsome than any use of a whip made of the straw lying around. The combative role of words in this episode is shown in the exchange of Jesus in the Gospel of John. When the alarmed authorities demand he give proof (a 'sign') of his authority to behave and to speak in this way, Jesus provokes them further: 'Destroy this house, and I will rebuild it in three days!'

---

[10] John Howard Yoder, *Politics*, 42.

[11] Josephus, *JW* 6.300–9. See Richard A. Horsley and John S. Hanson, *Bandits, Prophets, and Messiahs: Popular Movements at the Time of Jesus* (San Francisco, CA: Harper & Row, 1985), 160–89, esp. 172–5; on Jesus ben Hananiah and Jesus and the prophetic tradition, see Scot McKnight, *Jesus and His Death: Historiography, the Historical Jesus, and Atonement Theory* (Waco, TX: Baylor University Press, 2005), 189–205.

Such words are themselves acts, and were understood to be such. As Hosea 6 reminds readers: 'Therefore I have hewn them by the prophets, I have killed them by the words of my mouth' (Hos. 6.5, 6). A focus simply on the physical actions in this episode misses the far greater expression of power and force – violence? – in the words both spoken and recalled.

What did Jesus' temple action mean?

Whereas at one time some scholars viewed the event as a some-what camouflaged memory of a zealot-like revolutionary attack on the temple,[12] today there is general agreement that this action was a symbolic act, in line with the long tradition of prophetic demon-strations.[13] There is every reason to believe that Jesus' contemporar-ies would have understood such a dramatic representation of a divine message. Indeed, what seems to our eyes like violence and hostility might well have been understood as the grammar of urgency. The vehemence of the action and the words are within the 'language set' of biblical prophetic demonstrations.[14] John's account suggests as much when the authorities demand a 'sign' to verify Jesus' actions, even if, in John's view, they find it impossible to 'get it'.

If there is general agreement on the symbolic nature of the act, there is little on what it symbolized. A number of proposals have been made, some of them overlapping. The first is the one nearest at hand: like an enraged prophet, Jesus dramatized a long overdue purification of the temple, of which the commerce within its precincts – whether money changing or the sale of animals – was the most

---

[12] S. G. F. Brandon, *Jesus and the Zealots: A Study of the Political Factor in Primitive Christianity* (New York: Charles Scribner's Sons/Manchester: Manchester University Press, 1967). Brandon was critiqued heavily; e.g. George R. Edwards, *Jesus and the Politics of Violence* (New York and London: Harper & Row, 1972), and more recently by Horsley, *Spiral*, 77–89; William R. Herzog II, *Jesus, Justice, and the Reign of God: A Ministry of Liberation* (Louisville, KY: Westminster/John Knox, 2000), 134.

[13] Horsley and Hanson, *Bandits*, 135–89; Wright, *Jesus*, 413–28.

[14] E.g. Isaiah's walking about naked for three years (Isa. 20), Jeremiah's broken pottery (Jer. 18, 19) and his yoke (Jer. 27), Ezekiel's brick (Ezek. 4) or Hosea's marriage to the prostitute Gomer (Hos. 1—3). But see the essays collected in Julia M. O'Brien and Chris Franke, eds, *The Aesthetics of Violence in the Prophets* (New York/London: T&T Clark, 2010).

obvious symptom. Jesus' objective in this vehement confrontation was ultimately to restore temple worship to its rightful state, a house of prayer for 'all nations', and thus a fitting home for his Father. It is not the temple that is the problem, or its sacrificial cult, but its profanation through commerce.

Others disagree that this explains Jesus' actions, since commercial activity associated with the temple was necessary to facilitate worship. Commerce could hardly have been corrupting in and of itself, and there is little evidence that this was a major concern at the time.[15] The currency exchange existed precisely to secure the purity of the monies pouring into the temple. Relatedly, there is disagreement on whether animals such as oxen would have been permitted in the temple proper, and whether John's account is to be trusted.

Second, some scholars have focused less on the commercial degradation of the temple and more on the systemic economic injustices that massive undertakings such as temples represented in Jesus' day, and most assuredly also the one in Jerusalem, which was still undergoing Herod's extravagant rebuilding programme.[16] Furthermore, the temple tax, the half-shekel Jewish males were expected to pay annually had two effects: one, it concentrated wealth in the temple at the expense of the peasantry and, two, the temple system of sacrifices marginalized those who could not afford them. Jesus' action must then be seen as a forceful protest against the economic violence the temple represented. His symbolic act announced that with the kingdom's coming the judgement of God would fall on this centre of injustice and oppression. There is no thought here of reforming a system that is deemed antithetical to the very character of the kingdom as Jesus understood it.[17] Jesus' action should be seen as symbolic violence against the real violence of the temple 'system'.[18]

Third, while some see the temple as a symbol of the oppression of the poor by the economic and religious elite, and thus in some sense as a symbol of acquiescence to imperial power, N. T. Wright sees

---

[15] E.g. Fredriksen, *Jesus*, 209.

[16] E.g. Mark R. Bredin, 'John's Account of Jesus' Demonstration in the Temple: Violent or Nonviolent?', *BTB* 33/44 (2003), 44–50 (47); Herzog, *Jesus*, 136–8.

[17] Horsley calls the event a 'minimally violent prophetic demonstration symbolizing the imminent action by God' (*Jesus*, 299).

[18] Herzog, *Jesus*, 142–3.

Jesus' symbolic destruction of the temple to have been a prophetic and messianic act of judgement against its role as symbol of national resistance to Rome.[19] Jesus' symbolic act of destruction thus anticipated the deathly consequences of resistance to Rome, as would become calamitously clear only four decades later with the destruction of the temple by the Romans. But Jesus did more than show symbolically where resistance to the empire might lead; he declared the temple itself 'redundant' since, in line with John's understanding of Jesus' action, he himself would come to constitute the new temple. In Wright's take on the event, both violent resistance to Rome and the temple were being dramatically rejected by Jesus. Jesus' act was forcefully anti-violent, we might say.

Fourth, Wright's comments reflect the fact that for many scholars Jesus' action is only intelligible in the light of apocalyptic eschatology, with its intense anticipation of an imminent upheaval. Jesus was not 'cleansing' the temple. Jesus' eschatology was marked by his announcement of the imminent arrival of the reign of God, and with it the end of the Jerusalem temple. He was (symbolically) destroying the temple in anticipation of its actual destruction. As N. T. Wright puts it: 'He was not attempting a reform; he was symbolizing judgement.'[20]

Still within the framework of the imminent convulsion of the arrival of God's reign, Ed Sanders proposes that Jesus was acting out the destruction of Herod's temple, which would be replaced by a new one made by God himself.[21] It is not temple as temple that is the problem, but this temple, at this time, on this side of the great divide represented by the full appearing of the *basileia* of God. Jesus' action would have resonated with the views, for example, of those whose literature has been preserved at the Dead Sea, who yearned for a new temple and a new priesthood.[22]

Fifth, others like John Dominic Crossan, with less stress on eschatology, see Jesus symbolically destroying the temple because of its role as 'broker' between God and the people. Jesus offered instead an unmediated relationship with God. He symbolized this unbrokered

---

[19] Wright, *Jesus*, 423.
[20] Wright, *Jesus*, 423.
[21] Sanders, *Historical Figure of Jesus*, 256–62.
[22] As is illustrated in the longest of Qumran's scrolls, the famous Temple Scroll (11QTemple).

relationship with God throughout his brief career by eating and consorting with those not welcome in the temple. In other words, Jesus' prophetic assault was not on the perversion of the temple but on the very notion of 'temple' as restricted and controlled zone of access to God.[23]

Last, Jennifer Glancy views Jesus' hostility against the temple as reflecting a deeply violent disposition on the part of Jesus. She views Jesus as a man 'with some familiarity with a whip . . . who knows what he's doing'.[24] In her assessment Jesus' action in the temple was a violent and deliberate 'profanation' of the space held sacred by others.[25]

Was Jesus violent?

First, it is difficult to assess the physical realities involved. While the evangelists suggest a major impact on the workings of the temple (e.g. Mark 11.16; John 2.15), some scholars have suggested it cannot have been a major event if the Roman troops stationed at the adjacent Antonia fortress did not intervene, and if Jesus was not immediately arrested.[26] It is also not clear, contra Glancy, that Jesus used a whip made up of more than some strands of straw, or that he used it against human beings, or for more than shooing animals. There is thus some ambiguity in the accounts and in the circumstances as best we are able to discern them, as to whether Jesus' physical actions were violent.

Second, should we consider Jesus' words as violent? Certainly Jesus' words accompanying his actions can be seen as highly provocative, which they were no doubt intended to be, either in the mouth of Jesus or from the pen of the evangelists. What adds to the force of the words is that prophetic utterances and actions were understood by both Jesus and his audience to be connected to the divine will. Such words were never just words. In narrating this episode the evangelists clearly believed that there was a direct connection between

---

[23] John Dominic Crossan, *The Historical Jesus: The Life of a Mediterranean Jewish Peasant* (San Francisco, CA: HarperSanFrancisco, 1991), 355–60.

[24] Glancy, 'Violence as Sign', 112.

[25] Glancy, 'Violence as Sign', 104.

[26] E.g. Markus J. Borg, *Conflict, Holiness and Politics in the Teachings of Jesus* (Studies in the Bible and Early Christianity, Vol. 5; New York/Toronto: Edwin Mellen, 1984), 171–3; Fredriksen, *Jesus*, 231–2.

Jesus' words of warning and prediction and the actual destruction of Jerusalem and its temple by the Romans some decades later, even if at some points they ascribe that prophecy to false witnesses (Mark 14.57–58). From that perspective Jesus' words might be understood not as 'only words' and thus not 'real' violence but, given who is saying them, and to what power they are connected, as an exercise of violence itself.

However, biblical prophecy functions within a dynamic reality in which the apparent certainty of judgement is tempered by (desired for) repentance. Such 'turning' (Heb. *teshuvah*) or 'change of mind' (Gk *metanoia*) is sought on the part both of the recalcitrant people and of God (e.g. Jonah).[27] Said differently, Jesus' prophetic action can be seen as intended to avert the very destruction it dramatized, not to ensure that it would take place.[28] Only in hindsight and in the absence of repentance does the warning look like certain prediction. Jesus' actions, whether he was 'cleansing' or 'destroying', should be understood within a Jewish narrative in which dire warnings of judgement are part of a necessarily unscripted interaction between repentance and mercy, or resistance and judgement.[29] The evangelists rehearse this episode, of course, on the other side of Good Friday and Easter, and more than likely on the other side of the destruction of the temple in 70 CE, when the death of Jesus has taken central place within the narrative of salvation, when believers in Jesus have come to see Jesus and themselves as the new temple.[30] The give-and-take of the prophetic encounter has given way to the 'necessity' of hindsight.

What happens when this text is read by Gentiles distancing themselves from the Jewish roots of their faith? What happens when this episode is taken outside a Jewish matrix in which prophecy serves to elicit change rather than to predict a fait accompli, in which Jesus the Jew and his Jewish followers engage with their fellow Jews on the

---

[27] E.g. Walter Moberly, 'Jonah, God's Objectionable Mercy, and the Way of Wisdom', in *Reading Texts, Seeking Wisdom: Scripture and Theology* (ed. David F. Ford, Graham Stanton; Grand Rapids, MI/Cambridge: Eerdmans, 2003), 154–68.

[28] Wright seems to acknowledge this when he quotes Jer. 7.5–7, in which the possibility of repentance and thus a different future is held out (*Jesus*, 417–19).

[29] As the larger contexts of Isa. 56 and Jer. 7 well indicate. See also Pss. 50; 51; Hos. 6.

[30] E.g. Eph. 2.19–22.

matter of temple and worship?[31] Then the vehemence of Jesus' actions can become one more arrow in the quiver of anti-Judaism. Then it serves to delegitimize, even condemn, Jewish worship, as symbolized in the temple. It takes no special insight to see how this episode plays a role in the history of violence, in particular against Jews. In short, this is a dangerous text for Gentiles to read.

Third, in yet another twist on the question of violence, a number of scholars have wondered whether this incident reflects a kind of death wish on Jesus' part. Did he come to Jerusalem to die, deliberately choosing the tinderbox of Passover time to provoke the authorities into a violent response so as to make that happen? In his 1906 *The Quest of the Historical Jesus*, Albert Schweitzer comes close to suggesting this when he famously postulated that Jesus attempted to usher in the 'Kingdom of Heaven' by throwing himself on 'the wheel of the world', only to get crushed by it when it did turn.[32] Schweitzer clearly viewed this episode as reflecting Jesus' intense eschatological expectation of the imminent arrival of the kingdom. Others have suggested that Jesus knew his mission would reach its climax in his death 'for others' and thus that he did his part in bringing it about.[33] But does this mean that Jesus orchestrated his own murder – even if for the sake of a larger programme? Does such a scenario not render the authorities little more than unwitting pawns in a divinely orchestrated drama, and thus in some sense themselves victims of the violence into which they are drawn? Does that not make Jesus complicit in their violence against him?

Such rumination is motivated sometimes by theology, at other times by psychology. Donald Capps, for example, suggests that the temple action represents an 'impulsive' if symbolic act that finds its roots less in the confrontation between Jesus and the system of the

---

[31] There were other Jews who for reasons no less eschatological and no less radical dreamt of the demise of the temple in Jerusalem and the building of a new one (see, e.g., the famous Temple Scroll of Qumran, 4QTemple).

[32] Albert Schweitzer, *The Quest of the Historical Jesus: A Critical Study of Its Progress from Reimarus to Wrede* (trans. W. Montgomery; London: A. & C. Black, 1910), 368–9.

[33] Craig S. Keener, *The Gospel of John: A Commentary* (Peabody, MA: Hendrickson, 2003), 527–9; for survey of scholarship that emphasized Jesus' deliberate provoking of a lethal response to his action in the temple, see Scot McKnight, *Jesus and His Death: Historiography, the Historical Jesus, and Atonement Theory* (Waco, TX: Baylor University Press, 2005), 84–93.

temple, its cult and its hierarchy, less between Jesus' egalitarian programme and the patronal and patriarchal system of the Herodian
temple, than in Jesus' own effort to overcome the marginalization
and 'melancholia' he personally suffered because he was illegitimate.[34]
Psychoanalytically viewed, the temple came for Jesus to represent
his mother, defiled for having given birth to him illegitimately.
Through this one act Jesus both 'cleansed' his mother of her defilement
and rectified his own ostracization as a bastard by reclaiming the
temple as his own father's (Abba) 'house', 'destroying' that which had
treated him as fatherless.[35] 'The dispossessed son had come home,
and had done so with a vengeance.'[36] Rather than participating in
a world-transforming dawn of God's kingdom, rather than pre-
cipitating the events leading to the salvation of the world, Jesus' true
motivation (however unconscious) was to deal with his own broken
childhood.

J. Harold Ellens, more bluntly than Capps, views this episode
as Jesus having one of his 'fits of violence', engaging in 'situation-
inappropriate behavior, maybe even [suffering from] borderline
personality disorder'.[37] Feverish Jewish Apocalyptic expectations com-
bined with Jesus' 'melancholy' made for an incendiary mix, exploding
lethally (for Jesus) in the precincts of the temple in a 'kind of suicide'.[38]
Once Christianity became the imperial religion, however, what was
for Jesus a 'kind of suicide' became 'a prototype of genocidal attacks
first on pagans, then on heretical Christians, then on Jews, then on
Muslims'.[39] Ellens goes so far as to make links between the temple
incident and the attack on the World Trade Center on September 11,
2001. 'Was that not Christ's way? Obsessive fits of incongruous

---

[34] Donald Capps, *Jesus: A Psychological Biography* (St. Louis, MI: Chalice, 2000).

[35] Capps, *Jesus*, 57–60.

[36] Capps, *Jesus*, 260.

[37] J. Harold Ellens, 'The Violent Jesus', in *The Destructive Power of Religion: Violence in Judaism, Christianity, and Islam*; Vol. 3, *Models and Cases of Violence in Religion* (ed. J. Harold Ellens; Westport, CT/London: Praeger, 2004), 15–37 (16–17). In contrast, in a quite different psychological portrait of Jesus, John W. Miller sees Jesus' prophetic action as nothing other than an effort to prepare the temple to become a house of prayer for all nations: *Jesus at Thirty: A Psychological and Historical Portrait* (Minneapolis, MN: Fortress Press, 1997), 89.

[38] Ellens, 'Violent Jesus', 30.

[39] Ellens, 'Violent Jesus', 33.

violence!'[40] The temple cleansing should be demystified by 'calling it by its right name: Jesus' violence in the temple'.[41]

One should, in my opinion, be extremely cautious about mining the Gospels for psychological insights about Jesus. The evangelists show little if any interest in psychology. What shapes their narratives is what they believed God was doing in and through Jesus for the sake of humankind, and they drew on Scriptures to make that point as much as they drew on historical memory. Putting Jesus on the couch strikes me as an exercise in anachronism, moreover one in which the therapist does all of the talking.

A different way of assessing Jesus' own responsibility for the lethal outcome of this confrontation is to consider his actions and words as not so much responsible for his death as that they 'exposed' the depth of resistance and hostility to himself and his mission. To illustrate with examples from recent history, Martin Luther King, Jr., or Bishop Oscar Romero of El Salvador knew they were courting death even as they quite consciously and deliberately confronted the entrenched injustices and institutions of their own day. We do not thereby suspect them of having a death wish. In persisting in their confrontation with injustice and the powers behind it they knew full well that it might cost them their lives.[42] The typical fate of prophets and *tzaddikim* was all too familiar to the Jews of Jesus' day (see discussion in Chapter 2). If the evangelists could narrate Jesus' story with such a template in mind,[43] can we rule out that Jesus himself was fully aware of such a scenario? But that is not the same as engineering one's own death and provoking others to facilitate it.

Whether we attempt to understand the actions and words of Jesus in terms of prophetic activity or in terms of Jesus' psychology, the Gospel writers make things difficult for us by narrating the death of Jesus and the events leading up to it as both the result of human

---

[40] Ellens, 'Violent Jesus', 33–4.

[41] Ellens, 'Violent Jesus', 35.

[42] Does the fact that Martin Luther King's last speech anticipates his imminent death, much as did Bishop Oscar Romero, make him responsible for it? See also the example of Ken Saro-Wiwa of Nigeria in Thomas R. Yoder Neufeld, *Recovering Jesus: The Witness of the New Testament* (Grand Rapids, MI: Brazos; London: SPCK, 2007), 240.

[43] See, e.g., the role Ps. 22; Isa. 53; and Wisd. 2—5 apparently play in constructing the passion narratives.

treachery and thus human culpability and the workings of a sovereign God (more on that in Chapter 5). This temple episode is one instance of a growing confrontation between the reign of God and entrenched religious and political power, a confrontation that is seen, with the benefit of hindsight, to have led under the sovereignty of God to the death of Jesus, and thus ironically to have become an essential element in what Jesus' followers called 'good news'. Small wonder that the narratives veer occasionally in the direction of looking like a predetermined scenario. At the same time, it is also always 'news' – gospel.

What does the temple incident mean for us?

To ask about the violence in this episode is to do so typically with an eye to what kind of behaviour it warrants or encourages in those who claim Jesus in some sense to be their master, teacher and model. Do Jesus' actions in the temple serve as a model for his followers? If so, for what? For the use of violence in self-defence? For enlistment in the army? For armed revolution? For dramatic acts of civil disobedience? For leading civil rights or peace marches? Or perhaps for acts of symbolic 'terrorism'? And does such a Jesus conflict with the one who called for turning the cheek and loving the enemy?

First, the evangelists do not view Jesus as acting in a 'normal' fashion. He was functioning as a prophet, and more than a prophet. He was possessed, as they have the onlookers point out, by a kind of all-consuming 'zeal' befitting someone acting as God's pleni-potentiary. The evangelists give no indication that they wish this episode to be taken as an ethical 'teaching moment'. In keeping with the world view of the evangelists, those acting and speaking as Jesus does in this episode are chosen by God for the task, and do not appoint themselves. In Jesus' day 'Who does he think he is?!' was more important than 'What does he think he is doing?!' Christology and not violence is central to the evangelists' narratives.

Even so, the evangelists do not draw a firm line between Jesus and his followers, regardless of how lofty their view of Jesus is. Jesus 'calls' persons to follow him as students and imitators, and enjoins them to take up their cross (Mark 8.34–38 and par.). The evangelists understood the fearsome nature of emulating and following Jesus. Love for the enemy would not keep them out of trouble, nor from confrontation with the structures of power. So it is not wrong to ask whether and how Jesus models behaviour for his followers. While there is a well-grounded fear that such actions encourage the worst kind of violence, others see Jesus as warranting a resolutely non-violent albeit deliberately disturbing confrontation with corruption and injustice. Once again it seems that who is interpreting the episode and with what disposition they do so makes a world of difference as to whether this episode encourages violence or encourages resolute confrontation with violence.

We return, finally, to the question of how Jesus' behaviour in this episode comports with his strict instructions to turn the cheek and love the enemy (see Chapter 2). Readers will recall that cheek, shirt, second mile and open wallet are evocative mini-parables of ingenuity in the face of oppression. They are not pictures of acquiescence in the face of violence, even if they do also clearly imply a deliberate if 'defiant' vulnerability that might well bring with it further suffering. Jesus' brazen symbolic demonstration in the temple has aptly been called 'an acted parable of judgement'.[44] The gulf between the to be enacted parables of the Sermon on the Mount and the acted parable of the temple demonstration may not be as wide as first appears. The examples in Matthew 5 reflect the ingenuity of 'little people' in the face of humiliation, abuse and oppression. The narrations of the temple episode show Jesus as vulnerable but also sovereign in his dramatic initiative. However much the character revealed in the temple action would trouble the Church, the evangelists were honest enough to remember the event as one in which Jesus defiantly challenged the status quo.

While it is not stretching our imaginations to see Jesus' temple action as an 'acted parable' of a kingdom that would overturn the present order, in line with those 'parables of the *basileia*' that would overturn the predictable scenarios of abuse and oppression, can we square Jesus' action with his command to 'love the enemy'? If so, such is not a quiet and gentle love. Such love is intelligible only within biblical narratives in which prophetic anger and rage are

---

[44] Wright, *Jesus*, 334, 416.

experienced, even if only with the benefit of long hindsight, as the sometimes fierce and terrifying love of a divine covenant partner.[45] We saw this on full display in the last 'core-sample' of Matthew 18. We will see it again in the chapters to come.

---

[45] Notice Luke's introducing the episode in the temple with a moving lament over Jerusalem (19.41–44).

5

Atonement and the death of Jesus

The story of Jesus' death is suffused with violence. His death came by crucifixion, Roman brutality at its worst. The questions of why he died and who killed him are themselves drawn into the reality of violence. Who killed Jesus? Romans? Jews? Given the long history of charging Jews with deicide, this question is loaded with potential violence. Or did God kill Jesus? Christians often view Jesus' death as the very purpose of his brief life – 'Jesus came to die'. When Jesus' violent death is perceived to be an essential part of God's 'plan' or even God's *doing*, the question arises whether that makes suffering and death 'redemptive' and violence thereby intrinsic to 'good news'.

The specifics of Jesus' death by crucifixion are familiar.[1] We will explore, rather, the matter of ascribing responsibility for Jesus' death and the meaning that is accorded that death, keeping the issue of violence at the centre of our focus.

Who killed Jesus?

Determining who killed Jesus is not straightforward. The 'firm fact'[2] is that Jesus died by crucifixion. That clearly points the finger at the Roman imperial authorities. Jews did not crucify. Romans did. Crucifixion was imperial state terrorism intended to stem insurrection, both by punishing troublemakers and, just as importantly,

---

[1] See, e.g., Raymond E. Brown, *The Death of the Messiah* (2 vols; New York: Doubleday, 1999); James D. G. Dunn, *Jesus Remembered* (Christianity in the Making, Vol. 1; Grand Rapids, MI/Cambridge: Eerdmans, 2003), 765–81; Gerard Stephen Sloyan, *The Crucifixion of Jesus: History, Myth, Faith* (Minneapolis, MN: Fortress Press, 1995); see also Thomas R. Yoder Neufeld, *Recovering Jesus: The Witness of the New Testament* (Grand Rapids, MI: Brazos; London: SPCK, 2007), 229–65.

[2] E. P. Sanders, *Jesus and Judaism* (Philadelphia, PA: Fortress Press, 1985), 294; N. T. Wright, *Jesus and the Victory of God* (Christian Origins and the Question of God, Vol. 2; Minneapolis, MN: Fortress Press, 1997), 543–47.

intimidating subject peoples.[3] The *titulum* 'Jesus of Nazareth, King of the Jews', attached to the cross over his head (Matt. 27.37; Mark 15.26; Luke 23.38; John 19.19), indicates that Jesus was crucified as a Jewish rebel, indeed as a messianic claimant to power. Even if they appreciate the irony in that charge, the evangelists do not camouflage that fact.

The evangelists also claim, however, that Jewish authorities played a significant role in Jesus' ignominious death. The discussion of Jesus' prophetic demonstration in the temple in Chapter 4 already indicated this. Indeed, the accounts of Matthew and John are particularly notorious for placing blame for Jesus' death on Jews.[4] Given the long and dark history of blaming Jews for the death of Jesus, and thus for nothing less than deicide, we should not be surprised, especially on this side of the Holocaust, that this ascription of responsibility should have come under sharp review. In other words, is Jewish collusion in Jesus' death another part of the 'firm' reality, or is it calumny occasioned perhaps by the growing hostilities between believers in Jesus and their fellow Jews who rejected their claims as blasphemous? If so, are the accounts of Jesus' death as found in the Gospels themselves acts of violence?

Two issues thus intersect in assessing responsibility for Jesus' death: empire and anti-Judaism. Given that the narratives of Jesus' death were produced by a community whose leader was *crucified* for insurrection, on the one hand, and whose fellow Jews rejected them for their blasphemous claims about their leader, on the other, the passion narratives are more than likely to have been impacted by both the reality of Roman hegemony and troubled relations with fellow Jews.

First, 'empire' has come to receive a great deal of attention in biblical studies, both with respect to the role of Rome in the life of early believers in Jesus and its impact on their writing and in relation to the analysis of documents.[5] Rome, as 'empire' par excellence, has few if any defenders, and there is thus little hesitation to see the

---

[3] See esp. Martin Hengel, *Crucifixion in the Ancient World and the Folly of the Message of the Cross* (Philadelphia, PA: Fortress Press/London: SCM Press, 1977).

[4] Compare Matt. 27.24–26 with Mark 15.15 and Luke 23.24–25; John 19.1–15.

[5] E.g. John Dominic Crossan, *God and Empire: Jesus against Rome, Then and Now* (San Francisco, CA: HarperSanFrancisco, 2007); Richard A. Horsley, *Jesus and Empire: The Kingdom of God and the New World Order* (Minneapolis, MN: Fortress Press, 2003); '"By the Finger of God": Jesus and Imperial Violence', in *Violence in the New Testament* (ed. Shelley Matthews and E. Leigh Gibson; New York/London: T&T Clark, 2005), 51–80.

'empire' as culpable for the death of Jesus.[6] That is what one expects of empires. Given the way crosses have come to adorn ears, necks and church steeples, and celebrated in song as 'old and rugged' and thus to be 'cherished',[7] it may take some effort today at a popular level to recover some of the revulsion to such imperial brutality that first-century folk would have known in their bones. To be sure, scholars such as Paula Fredriksen have their doubts about whether Jesus would have been viewed by Rome as a threat. Why did Pilate not arrest and crucify Jesus' followers along with him? Fredriksen draws the conclusion that Pilate, at least, probably did not think Jesus to have been much of an insurrectionist.[8] Even were she to be right, that Pilate had Jesus crucified only adds to the casual brutality of the empire as experienced in the colonies.

How do we then assess the blaming of 'the Jews' in the accounts? First, we should remember that the narrators were themselves, perhaps without exception, 'Jews'. Do they mean 'Judaeans', whom they view as culpable in handing over the Galilean to the Romans? Or do they have in mind Jewish leaders? Adding to the complexity of whom to blame for Jesus' death is that while the evangelists shared in the marginalization of Jews generally within the Roman Empire, they were further marginalized by their own Jewish community for their adherence to Jesus as Messiah and Son of God. At the time of the writing of the Gospels the Jesus movement was a fringe phenomenon on the edges of a large and diverse Jewish community, which was negotiating its own often fragile place within the empire. A good case can be made that the downplaying of the role of Pilate, for example, and the highlighting of the role of the Jewish authorities was an effort by the evangelists to protect the Jesus movement from imperial suspicion and brutality. In short, affecting the narratives was the movement's own vulnerability vis-à-vis Rome, even as they also reflect the internecine battles among Jews over Jesus.

---

[6] Crossan's accounts are particularly evocative of imperial callousness (e.g. John Dominic Crossan, *Jesus: A Revolutionary Biography* (San Francisco, CA: HarperSanFrancisco, 1994), 123–7).

[7] 'The Old Rugged Cross', composed by George Bennard in 1912.

[8] Paula Fredriksen, *Jesus of Nazareth, King of the Jews: A Jewish Life and the Emergence of Christianity* (New York: Vintage, 1999), 241–59. Recall from Chapter 4 her characterization of Jesus' temple demonstration as having been exaggerated by the evangelists. But see Wright, *Jesus*, 543–7.

When Christianity became the imperial religion in the fourth century, however, it was Jews who were marginalized. The passion narratives would come to be read no longer 'from the margins' but from the centre, from a position of power. Blaming 'Jews' for Jesus' death would subsequently play a pernicious and often lethal role, to the present day. It matters enormously for the question of violence who is reading the accounts of Jesus' death, from what position of marginalization or of power and privilege, and to what end they are doing so. Scholars today rightly bear the burden of that history as they assess the accounts.

That said, there are many scholars who view the accounts as containing historical memory, however tragic, even if there may be exaggeration of Jewish participation by the evangelists. It is entirely plausible that some of Jesus' main detractors would have been at least some of the Jewish authorities. He would not be the last to experience such hostility.[9] That these leaders would have been nervous about Jesus' activities to the point of lethal hostility seems entirely plausible (see Chapter 4).[10] There are plenty of reasons. The Gospels consistently remember Jesus as provoking suspicion and outright hostility through his practice of consorting with 'tax collectors and sinners' as a 'drunkard and glutton' (e.g. Matt. 11.19//Luke 7.34). Charges of blasphemy and of drawing on evil power for his miracles and exorcisms seem to have dogged his brief ministry from the start. As we have seen, his stance on the temple was such that it at least caused serious consternation, as reflected in the charges brought against him that he intended its destruction. Perhaps most immediately relevant was the messianic buzz surrounding Jesus, if we may call it that.[11] We can add to this that Jewish leaders were constantly negotiating the volatile relationship

---

[9] Recall from Chapter 4 Josephus' account of Jesus ben Hananiah. His fellow Jews became so upset with his constant predictions of ruin for Jerusalem and the temple before the first Jewish war with Rome that they handed him over to the Roman governor to be beaten within an inch of his life. Even then he refused to be silenced (Josephus, *JW*, 600–9). Intra-Jewish hostility and violence is part of the story of the 'Jesus movement', not least as Paul experienced it (e.g. 2 Cor. 11.22–25, and as recalled in Acts 14.19; 17.1–9; 18.5–17; 21.17—26.32).

[10] Sanders, *Jesus*, 309–18; Wright, *Jesus*, 547–52.

[11] Jesus' 'messianic self consciousness' is a matter of dispute. I find it entirely plausible that Jesus might well have been seen as a messianic pretender by others, even if the tradition shows him to be quite nervous about that. That does not rule out that he saw himself in some continuity with what his followers would later confess him to be. See Yoder Neufeld, *Recovering Jesus*, 295–97; Wright, *Jesus*, 477–611.

between themselves, their people, their religion as centred in the temple, and the imperial authorities on constant lookout for insurrection. What looks like collusion between at least some authorities and Roman imperial overlords is entirely plausible. Given such a heap of dry kindling, it is not difficult that it caught fire on that Passover feast, ending in the crucifixion.

With respect to the violence of crucifixion itself, the reticence of the NT writers to indulge voyeuristic or even pietistic fascination with violence is noteworthy. This is in rather marked contrast to a great deal of piety that focuses on the physicality of Jesus' suffering.[12] There was of course no need for the evangelists to depict the torment in detail or to evoke what crucifixion entailed. Crucifixion had not yet entered the world of religious symbol or adornment. There is no evidence that Jesus' physical suffering itself was deemed to be uniquely horrible. The scene is depicted, rather, with references to Scripture, to such an extent that we might well wonder whether the depiction of the crucifixion and its attending circumstances is Scripture historicized or history 'Scripturized'.[13]

Put plainly, by the time the evangelists narrate the death of Jesus they are interested chiefly in telling us what it is about. Scripture serves them best for such a purpose. On the one hand, they are unambiguous in telling the story of an innocent having fallen victim to human treachery and brutality. Some of the Scriptures they cite serve to identify Jesus with the suffering of the innocent righteous ones.[14] On the other hand, allusions to Scriptures such as Isaiah 53[15] serve to give notice that God is also at work as an actor in this event, in that Jesus' death comes to be a central part of divinely worked atonement.

The death of Jesus as atonement

For the Christian religion 'the cross' has come to represent nothing less than 'the power of God' for those who are being saved, as

---

[12] E.g. Mel Gibson's fusion of a piety focused on Jesus' physical suffering with Hollywood pornography of violence in his *The Passion of the Christ* (2004).

[13] Crossan proposes that the Gospel narratives are 'not *history remembered* but *prophecy historicized*' (*Jesus*, 145). To recognize that does not rule out the memory behind the 'Scripturized' account (e.g. Dunn, *Jesus Remembered*, 777–81).

[14] See Ps. 22.1, 7–8, 18; 69.21; and echoes of Wisd. 2.16–20.

[15] E.g. Isa. 53.3 (Mark 9.12); 53.12 (Luke 22.37; Mark 10.45; 14.24).

Paul puts it unforgettably in 1 Corinthians 1.18. Brutal violence and liberating power: a perfect recipe for trouble for those on the lookout for violence. We begin with a brief detour into the most important theories of atonement, since they have largely provided the lenses through which the New Testament is read, and provide much of the fuel for the contemporary debate.[16]

Theories of atonement

One can do the taxonomy of atonement theories in various ways. I've simplified them for our purposes into three: substitution or satisfaction; moral influence; and *Christus Victor*, which entails both the motifs of rescue and recapitulation 'in Christ'.

The presently most widely held and at the same time most contentious is the substitutionary or penal satisfaction theory of atonement, usually identified with Anselm of Canterbury (1033–1109). In his famous *Cur Deus Homo* (Why God became Human), Anselm sets out to explain to his conversation partner, Boso, why it is that God had to become human. He 'explains' a thousand-year-old event in the categories of feudal Europe. Humanity sinned against God, Anselm explains, and thus wounded God's honour. The offence has put

---

[16] There are many excellent surveys and engagements with theories of atonement from various perspectives, many of them touching base with the New Testament. E.g. Hans Boersma, *Violence, Hospitality, and the Cross: Reappropriating the Atonement Tradition* (Grand Rapids, MI: Baker Academic, 2004); John C. Driver, *Understanding the Atonement for the Mission of the Church* (Scottdale, PA/Kitchener, ON: Herald Press, 1986); Stephen Finlan, *Options on Atonement in Christian Thought* (Collegeville, MN: Liturgical Press, 2007); Finlan, *Problems with Atonement: The Origins of, and Controversy about, the Atonement Doctrine* (Collegeville, MN: Liturgical Press, 2005); Joel B. Green and Mark D. Baker, *Recovering the Scandal of the Cross: Atonement in New Testament and Contemporary Contexts* (Downers Grove, IL: InterVarsity, 2000); Brad Jersak and Michael Hardin, eds, *Stricken by God? Nonviolent Identification and the Victory of Christ* (Grand Rapids, MI/Cambridge: Eerdmans, 2007); Gregory Anderson Love, *Love, Violence, and the Cross: How the Nonviolent God Saves Us through the Cross of Christ* (Eugene, OR: Cascade Books, 2010); Scot McKnight, *Jesus and His Death: Historiography, the Historical Jesus, and Atonement Theory* (Waco, TX: Baylor University Press, 2005); McKnight, *A Community Called Atonement* (Nashville, TN: Abingdon, 2007); Sally B. Purvis, *The Power of the Cross: Foundations for a Christian Feminist Ethic of Community* (Nashville, TN: Abingdon, 1993); Peter Schmiechen, *Saving Power: Theories of Atonement and Forms of the Church* (Grand Rapids, MI/Cambridge: Eerdmans, 2005); J. Denny Weaver, *The Nonviolent Atonement* (2nd edn; Grand Rapids, MI/Cambridge: Eerdmans, 2011).

humanity in God's debt, a debt it cannot possibly pay (we cannot help hearing an echo to the parable of the Unforgiving Slave discussed in Chapter 3). It is a debt, however, which a human being *must* pay. Now Anselm draws on his Trinitarian understanding of God. The Father, who is just and loving in equal measure, offers Jesus, the incarnate Son, since through his death alone can the debt be paid. It is because Jesus is fully *divine* that his death has the capacity to pay the debt; it is because Jesus is fully *human* that only he can pay it. Through the death of the God-man the love of God meets the requirements of the justice of God. The atoning transaction to solve humanity's problem takes place within the Godhead, as it were, between the will of the Father and the obedience of the Son.

Having laid that out quite neatly, Anselm acknowledges to his interlocutor, Boso, that all theorizing of the event is at best only an attempt after the fact to trace the inscrutable ways of an atoning God. 'We must understand that for all that a man can say or know, still deeper grounds of so great a truth lie concealed.'[17]

The force and clarity of his logic has resonated over the centuries, even if his caution about humility regarding mystery has too often gone unheeded. Anselm's way of construing atonement made an enormous impact on the sixteenth-century Reformers and their offspring, up to the present, most especially in Evangelical theology, where it holds pride of place in connecting Jesus' death to atonement. In the process, however, the context shifted from the royal court to the court of law, from a question of how honour can be restored to how justice or even divine 'wrath' can be satisfied.

Anselm's younger contemporary, Peter Abelard (1079–1142), more famous to many for his poetry to his beloved Eloise, offered an alternative to Anselm's 'substitution' or 'satisfaction' understanding of atonement. In Abelard's view God does not need to be placated, God's honour does not need to be restored, nor does justice need to be served in a kind of exchange. Sin is less objective offence for which payment is required than intention gone awry, a relationship broken. Rather than Jesus' death constituting an objective transaction

---

[17] St Anselm, *Basic Writings: Proslogium, Monologium, Gaunilon's On Behalf of a Fool, Cur Deus Homo* (trans. S. W. Deane; 2nd edn; La Salle, IL: Open Court, 1962), 181.

(payment for offence), it should be viewed as a demonstration of God's fathomless love, intended to atone by eliciting a response of love and repentance, thus bringing about reconciliation. Abelard's understanding of atonement is often referred to as the 'moral influence' or 'subjective' theory of atonement.

The last of the atonement theories identified in this all-too-brief survey is known by its Latin moniker, *Christus Victor* (Christ the victor). In 1931, the Swedish scholar Gustav Aulén published a book, *Christus Victor*,[18] in which he argued that for the first half millennium of Christianity the main way atonement was 'explained' was as Christ's successful cosmic victory over Satan who held humanity in thrall. Aulén called this the 'classic' or 'dramatic' view of the atonement. At the centre of what is less theory than tradition is not sacrifice, nor a demonstration of love, but Christ's victory over Satan and the forces of evil.

Several themes come together in this varied tradition. First, through his own death Christ won the victory over the powers that held humanity captive. His life becomes a ransom paid to Satan to release humanity. In other words, atonement is a kind of kidnapping drama in which God offered his son's life as ransom. Sometimes this is depicted as a sort of subterfuge. Satan is tricked into freeing his captives because he and his powers did not know that the one whose life they took was the God-man, Jesus. They were deceived by Jesus' apparent vulnerability. Resurrection proved them ignorant and defeated. Resurrection thus becomes an intrinsic part of the atonement drama, in that death or Satan could not hold this hostage or those he came to ransom. God raised Jesus from the dead and with him those held captive to evil.

A second feature is 'recapitulation'. This is different from Anselm's 'substitution', in that here sinful humanity is recapitulated, subsumed in or identified with Christ's death, and thus also with his victory and exaltation. Some ancient (and recent Orthodox) theologians speak of atonement as finding its ultimate goal in this identification with the risen and exalted Christ, in the 'apotheosis' or 'deification' of humanity in and through Christ.

---

[18] Gustav Aulén, *Christus Victor: An Historical Study of the Three Main Types of the Idea of the Atonement* (Eugene, OR: Wipf & Stock, (1931) 2003).

Theories of atonement and violence

Each of these theories has come under sharp scrutiny with respect to whether and in what ways they are violent, or make violence a necessary part of the atonement.

First, Anselm's theory has drawn the most fire, to put it indelicately. Some are not critical of the notion of substitution or satisfaction so much as they lament the degree to which this theory has come over the centuries to crowd out other equally biblical and perhaps more fitting ways of accounting for the atoning significance of Jesus' death. In other words, it is the exclusivity of substitution or satisfaction that distorts the image of God and the meaning of Christ's death for the Christian faith.[19]

Others, however, wish to expunge it outright, in some cases on biblical grounds, in more cases on moral, ideological or theological grounds. They object that this construal of atonement puts God in the position of a vengeful judge who needs to be appeased. What Anselm viewed as love finding a way to serve justice to the benefit of humanity is viewed instead as the worst kind of violence, precisely when it is presented as 'redemptive'. It may not be fair to let Harold Ellens speak for such critics, but he certainly illustrates the vehemence and rhetorical pugilism with which the criticism is frequently made. The irony should not go unnoticed. In Anselm's construct of atonement, according to Ellens, God's options were to

> destroy us or substitute a sacrifice to pay for our sins. He did the latter. He killed Christ. This has been elaborated in sentimental and well-frosted theological terms, and interpreted so as to make the cross, as substitutionary atonement, appear to be a remarkable act of grace. However, at the unconscious level it is, in fact, a metaphor of the worst kind of violence, infanticide or child sacrifice. [The only way God] can get his head screwed back on right is to kill somebody, us or Christ.[20]

---

[19] E.g. Boersma, *Violence*; Green and Baker, *Recovering the Scandal*; Driver, *Understanding the Atonement*.

[20] J. Harold Ellens, 'Religious Metaphors Can Kill', in *The Destructive Power of Religion: Violence in Judaism, Christianity, and Islam*; Vol. 1, *Sacred Scriptures, Ideology, and Violence* (ed. J. Harold Ellens; Westport, CT/London: Praeger, 2004), 255–72 (263).

The charge of infanticide and child sacrifice or, as they prefer to put it, 'divine child abuse', has been levelled also by some feminist critics.[21] Not all feminist criticism is that harsh, to be sure. But there is a widely shared concern that any theory of atonement that makes death its centrepiece makes suffering 'redemptive', thus spawns violence, or minimally undermines resistance to it.[22]

Not only feminists have taken exception to the mix of sacrifice, suffering and redemption, of course. Anselmian atonement is but one instance of what is dubbed 'redemptive violence' and is thus seen as inscribing violence into the heart of the Christian understanding of justice and salvation, in the process buttressing a retributive justice system, including the death penalty. J. Denny Weaver's *The Nonviolent Atonement* critiques Anselm with particular sharpness. Given his desire to be consistently non-violent, Weaver denies God any active role in the death of Jesus, since that would implicate God in violence. Jesus did not come to die in any sense other than willingly undergoing the resistance to his mission. He died tragically because of how he lived and what he taught. There was nothing redemptive or saving about any of this violence. God's involvement is seen not in the cross but in the resurrection. The cross becomes a model of non-violent suffering, not of divinely willed saving suffering. Forgiveness requires no price to be paid; God's honour does not need to be restored through the sacrifice of a life; God's justice is 'satisfied' not by punishment but by the act of forgiveness; being 'saved' means participating in Jesus' non-violent mission of announcing and living the reign of God. Atonement is God's choosing and inviting persons to participate in the transformation of the cosmos. If it was costly for Jesus, it will be costly for his followers.[23]

Many of these critics have been heavily influenced in their aversion to the notion of sacrifice and 'redemptive violence' by the work of

---

[21] E.g. Joanne Carlson Brown and Rebecca Parker, 'For God so Loved the World?', in *Christianity, Patriarchy, and Abuse: A Feminist Critique* (ed. Joanne Carlson Brown and Carole R. Bohn; New York: Pilgrim, 1989), 1–30.

[22] For a particularly trenchant discussion of the problem and the power of the cross, see Purvis, *Power of the Cross*; see also Ched Myers and Elaine Enns, *Ambassadors of Reconciliation; Vol. 1, New Testament Reflections on Restorative Justice and Peacemaking* (Maryknoll, NY: Orbis Books, 2009), 93–5; Weaver, *Nonviolent Atonement*, 151–217.

[23] Weaver, *Nonviolent Atonement*, 306–20.

French anthropologist and literary critic, René Girard.[24] Girard's work has focused on '*mimesis*' (imitation) or 'rivalry' as the root of violence. Human beings, briefly, are caught in a mimetic cycle of wanting what the other wants, a competition that generates violence. Human culture was and is born out of attempting to control such violence through the murder of a scapegoat, on whom the violence is blamed. This 'founding murder' is then masked by creating a myth in which the victim is deified. Sacrifice and scapegoating become rituals by which this myth sustains society. Culture is thus premised on violence.

Girard sees the Gospels' account of Jesus' death not, interestingly, as an instance of such a scapegoat myth but its only and also its final unmasking. The true nature of this mechanism is laid bare for all to see, and thus its lie is brought to an end. Wherever sacrifice and victimage play a role, whether in the Hebrew Bible or in New Testament writings still imbued with sacrificial thinking, and most especially in Christian theories of atonement that work with sacrificial understandings, as does Anselm's, the gospel of the end of victimage has not yet taken hold.[25]

Second, while Abelard does not draw the intensity of ire, his theory too runs into criticism, in that it is seen as idealizing self-denial to the point of death as the full and transformative – atoning – expression of love. We might observe certain affinities to Girard's theory of Jesus' death as exposing the scapegoat mechanism. In both Abelard and Girard, Jesus' death serves not so much to 'do something' as to 'show something', fully 'exposing' God's love or the violence of the scapegoat mechanism, as the case may be.

Third, despite the motifs of combat and victory, *Christus Victor* enjoys more favour, especially among those whose theology is centred

---

[24] Some of René Girard's best-known works are: *The Scapegoat* (trans. Yvonne Freccero; Baltimore: Johns Hopkins University Press, 1986); *Things Hidden since the Foundation of the World* (trans. Stephen Bann and Michael Metteer; Stanford, CA: Stanford University Press, 1987); *Violence and the Sacred* (trans. Patrick Gregory; Baltimore, MD: Johns Hopkins University Press, 1977). See contributions by many scholars who have been influenced by Girard in Jersak and Hardin, *Stricken by God?* and Willard M. Swartley, ed., *Violence Renounced: René Girard, Biblical Studies, and Peacemaking* (Telford, PA: Pandora Press; Scottdale, PA: Herald Press, 2000). For a critical assessment of Girard, see Boersma, *Violence*, 133–51.

[25] See here in particular the articles gathered in Brad Jersak and Hardin's *Stricken by God?*

on liberation. Humanity is not so much 'bad' as 'captive', not so much perpetrator as victim. Humanity is thus less in need of punishment than of liberation or salvation. Humanity is not saved from God's wrath but from Satan's hold on it. Clearly the issues of violence take on a very different hue. It is the 'violence' of the divine response to the primal violence of the powers holding humanity in their grip.

What commends this theory to many is that it doesn't set guilt and sacrifice at the centre of the drama of atonement. Nor does it, secondly, make atonement dependent on the subjective response of rebellious humanity. Finally, it does not restrict atonement to the death of Jesus but sees the resurrection as central to the drama of atonement. Jesus as Messiah is not the sacrificial lamb who takes away the sins of the world so much as the victorious warrior who liberates humanity from the 'powers'.

Even here, however, the metaphorical presence of combat, victory and defeat draws criticism, most especially when it implicates God. For example, J. Denny Weaver considers the 'classic' *Christus Victor* view as still implicating God in violence. He thus proposes an alternative to *Christus Victor*, calling it 'narrative Christus Victor'.[26] He proposes that the narrative of Jesus' life as a non-violent proclaimer and practitioner of the kingdom is the essential and defining centre of the account of atonement. Jesus dies tragically even if inevitably – given the resistance of the 'powers' and of human beings colluding with them – because of his non-violent proclamation and enactment of the God's reign. Christ does not die for us, nor on our behalf, but at 'our' hands. God's 'active' role in the drama of atonement is in raising Jesus non-violently. Atonement happens when persons heed Jesus' proclamation and follow him by imitating him in his non-violence vis-à-vis enemies. 'Grace' is not so much forgiveness as enablement to participate in the non-violent 'saved life of witnessing to the reign of God'.[27]

To be sure, many scholars continue to insist on the importance of traditional atonement theories. One intrepid scholar, Hans Boersma,

---

[26] Weaver, *Nonviolent Atonement*, 20–85, 306–20; for a concise summary of his argument, see J. Denny Weaver, 'The Nonviolent Atonement: Human Violence, Discipleship and God', in *Stricken by God? Nonviolent Identification and the Victory of Christ* (ed. Brad Jersak and Michael Hardin; Grand Rapids, MI/Cambridge: Eerdmans, 2007), 316–55.

[27] Weaver, 'Nonviolent Atonement', 336.

engages the issue of violence head on by arguing that we need all three historic theories of atonement, that 'redemptive violence' is a necessary reality in the service of a loving God's 'hospitality', shown in an unprecedented way in the death of Jesus, and in an absolute way as anticipated in the defeat of death itself in the resurrection and the reconstitution of the cosmos.[28]

New Testament and atonement

These various atonement theories have influenced and continue to influence how the New Testament is read on the death of Jesus. Conversely, it is also true that there is plenty in the New Testament that gives each theory grist for its mill. To be sure, Jesus' followers did not stand by at his crucifixion rejoicing at the fashioning of atonement. Since New Testament writers view the death of Jesus as taking place within an unfolding story full of surprises, the New Testament does not contain *a* theory of atonement, let alone theories of atonement. We find, rather, metaphors and scriptural connections and allusions that point, *after the fact*, to how it could possibly be that the scene of humanity's worst crime could also be the moment of God's reconciling embrace of precisely that hostile humanity. The various metaphors are a way of naming the surprise of grace.

We must state first that what we call 'atonement', a term not used often in New Testament translations,[29] encompasses such rich and suggestive terms as 'reconciliation', 'redemption', 'liberation' or 'salvation', 'forgiveness', 'justification' and no doubt yet others. Indeed, Jesus' whole life, teachings, healings, announcing and enacting of the reign of God, resurrection and *parousia* are all part of the drama of 'at-one-ment' that began at the first sin and will culminate with the final mending of the broken cosmos. New Testament writers viewed the death of Jesus as central to this unfolding story, even if in different ways and vocabulary. That is what 'cross' implied to the New

---

[28] Boersma, *Violence*, 200–1 and *passim*. For an attempt to view Anselm appreciatively through the lens of 'peace theology', see Rachel Reesor-Taylor, 'Anselm's Cur Deus Homo for a Peace Theology: On the Compatibility of Non-violence and Sacrificial Atonement' (PhD; Montreal: McGill University, 2007).

[29] Some translations use 'atonement' for what older versions translate as 'propitiation' (e.g. NRSV at Rom. 3.25; Heb. 2.17; 1 John 2.2; 4.10; NIV adds to those Heb. 9.5).

Testament writers – the site of the most concentrated rebellion against God's initiatives, and the most concentrated response of God's efforts at making peace with these rebels.

Many of the metaphors, turns of phrase and scriptural allusions have provided the theorists of atonement with the raw materials. First, Jesus' death is spoken of repeatedly as a sacrifice. While this is most prominent in Hebrews (see especially chs 7; 9—10), the motif is not restricted to that letter. It is implied in the connection the evangelists make between Jesus' death and the celebration of the Passover and the ritual of the sacrifice of the lamb.[30] John the Baptist identifies Jesus as the 'lamb of God that takes away the sin of the world' in John 1.29, 36. In Romans 3.25 Paul makes a connection between Jesus' 'blood' and the *hilastērion*, variously translated as 'expiation', 'propitiation', 'mercy seat' or 'sacrifice of atonement' (compare also Heb. 9.22; Lev. 17.11). There is little doubt that underlying this is that sin is indebtedness (see Chapter 3). If the offender does not 'pay' then the one harmed bears the weight of the loss. That is one meaning of forgiveness (see Chapter 3). What would have struck every first-century reader is that it is *God* who does the presenting or the offering (*protithēmi*) and not the sinner. More, this initiative of grace and reconciliation is seen as God's justice or righteousness (*dikaiosunē*) on full display or, better, fully at work. Justice and mercy are in this moment indistinguishable. To speak of the 'faith(fulness) of Jesus Christ' in Romans 3.22 and 26 acknowledges the element of obedience on the part of Jesus to God's righteous or just, and thereby saving, will.[31]

There is at the same time a certain reticence about sacrifice in the New Testament. The New Testament writers share in the prophetic and wisdom suspicion of sacrifice unmatched by a life of justice, that is, conformity to God's will. Matthew twice has Jesus allude to Hosea 6.6, 'I desire mercy, not sacrifice' (9.13; 12.7). Hebrews too

---

[30] This is true in the Synoptic Gospels where Jesus celebrates the last supper with his disciples as a Passover meal (Matt. 26.17–19//Mark 14.12–16//Luke 22.7–13) and in John 19.14, where it is stated that Jesus' death was on the Passover. See Scot McKnight, *Jesus and His Death: Historiography, the Historical Jesus, and Atonement Theory* (Waco, TX: Baylor University Press, 2005), 259–73; Wright, *Jesus*, 554–63.

[31] See, e.g., Richard B. Hays, *The Faith of Jesus Christ: An Investigation into the Narrative Substructure of Galatians 3.1—4.11* (2nd edn; Grand Rapids, MI: Eerdmans, 2002); John E. Toews, *Romans* (BCBC; Scottdale, PA/Waterloo, ON: Herald, 2004), 108–111.

recalls Psalm 40.6, to the effect that God does not desire sacrifice, all the while applying that to why, after Christ's 'final' sacrifice, sacrifices are no longer needed (see also Pss. 50 and 51). Which means that along with such reticence, Jesus' death is spoken of in sacrificial terms, not only in terms of what Jesus has done on behalf of humanity and its sin but also as a model to be emulated (e.g. Eph. 5.2).

Closely related is the repeated stress on Jesus' dying 'for us'. In short, there appears to be a recognition that sinful humanity deserves death (e.g. Rom. 1.32), but that Jesus died on behalf of sinners, in their stead. Romans 5.8 states it succinctly: 'But God proves his love for us in that while we were still sinners Christ died for us.' Sometimes the suffering of Christ is not so much a matter of 'taking it for us' as an expression of solidarity for those who themselves suffer (e.g. 2 Cor. 1.5). Even so, the motif of Jesus' death as a death 'for us' is widespread in the New Testament. It may be that 'representation' is better than 'substitution',[32] allowing for resonance in both Anselmian and *Christus Victor* understandings of Jesus' death.

The imagery of sacrifice is derived from the long history of reconciliation and worship rituals, which would have found immediate resonance even among the non-Jewish believers in Jesus, and in the New Testament serves to highlight the irony that it is *God* who takes the initiative to bridge the chasm of estrangement and offers the means to do so. That is what makes it 'gospel' – 'good news'. Yes, sin as offence against fellow human beings and especially against God is viewed against the backdrop of judgement, even severe judgement (see Chapter 3). All the more 'news' then that the judge should love sinners to such an extent that God himself provides the lamb, the offering, the sacrifice to end all sacrifice. But God's agency is never allowed to stand apart from the fact that Jesus is repeatedly said to be a victim of human beings, suffering the (typical) violence of rebellious humanity against God's messenger, and that with respect to God, Jesus is always a full and willing participant in the drama of salvation (Gethsemane notwithstanding).

To remove Anselm and his theory from the debate thus does not remove the stone of stumbling. The New Testament provides plenty

---

[32] Boersma, *Violence*, 177; Christopher D. Marshall, *Beyond Retribution: A New Testament Vision for Justice, Crime, and Punishment* (Grand Rapids, MI: Eerdmans, 2001), 61.

of boulders over which to trip.[33] Critics might thus want to be cautious not to make Anselm the scapegoat, thinking that to reject him is to have sent with him the troublesome images of sacrifice, wrath, judgement, payment and blood. They are constituent elements in the metaphors with which the evangelists and apostles depict the wonder of God's love on full display and fully at work. Revulsion to images of violence should not be allowed to obscure that terrible beauty.

There is plenty of support for the other theories of atonement as well. As already intimated, evangelists and apostles alike knew well that the self-giving of Christ was a model of what it means to love selflessly, and thus a demonstration of love. It both demonstrated the love of God, and serves as a model to be imitated by those who are transformed thereby. 1 John 4.7–11 illustrates this perfectly (see also Rom. 5.8):

> ₇ Beloved, let us love one another, because love is from God; everyone who loves is born of God and knows God. ₈ Whoever does not love does not know God, for God is love. ₉ God's love was revealed among us in this way: God sent his only Son into the world so that we might live through him. ₁₀ In this is love, not that we loved God but that he loved us and sent his Son to be the atoning sacrifice (*hilasmos*) for our sins. ₁₁ Beloved, since God loved us so much, we also ought to love one another.

In addition, there is also the imagery of ransom, liberation from bondage and identification with the dying and rising Messiah, constitutive of the *Christus Victor* understanding of atonement. It is clear that sometimes the term 'saved' relates to (divine) wrath or the judgement to come (e.g. 1 Thess. 1.9). But there are clear instances where being saved or liberated means being freed from the captivity to sin, or of death, or of the 'evil one' or the devil. However the captor is identified, such captivity is envisioned as humanity being both culpable and helpless in captivity, and thus in need of rescue. We have already seen that in Romans 5, where the 'enemies' are at the same time 'sinners' and 'weak' (vv. 6, 8, 10), ruled by death itself (v. 17).

---

[33] See Finlan, *Options*, 18–42, for a survey of Paul's metaphors, which, Finlan insists, have nothing to do with how Jesus himself thought. He suggests not taking them 'literally' and thus lessening their hold on theology and imagination.

This construal of atonement comes to clear expression in the later Pauline writings of Colossians and Ephesians. Colossians 2.13–15, for example, depicts God as a Roman victor and executioner, except that God does not kill, but brings the dead – dead because of their sin! – to life, forgiving all offences, and then, like Pilate with the *titulum*, nails the charges against the condemned to the cross, in the process stripping the powers of their force and authority and parading them as defeated foes in a victory procession. No one in the first century could have mistaken the remarkable recasting of images of imperial and spiritual oppression into an image of divine love at work in liberating those in slavery.

Ephesians 2.1–10 likewise, in possible dependence on Colossians, depicts humanity as the walking dead in the thrall of the 'prince of the power of the air' (vv. 1–2).[34] But God, full of love, mercy and grace, liberates these captives from this death camp and raises them up together with the Messiah, the victorious liberator, and seats them with him in the 'heavenlies', so as to demonstrate God's great wealth in grace and kindness (vv. 4–7).[35] Indeed, God 'saves by grace' precisely to demonstrate or 'show off' to the coming aeons the immeasurable wealth of his grace in the kindness shown rescued humanity. This is a rescue mission on the grandest possible scale; hence the vocabulary of being 'saved' or 'liberated'.

Ephesians 2 likewise illustrates the 'identification' or 'recapitulation' aspect of the 'classic' view of atonement. Those who have been 'saved by grace' (vv. 5, 8) – not from the wrath of God but from captivity to sin and evil – become part of the One who died, was raised and, as we see in verse 6, exalted to the 'heavenlies'. Nowhere is this idea of 'recapitulation' as clearly expressed as in Ephesians 1.10, where God is said to 'gather up' or 'bring under one heading' all things in heaven and on earth. The term there is quite literally 'recapitulation' (Greek: *anakephalaiōsasthai*). 'All things' (*ta panta*) thus become members of his 'body', as is expressed frequently in the Pauline

---

[34] See a more extensive discussion of the Ephesians references in Thomas R. Yoder Neufeld, *Ephesians* (BCBC; Scottdale, PA/Waterloo, ON: Herald, 2002).

[35] With respect to the theme of the rescue from the realm of death we are reminded also of the tradition of the Messiah descending into the realm of the dead there to preach the good news (1 Pet. 4.6).

writings.[36] They are branches on the one vine, as John 15.1–11 has it. They are drawn into the 'oneness' of the Father and the Son, as the so-called 'high priestly prayer' of Jesus suggests in John 17. The faithful share the fate, both in suffering and in exaltation, of the Messiah. Here the guiding thought regarding atonement is less payment than 'at-one-ment'.

The metaphors of rescue, victory and mortal combat are very much part of this understanding of atonement. And, as we see in the second half of Ephesians 2, where the Messiah is depicted as 'killing the enmity' between erstwhile enemies and between them and God, doing so through his own death on the cross (2.16), Jesus' death no less than his resurrection is central to this 'gathering up' of all things. 'Recapitulation' comes at the price of the liberator's life (Eph. 1.7–10). Just so, atonement is not complete without the recapitulation of all things and the identification of the faithful through and in the risen Christ.

To view this as valorizing violence reflects a very different under-standing of the human plight than that held by the writers of the New Testament. For them sin is real and much more than infractions of rules and laws. Sin is a power and force that holds humanity in a deathly grip. To call Jesus 'Messiah' is to make the claim that divine intervention was and is needed to liberate humanity from this death camp. Images and motifs of combat, rescue, liberation, defeat and victory were readily available for New Testament writers, both from their Scriptures and from their imperial context. Most relevant to the issue of violence is the irony that it was the *cross*, imperial brutality at its most naked, that was drawn into the victorious defeat of the power(s)[37] – not, importantly, by putting, even metaphorically, the Romans on their own cross, but their (ostensible) victim, Jesus. This is nothing less than thumbing the nose at imperial power, and most especially at the powers behind the imperial throne.[38] But it is

---

[36] As Eph. 1.23 and 4.4, 12–16 illustrate, the 'body' (*sōma*) serves to strengthen this sense of being drawn into and identified with the 'head' (*kephalē*; 4.15), as does in a very different way the image of husband and wife as an analogy for Christ and the *ekklēsia* in 5.28–32. See also Rom. 12.4, 5; 1 Cor. 12.12–27; Col. 1.18; 2.9, 10; 3.15.

[37] The cross must not be separated from the resurrection within a biblical account of atonement.

[38] Note the ambiguity in 1 Cor. 2.8. Who are the 'rulers (*archons*) of this age'? Human or spiritual powers, or both?

so much more: for those being liberated the cross 'is the power of God' (1 Cor. 1.18).

Our focus here has been on the death of Jesus, given that violence is the focus of our study, and where it is most highly concentrated. But even this brief survey of New Testament motifs, metaphors and images of atonement shows clearly that atonement goes well beyond Golgotha in its scope. The cross is one element in a large and variegated divine enterprise of atonement.

Violence and atonement revisited: 'What does it take?' versus 'What did it take?'

It is clear that no one theory, however 'classic', 'orthodox' or 'non-violent', can *by itself* lay claim to the witness of the New Testament. Joel Green has thus suggested that a 'kaleidoscopic' reading of the New Testament captures its understanding of atonement far better than the privileging of any one of the theories.[39] I would go further and ask whether the search for 'theories' might not be part of the problem. Efforts to fashion theories of atonement typically ask: 'What *does* it take?' In terms of our focus, we might put it crudely: 'How much violence does it or does it not take to effect atonement?' This or that is what makes for atonement, for justice not to be compromised, for the power of evil to be broken, for love to be fully demonstrated and so on. But that is precisely not how the writers of the New Testament think. They ask rather: 'What *did* it take?'

Let me use an analogy from common experience, one that serves as well as a biblical metaphor for the relationship God has with humanity. To ask 'what it took' to save a particular marriage shattered by a spouse's infidelity is quite different from asking 'what it takes' to make a strong marriage. 'What it took' might have been very messy and might have included desperate measures to save it. But no one would argue that an affair is the key to a perfect marriage. But that is too often what the atonement debate is like with respect to the role

---

[39] Joel B. Green, 'Kaleidoscopic View', in *The Nature of the Atonement: Four Views* (ed. James Beilby and Paul R. Eddy; Downers Grove, IL: InterVarsity Press, 2006), 157–85. See also Green and Baker, *Recovering the Scandal*, 15; Driver, *Understanding the Atonement*; Perry Yoder, *Shalom: The Bible's Word for Salvation, Justice, and Peace* (Newton, KS: Faith and Life, 1987), 53–70.

of violence. The New Testament writers witness to 'what it took' to save this failed relationship between God and humanity, failing precisely at the moment of the lover's most intense and vulnerable initiative. It was messy and costly beyond words. What made it 'necessary' is that 'they' killed Jesus. Making Jesus' death God's atoning gift, however inadequately any metaphor will capture the mystery of that gesture, was what God 'had to do' to reconcile with humanity. That is what it 'took' to 'kill enmity', not what it 'takes'.

Biblical writers, without exception, see themselves living within an unfolding story. The ultimate outcome is assured by the gracious sovereignty of God, but the course of it is full of surprises – as it has ever been. But God's sovereignty never renders the story a simple unfolding of a set play. Human beings were and are actors, not marionettes. Jesus died at a particular moment in time because of the hostilities of his contemporaries. Is it impertinent to ask whether God would have been disappointed, to speak anthropomorphically, had Jesus' contemporaries heeded his summons to turn toward the arriving reign of God? Would God's 'plan' have been subverted by an enthusiastic reception of Jesus' announcing of the kingdom? Did the evangelists believe Jesus only feigned grief in his lament over Jerusalem (Matt. 23.37//Luke 13.34)?[40]

Jesus' insistent and genuine summons to repentance, to 'turning' toward the coming of God's reign, was, as the evangelists tell us, largely rebuffed, to the point where he lost his life – a fate typical, perhaps even predictable, but never inevitable, for the messengers of God throughout biblical history. Jesus' death was a calamity, as the Gospel writers make plain simply by narrating the story of his death as that of a prophet and innocent Just One, as a result of human machinations and thus as a cruel response to his ministry.

That such a calamitous death should become 'good news' (*euangelion*) for criminals, collaborators, callous bystanders and cowardly followers came as a profound surprise, and is perceived as such by the writers of the New Testament. As they depict it, there could have been no greater, more unforgivable crime than to hand over God's anointed, God's Son, to the imperial authorities for torture and execution. The script that should now have played itself out is captured

---

[40] Wright, *Jesus*, 14.

in the parable of the Vineyard (Matt. 21.33–46//Mark 12.1–12//Luke 20.9–19): repeated entreaties are rebuffed, finally by killing the vineyard owner's own son. In the parable, vengeance is wreaked on the perpetrators of the crime. But in the story the New Testament writers tell, that is exactly what did *not* happen in the real-life case of Jesus' being killed.[41] To re-imagine the parable in the light of the death of Jesus and the interpretation the New Testament gives it is to have the vineyard owner carry the body of his son to the gates of his own vineyard as an offering of peace.

How could the followers of Jesus make sense of and give expression to this non sequitur of grace? It is exactly here that we need to locate the various efforts of New Testament writers to find vocabulary, motifs, images and metaphors for what is *news*. All of these metaphors emerge out of the euphoria of gratitude and worship, not the desire to figure out the mathematics or the chemistry of atonement. New Testament authors reach back to the traditions of Israel, to the Scriptures and to the highly resonant images familiar to their contemporaries, Jewish or not, in order to give voice to their gratitude and intelligibility to their witness. This creativity accounts for why diverse images and metaphors sit alongside each other with little need to sort out their various implications. The writers of the New Testament are witnesses to a surprise, not theoreticians of atonement. Royal court, legal court, sacrificial ritual, commercial transaction, kidnapping, invasion, giving one's life for another, becoming one with the object of love – all of these *together* offer a glimpse at the wonder of a God who forgives, who pays the inestimable debt, who loves even his enemies, who raises them up to sit with his own son on the throne, who gathers everything and everyone together into his Anointed in a cosmic embrace. As Green and Baker put it, the New Testament offers not a theory but a 'many-hued mural interpreting Jesus' death'.[42] Even the image of a mural may be too static, however, since New Testament writers account for the importance of Jesus'

---

[41] This does not preclude that the parable was later interpreted as God having given the vineyard to the Gentiles. For a full discussion of this text and its interpretation, including that it was seen as announcing judgement on those rejecting Jesus, see Klyne R. Snodgrass, *Stories with Intent: A Comprehensive Guide to the Parables of Jesus* (Grand Rapids, MI/Cambridge: Eerdmans, 2008), 276–99.

[42] Green and Baker, *Recovering the Scandal*, 15.

death only as part of a grand narrative that has not yet ended, and that has yet more surprises in store.[43]

Weaver is thus absolutely right in insisting on the narrative nature of atonement in the New Testament, and that the story encompasses Jesus' life and ministry leading up to his death, and followed by the resurrection and the ongoing 'incarnation', as it were, of his body. Weaver is wrong, however, to leave God out of it when it comes to this darkest, most violent hour.[44] Evangelists and apostles alike insist that it was *God* who retrieved from the event of the death of Jesus the means of reconciliation precisely with those who killed him. That is why it is impossible for the evangelists, who tell the story of Jesus' death as that of an innocent man caught up in the treachery of a miscarriage of justice, not *also* to tell it as the story of *God*'s initiative.

Admittedly, the lively Jewish sense of God's sovereignty lends to the narratives of the evangelists and the reflections of the apostles a certain ambience of necessity.[45] The use of Scripture to show fulfilment (1 Cor. 15.3), the repeated predictions of the suffering and death of the Son of man (e.g. Mark 8.31; 9.31; 10.33–34 and par.), Jesus' wrestling in Gethsemane with the 'will' of his Father (Matt. 26.39// Mark 14.36//Luke 22.42), and the character of Judas (e.g. John 17.12), can be read as implying a foreordained or predetermined script. But the evangelists and apostles never obscure the fully human story of Jesus' death. God's agency in rendering the crime scene a place of mercy and grace was the surprise love sprang on humanity caught in the act of rebuffing the messenger of God's *basileia*. Remarkably, such love is nothing other than God's justice (*dikaoisunē*) at work in the faithfulness of Jesus (Rom. 3.21–26). Hence it is in the New Testament always storied *gospel* – 'good news' and never 'system' or 'theory'.

It is precisely the mysterious foolishness of the 'power of God' at work within the abject weakness and scandal of Jesus' death (1 Cor. 1.18–25) that makes any closed theory suspect or any one metaphor

---

[43] For the importance of a 'storied' reading of the death of Jesus and all else, see Wright, *Jesus*, 540–611.

[44] So also Christopher D. Marshall, 'Atonement, Violence and the Will of God: A Sympathetic Response to J. Denny Weaver's The Nonviolent Atonement', *MQR* 77 (2003), 69–92. See also Marshall, *Beyond Retribution*, 38–69.

[45] Yoder Neufeld, *Recovering Jesus*, 256–8.

inadequate. The insistence on this as *both* a human and a divine story also makes an ideologically or even theologically driven assessment of violence highly problematic. When the human story is relegated to secondary status, the issue of violence and its 'necessity' is placed at the feet of God, as atonement theorists and their critics are wont to do. New Testament writers are interested neither in making violence good news nor in denying God access to the scene of the crime, precisely there to make peace with that violent community.

Compounding the difficulties for assessing the issue of violence is that metaphors are inherently unstable. They function both within the context of a 'shared encyclopedia'[46] and at the same time are taken up by highly diverse imaginations sharing that very same encyclopedia. Let me illustrate. When Mel Gibson's *The Passion of the Christ* appeared on the screen, I was asked to meet with a group of students. Even within that relatively homogeneous circle of students the reactions to the film were anything but homogeneous. Some were repulsed by what they saw as a voyeuristic focus of violence (as was I), while others had not been able to stop crying during the viewing of the film and not because of monstrous sadism. They saw, instead, fathomless love. Just as in the case of Anselm's construal of atonement, some see divine child abuse, even murder, where others see the saving love and justice of God. To paraphrase the words of Goethe's *Harzreise im Winter*,[47] what to one is the balm of fathomless love is for another the poison of misanthropic violence.

When such radically different takes on the death of Jesus emerge out of ideology or theology, pro or con, we must ask whether that ideology or theology illuminates or obscures the saving power of God at work in the event of human violence in the crucifixion of Jesus. A 'Gotcha!' approach to violence within the biblical narrative is prone to miss the ingenuity of love the evangelists saw in the cross. When such radically diverse assessments emerge out of experience, corporate or individual, whether profoundly healing or terribly damaging, we

---

[46] Green and Baker, *Recovering the Scandal*, 20.

[47] Johann Wolfgang von Goethe, 'Winter journey in the Harz mountains' (1777).

> *Ach wer heilet die Schmerzen* / O, who will heal the pain
> *des, dem Balsam zu Gift ward ?* / of one for whom balm became poison,
> *Der sich Menschenhass* / who drank human hatred (or who imbibed misanthropy)
> *aus der Fülle der Liebe trank ?* / from the fullness of love?

are on holy ground, and should exercise great respect for such experience, most especially if we do not share it.[48] As one who has drunk love from the chalice of the story of Jesus' death, I need precisely for that reason to have empathy with those for whom the cross has become yet again a scene of violence – against them. Even so, the cross is and will remain offensive, inconvenient, scandalous and idiotic (1 Cor. 1.18–25). One should just be concerned to get the scandal right.

It is fitting, in conclusion, to recall Anselm's caveat that after all efforts at grasping atonement have been expended, 'still deeper grounds of so great a truth lie concealed'.[49] Anselm's words echo Paul's wonder and humility at the end of his peerless rehearsal of God's reconciling with humanity (Rom. 11.33–36).

> ₃₃ O the depth of the riches and wisdom and knowledge of God! How unsearchable are his judgements and how inscrutable his ways!
> ₃₄ 'For who has known the mind of the Lord?
> Or who has been his counsellor?'
> ₃₅ 'Or who has given a gift to him,
> to receive a gift in return?'
> ₃₆ For from him and through him and to him are all things. To him be the glory for ever. Amen.

---

[48] Green and Baker, *Recovering the Scandal*, 199–221.
[49] Anselm, *Basic Writings*, 181.

6

Subordination and violence

Subordination has become an important part of the violence debate, most particularly when a 'broad' definition of violence is employed (see Chapter 1). The acquiescence to or endorsement of the domination of some over others is an obvious flashpoint, as is the door that that opens to violence of the strong against the vulnerable, even when that violence is not physical but 'only' social. This is relevant particularly to relations between the sexes. Another point of controversy is the relationship of persons to the demands the state places on them. For both contexts there are specific traditions within the New Testament – the Household Codes and 'Romans 13' – that have become the arenas of controversy.

I will consistently use the word 'subordination' rather than the more common 'subjection', 'submission' or 'obedience'. 'Subordination' or 'to subordinate (oneself)' best translates the Greek noun *hupotagē* and verb *hupotassō* (*hupo* – 'under', *tassō* – 'order'). I wish to leave the question open as to whether that implies subjection and obedience, and allow the reader to join in the interpretive process of discerning its meaning and implications for the topic of violence.

Subordination is part of a wider pattern in the New Testament. The Synoptic tradition has Jesus pitting himself against the 'Gentile' notion of status and power by demanding that his followers imitate him in becoming slaves to each other (Matt. 20.25–28//Mark 10.42–45//Luke 22.24–27). In the minds of the evangelists this clearly anticipates the ultimate offering of Jesus' own life as God's 'slave' or 'servant' (see Chapter 5). Readers will recall that in answer to the disciples' question as to who is the greatest in the kingdom, Jesus puts a child (or little slave boy; *paidion*) before them as representative of greatness in the *basileia* of God (Matt. 18.3–5). In the Gospel of John Jesus scandalizes his followers at their final meal together by washing their feet, a task typically assigned to a slave (John 13.1–20). We see it as well in the humility, meekness, and deliberate powerlessness that Paul demands both of himself and his congregations in imitation of

Christic.[1] Disciples of Jesus are to be deliberately slave-like in placing others before themselves.

Humility, servanthood and putting the needs of others before your own can be viewed as resolute forms of non-violence. As we saw in Chapters 2 and 3, they are decidedly anti-domineering and intentionally subversive of status and power. They are in that sense truly counter-cultural in their first-century setting, as they still are in our day.

But that is not all there is to this topic in the New Testament. There are texts that ask wives, children and slaves to be subordinate to hus-bands, fathers and masters, respectively, and all of them together to the authorities. This looks an awful lot like one-sided servitude and decidedly not the subversion of social power and privilege we have just noted. This strain of tradition in the New Testament is perceived by many to have aided and abetted the violence against the most vulnerable in society.

The Household Code

The ancient household or family, indeed society generally, was organ-ized like a pyramid, with the father at the top, then the mother, children, freed-persons and finally slaves at the bottom, even if actual social expression of this 'ideal' varied from time to time and place to place. The (in)famous Household Code[2] addresses both the microcosm of family and, implicitly, the macrocosm of society.

We find the Household Code in its clearest form in Colossians 3.18—4.1 and Ephesians 5.21—6.9. It is present in looser form in

---

[1] E.g. 1 Cor. 1; 4; 2 Cor. 4; 12; Phil. 2.1–11; Eph. 4.1–3.

[2] I have discussed the Household Code at considerable length and depth in my commen-tary (Thomas R. Yoder Neufeld, *Ephesians* (BCBC; Scottdale, PA/Waterloo, ON: Herald, 2002), 253–89. The term is derived from Martin Luther's *Haustafel*, and sometimes also called 'station code' (David Schroeder, 'Lists, Ethical', *IDBSup.*, 546–7) or 'Domestic Code' (e.g. David J. Balch, *Let Wives be Submissive: The Domestic Code in 1 Peter* (Chico, CA: Scholars Press, 1981); Ernest D. Martin, *Colossians* (BCBC; Scottdale, PA/Waterloo, ON: Herald, 1993), 181). See, apart from the many commentaries on Colossians, Ephesians and 1 Peter, also Balch, 'Household Code', *ABD* 3.318–20; James E. Crouch, *The Origin and Intention of the Colossian Haustafel* (Göttingen: Vandenhoeck & Ruprecht, 1971); John H. Elliott, *A Home for the Homeless: A Sociological Exegesis of 1 Peter, Its Situation and Strategy* (Philadelphia, PA: Fortress Press, 1981); Elisabeth Schüssler Fiorenza, *In Memory of Her: A Feminist Theological Reconstruction of Christian Origins* (New York: Crossroad, 1983), 251–84; John Howard Yoder, *The Politics of Jesus: Vicit Agnus Noster* (2nd edn; Grand Rapids, MI: Eerdmans/Carlisle: Paternoster, 1994), 162–92.

1 Peter 2.13—3.7, looser yet in 1 Timothy 2.8–15; 5.1–2; 6.1–2 and Titus 2.1–10; 3.1. The tradition as found in 1 Peter 2.13–17 begins with a call to be subordinate to 'every human creation', typically understood as a reference to governments. The similarities to Romans 13.1–7 will be taken up in the second half of this chapter.

Many scholars today consider Colossians, Ephesians, 1 Peter and especially the Pastoral Letters to have been attributed to Paul and Peter after their death, which I too find most likely. This suggests to many that at least some communities within the Jesus movement grew increasingly conservative,[3] with a gradual waning of the counter-cultural impulses shaping life in the early years. The Household Code is typically seen as reflecting a return to the long tradition of a patriarchal ordering of social relations within family and society. For example, Aristotle's teaching on 'household management' anticipates roughly the structure of the Household Code in Colossians and Ephesians.

> [T]he investigation of everything should begin with the smallest parts, and the primary and smallest parts of the household are master and slave, husband and wife, father and children; we ought therefore to examine the proper constitution and character of each of these three relationships. (*Politics* 1.1253b)

It is thus quite common to see a widening gulf between the traditions of Jesus and the Paul (and Peter) of the Household Code, reflective of social mores prevalent in the Graeco-Roman world.

While there is an obvious structure to the Code, it has been adapted and fitted to the particular interests of each of the writers. There appears to be most similarity between Colossians and Ephesians, perhaps even literary dependence.[4] We notice, first, that in all instances it is the wives who are to be subordinate to their husbands. In 1 Peter wives are to be subordinate to husbands who may not be believers, in which case their motivation is to be one of quiet evangelism. Further, in contrast to Colossians, Ephesians greatly expands the husband–wife relationship into a reflection on the relationship between Christ and the *ekklēsia*, to the point where it

---

[3] Perhaps other parts of the communities grew more radical, as the second-century struggles with Gnosticism, for example, illustrate.

[4] For a history of the relationship, see Yoder Neufeld, *Ephesians*, 275–83, and the many commentaries on Colossians and especially Ephesians.

is not always clear which relationship is being illuminated by the other (5.32). The instructions to children and parents (fathers) are present in both Colossians and Ephesians but not in 1 Peter. In 1 Peter, the address to slaves precedes that directed to wives and husbands. What we note in the two Pauline letters is that slaves are told that they are to perform their duties 'as slaves of Christ' (Eph. 6.6) or 'fearing the Lord' (Col. 3.22). Christ is their actual owner and master. Slave holders are in turn enjoined to be just and fair, since they too have a 'master in heaven'. Just to make that point crystal clear, Ephesians makes the instructions just given to slaves the template for the slave owner's own behaviour (6.9). Notably, in 1 Peter there are no instructions for masters. Nor is Jesus appealed to as a model slave owner or master, as in Colossians and Ephesians, but rather as a fellow slave, willingly suffering the abuse to which slaves are routinely subjected. 1 Peter seems to reflect the marginal status of the community to which it is addressed: wives are likely to be married to unbelievers and slaves are 'house servants' (*oiketai*) who suffer the abuse of their owners.[5] While there is a certain amount of mutuality in each instance of the code, only Ephesians makes it explicit in 5.21.

The Household Code as violent

The question of whether and how the Household Code is complicit in violence is complex, depending on which instance of the code one is considering, and through which lens it is read.

While 1 Peter utilizes the tradition of the Household Code, it is apparent that the author views domestic and economic relationships as marked by suffering (2.20). After the general instruction to all to be subordinate to the 'human creations' (2.13–17), slaves are mentioned first, without a corresponding word to masters. In contrast to Colossians and Ephesians, Christ is not put forward as a master or lord so much as one who stands in solidarity with sufferers, in particular with vulnerable slaves. Importantly, such suffering is interpreted in the light of the Fourth Servant Song of Isaiah 53,

---

[5] This is the essential argument of Elliott, *Home for the Homeless*. See also Mary H. Schertz, 'Nonretaliation and the Haustafeln in 1 Peter', in *The Love of Enemy and Nonretaliation in the New Testament* (ed. Willard M. Swartley; Studies of Peace and Scripture, Institute of Mennonite Studies; Louisville, KY: Westminster/John Knox, 1992), 258–86.

where the Slave of God bears the sins of others and brings healing (1 Pet. 2.21–25). Violence and abuse are thus not simply to be suffered stoically and fatalistically, but in effect as the imitation of Christ, their fellow slave, liberator and guardian. Wives are told that through their patient conduct they might just 'win' their husbands (1 Pet. 3.1–2). Such suffering takes place against the backdrop of divine judgement and vindication. Given the high degree of eschatological expectation, suffering is therefore neither trivialized nor given permanence (4.7–19).

Many critics will have the same difficulty with the code in 1 Peter as they have with the call to turn the cheek and love the enemy we saw in Matthew 5 (see Chapter 2). It is too vulnerable to leaving the door open to abuse and violence, and undercutting resistance to it, particularly in the realm of domestic relationships, where privacy serves to keep abuse and violence out of sight, most especially when enforced by a patriarchal Church. To strip 1 Peter's Household Code of its eschatology and its identification with the suffering Messiah does indeed render it vulnerable to the charge of passivity in the face of violence, and thus of collusion with it. The Household Code as found in 1 Peter thus shares with the Sermon on the Mount the perspective that willing, suffering vulnerability constitutes a form of enemy love. It also shares with the Sermon the conviction that such subordination, such deliberately vulnerable love, will be vindicated by God.

In contrast to what we observe in 1 Peter, the Household Code in Colossians and Ephesians makes subordination of social inferiors to social superiors a *positive* vision of domestic and socio-economic relations and not an instance of suffering. From a contemporary egalitarian perspective such discrimination on the basis of sex, age and class is viewed as inherently violent. Moreover, it provides space and sanction for physical and psychological violence. When such a social structure is supported by making Jesus the model for *super*-ordinated husbands, fathers and slaveholders, patriarchy is seen to be given a solidity it did not have with Jesus.[6] Patriarchal inequalities are thereby 'cemented'[7] christologically and ecclesiologically. Indeed,

---

[6] Recall Jesus' harsh words regarding family (Luke 12.51//Matt. 10.34–39; Luke 14.26). See also Gal. 3.28.

[7] Fiorenza, *In Memory of Her*, 270.

the higher the Christology the greater the *sub*ordination of wife, child and slave. There can, after all, be no firmer foundation than Christ, to paraphrase Paul in 1 Corinthians 3.11. To place a patriarchal and thus hierarchical ordering of society on such a foundation is seen as either 'baptizing' what had already been rejected (unequal gender relationships and, most unambiguously, slavery) or destabilizing the foundation itself. Viewed in this light, Jesus and the Household Code are thus fundamentally at odds with each other.

Feminists have understandably been sharpest in their criticism, deeming the Household Code to be 'dangerous to [women's] health'.[8] What adds to the criticism is the frequently expressed suspicion that the introduction of the Household Code was an attempt to reign in freedom, to put the Spirit back in the bottle, as it were, among sectors evidently too energetic in making real a community in which there were no longer slave or free, male or female (Gal. 3.28).

Mitigating this, it is sometimes pointed out, is that there is recognition in the codes themselves of the abusive potential in patriarchal relationships, one in which wives 'fear' their husbands and slaves serve their masters with 'fear and trembling' (Eph. 5.33; 6.5). Husbands are to 'love' their wives and to treat them considerately (Eph. 5.25–33; Col. 3.19; 1 Pet. 3.7). Fathers are not to enrage their children, and masters are not to threaten their slaves. Some have dubbed this 'love patriarchalism' or 'benevolent patriarchy'.[9] In other words, privilege is tempered by love. For those who see patriarchy itself as a violation of the full humanity of women, children and slaves, such amelioration only exacerbates the oppressiveness of the Household Code in that it offers not emancipation, but at best 'a modified plan of business as usual'.[10]

---

[8] Letty M. Russell, 'Authority and the Challenge of Feminist Interpretation', in *Feminist Interpretation of the Bible* (ed. Letty M. Russell; Philadelphia, PA: Fortress Press, 1985), 137–46 (141). See also Catherine Clark Kroeger and James R. Beck, eds, *Women, Abuse, and the Bible: How Scripture Can Be Used to Hurt or to Heal* (Grand Rapids, MI: Baker Books, 1996), and the articles included there. See also the articles by Gail Gerber Koontz, Carol Penner and Mary Schertz, in Elizabeth G. Yoder, ed., *Peace Theology and Violence against Women* (Occasional Papers, 16; Elkhart, IN: Institute of Mennonite Studies, 1992).

[9] Cf. e.g. Andrew T. Lincoln, *Ephesians* (WBC 42; Dallas, TX: Word Books, 1990), 391; Fiorenza, *In Memory of Her*, 269–70.

[10] Letty M. Russell, *Imitators of God: A Study Book on Ephesians* (New York: Mission Education and Cultivation Program Department, General Board of Global Ministries, 1984), 100.

Other factors mitigating the potential for violence are witness and apology.[11] 1 Peter makes clear the role of 'good behaviour' in the community's witness to a largely hostile world (2.12; 3.13–17). That may have played a role in Colossians and Ephesians as well.[12] The inherently tactical nature, then, would make of subordination either a means of survival or a kind of 'stealth' operation in which the 'revolution' could continue under cover, as it were. If so, this sense of witness was tragically lost sight of, and the Household Code too quickly served to entrench patriarchy.

Not surprisingly, some scholars have sought to remove the offence by proposing that the Household Code in Colossians and Ephesians is an interpolation. Winsome Munro, for example, has argued that the Household Code has its home in the patriarchal world of the Pastoral Letters, and that the Household Code was inserted into both Colossians and Ephesians, as well as 1 Corinthians 14.33–35 and, notably, Romans 13.1–7.[13]

It is difficult to shake the sense that a good deal of what fuels the criticism of the Household Code derives from the way it has been used over the centuries, both in home and church. Thus while these texts continue to be the source of controversy in conservative or evangelical circles, where the normativity of the Scriptures continues to intersect with social change, in many parts of the more 'liberal' Church these texts have largely fallen into disuse. There is little interest in investigating whether the texts permit something other than a 'violent' reading.

'Non-violent' readings of the Household Code

There are many interpreters who continue to read the Household Code 'straight up' as an endorsement of patriarchy as the God-intended order for social relations. But there are interpreters who share with the critics a rejection of the inherent violence of

---

[11] E.g. Thomas R. Yoder Neufeld, 'Paul, Women, and Ministry in the Church', *Conrad Grebel Review* 8 (1990), 289–99.

[12] E.g. Angela Standhartinger, 'The Origin and Intention of the Household Code in the Letter to the Colossians', *JSNT* 79 (2000), 117–30.

[13] Winsome Munro, *Authority in Paul and Peter: The Identification of a Pastoral Stratum in the Pauline Corpus and 1 Peter* (Cambridge: Cambridge University Press, 1983); Sarah J. Tanzer, 'Ephesians,' in *Searching the Scriptures; Vol. 2, A Feminist Commentary* (ed. Elisabeth Schüssler Fiorenza; New York: Crossroad, 1994), 325–48.

one-sided subordination and thus also domination, while also seeing precisely in the manner in which the Household Code is taken up in the New Testament the influence of Jesus' legacy on social and familial relationships within the nascent Christian movement. Already in a 1959 University of Hamburg dissertation, David Schroeder argued against the grain that the character of the Household Code as present in the New Testament goes back to Jesus' own approach to human relationships.[14] Schroeder was followed by John Howard Yoder in his *Politics of Jesus*, who discusses the Code under the chapter title 'Revolutionary Subordination'.[15] More recently, a number of scholars have each in their own way raised questions as to whether the Household Code might not be something other than an effort to entrench patriarchy in the church communities.[16]

Patriarchal social arrangements would have been largely taken as a given by first readers of these texts. Given that, let me identify a number of features that might have alerted the reader to read the Household Code against the grain of common assumptions.

First, those in subordinate positions are addressed first and directly.[17] The contrast can be seen most clearly when comparing the New Testament Household Code with ancient texts in which it is the *pater familias*, the 'father of the family' as head of the household, who is to see to it that everyone knows their place or 'station'.[18] That women

---

[14] David Schroeder, 'Die Haustafeln des Neuen Testaments: Ihre Herkunft und ihr theologischer Sinn' (DTheol. dissertation; University of Hamburg, 1959); Schroeder, 'Lists, Ethics', 547.

[15] John Howard Yoder, *Politics*, 178–9, 187.

[16] Ronald R. Clark, Jr., 'Submit or Else! Intimate Partner Violence, Aggression, Abusers, and the Bible', in *A Cry Instead of Justice: The Bible and Cultures of Violence in Psychological Perspective* (ed. Dereck Daschke and Andrew Kille; New York/London: T&T Clark, 2010), 87–106; Suzanne Watts Henderson, 'Taking Liberties with the Text: The Colossians Household Code as Hermeneutical Paradigm', *Interpretation* 60/4 (2006), 420–32; James P. Hering, *The Colossian and Ephesians Haustafeln in Theological Context: An Analysis of Their Origins, Relationship, and Message* (New York/Frankfurt am Main: Peter Lang, 2007); Andrew T. Lincoln, 'The Household Code and Wisdom Mode of Colossians', *JSNT* 74 (1999), 93–112; Standhartinger, 'Origin and Intention'; Brian J. Walsh and Sylvia C. Keesmaat, *Colossians Remixed: Subverting the Empire* (Downers Grove, IL: InterVarsity Press, 2004) (they call the relevant chapter 'An Ethic of Liberation', 201–19).

[17] The directness of the injunction is a bit ambiguous in Eph. 5.22, since the specification of wives follows after the general appeal to all to 'mutual' subordination in v. 21.

[18] As in, e.g., the Pastoral Letters.

and slaves are asked to be subordinate to their husbands and bosses means that they presumably can choose not to. Schroeder, and those who follow his lead, thus view the Household Code as reflecting the ongoing struggle to get people to choose servanthood in imitation of Christ voluntarily.[19] To the degree to which the Household Code is intended to inject Jesus-the-servant into everyday domestic relationships, it has the potential of being, in Yoder's word, 'revolutionary'.[20]

Second, the relationships within the household are addressed as reciprocal. That is reflected already in the structure of the code. Ephesians takes it one step further, however, by restructuring the first injunction directed to women (5.22) by moving the command to 'be subordinate' into a preceding phrase in which all are to be 'mutually' (*allēlōn*) subordinate, essentially framing the whole of the Household Code as one of mutual subordination (5.21).[21]

Third, instead of seeing the appeal to Christ as 'lord' in both the Colossian and Ephesian Code as a means of 'cementing' patriarchy, it should be seen as a way of reframing any and all social relationships in light of Jesus the Messiah.[22] The household was understood to be a microcosm of society. To demand that readers subject their everyday domestic relationships and structures to the 'lordship' of Christ was to subject them to one who still within living memory had been crucified for insurrection, and who had repeatedly scandalized his contemporaries with his hostility to status and conventional power. We should notice that in 1 Peter, Jesus is in full solidarity with slaves as a fellow sufferer. In Colossians slaves have an inheritance promised them (3.24), and slave owners are reminded of their equality (*isotēs*) with their slaves (4.1).[23] Ephesians does that dramatically simply by telling the masters that they receive the same instructions as their slaves (6.9).

---

[19] Schroeder, 'Haustafeln', 151.

[20] John Howard Yoder, *Politics*, 162–92.

[21] Yoder Neufeld, *Ephesians*, 255. See also Clinton E. Arnold, *Ephesians* (ZECNT; Grand Rapids, MI: Zondervan, 2010), 363; Harold W. Hoehner, *Ephesians: An Exegetical Commentary* (Grand Rapids, MI: Baker Academic, 2002), 716–17; Frank Thielman, *Ephesians* (BECNT; Grand Rapids, MI: Baker Academic, 2010), 365.

[22] See Henderson, 'Taking Liberties', and Lincoln, 'Household Code', who makes a link between the wisdom hymn to Christ and the Household Code.

[23] Standhartinger, 'Origin and Intention', 128.

Most troubling to many critics is Ephesians' identification of Christ and *ekklēsia* with husband and wife. Might that identification be seen as an effort to refashion conventionally understood relationships? True, Christ is the 'lord' and 'head'[24] to be obeyed out of 'fear' (5.21). He thus serves as role model for the *super*ordinated husband. But his 'lordship' has a remarkable affinity with the 'master' at the Last Supper in John: he washes and gives his life for his beloved (Eph. 5.25–27; John 13.1–20). This sheds light also on the love-of-one's-own-body in Eph. 5.28. Given the indicated relationship of Christ to the *ekklēsia* and his body, 'self-love' becomes, ironically, self*less* love for the other, the *ekklēsia*. There is surely a deliberate allusion to the love of neighbour in Leviticus 19.17, where the love-of-self is taken to be the measure for the love of the other, which, if enacted within the domestic setting, amounts to the opposite of privileging the husband over the wife.[25] Finally, when Genesis 2.24 is applied to Christ it both serves to denote desire for the spouse and also a way of alluding to the entry of Messiah/Wisdom into the world for the sake of humanity in need of divine companionship and rescue.[26] In no way is Christ put forward in a dominating way. Rather, husbands and wives are invited to view their own relationship as a dramatic enactment of the drama of liberation.[27] It is not clear what there is to 'fear' from the Christ depicted in the Household Code. While the identification of Christ and *ekklēsia* is not made within the Colossian Household Code, it is preceded by a moving call to mutual love and deference, strikingly evocative of what we have seen in the Sermon on the Mount and Matthew 18.[28] In Ephesians the Household Code is preceded by a call to thoroughgoing identification with the kindness of God and the self-giving of Christ (5.2), radical noncon-formity, and finally wise, worshipful, grateful and empowered living; and the Household Code is followed by a call to militancy (6.10–20; see Chapter 7).

---

[24] On 'head', see Yoder Neufeld, *Ephesians*, 347–50.

[25] Notice that in Luke 10.25 the double commandment ushers in the parable of the Good Samaritan; cf. also John 15.12–17. See also the 'love of enemy' as an intensification of precisely this command (see Chapter 2). Recall its presence in Matt. 18.15–20 in Chapter 3.

[26] E.g. Ecclus. 24; Phil. 2; and John 1.

[27] Yoder Neufeld, *Ephesians*, 286–7.

[28] The baptismal imagery of putting on the 'new human', i.e. Christ, pervades Col. 3.

Is the Household Code violent?

Is the Household Code violent? If so, has the Household Code tradition been complicit in violence because it has been heeded, or because it has not? Is it 'revolutionary', as Yoder claims, or is it the means by which the revolution of Jesus was and is subverted, possessing at most a Christianizing veneer, and thus 'in no sense revolutionary'.[29] The answer depends on the way the textual evidence is handled, certainly. But it depends finally less on the parsing of the texts than in the living out of the identification with the Christ to whom appeal is made. Texts live by how they are used and abused, by who is reading them, from what social location and to what end. The relationship of the Household Code to violence thus depends on the disposition and experience of those reading it, their take on Jesus, and on the everyday choices made in intimate closeness with those with whom they are in the body of Christ. With respect to 1 Peter it depends on whether deliberate, patient and sometimes defiant vulnerability is in fact the 'weakness' through which the power of God is active. If that is not so, then all who claim the crucified one as lord are 'most to be pitied', to echo the words of Paul in 1 Corinthians 15. With respect to Colossians and Ephesians, the answer depends on whether husbands, fathers and bosses – today we would say heads of households, parents and bosses regardless of sex – can summon the courage to emulate a master who, in the words of the Philippian hymn, took on the role of a slave as the form of his lordship, for the sake of the object of his or her love. In contrast to 1 Peter, this is revolution or at least transformation 'from above'.[30]

One must respect angry criticism of the Household Code when it shares in Jesus' own rage at the abuse of the 'little ones' in Matthew 18 (see Chapter 3). It is better not to read the Household Code at all than to read it as a privileged, self-assured male, who takes it as

---

[29] Ernest Best, *Ephesians* (New Testament Guides; Sheffield: JSOT Press, 1993), 85; Best, *Ephesians* (ICC; Edinburgh: T&T Clark, 1998), 583.

[30] Myers and Enns refer to the Ephesian Household Code as potentially 'an ethic of nonviolent transformation from below' (Ched Myers and Elaine Enns, *Ambassadors of Reconciliation; Vol. 1, New Testament Reflections on Restorative Justice and Peacemaking* (Maryknoll, NY: Orbis Books, 2009), 111. While substantially correct with respect to its potential, what makes the Colossian and the Ephesian *Haustafeln* so challenging is that they demand the relinquishing of power and privilege within a patriarchal social arrangement by those in the *super*ordinate position.

permission to dominate and abuse with impunity. Better too not to read it if it leads to accepting one's own oppression as part of the divinely willed order. But, we might ask, is it unfaithful to the text if the appeal to Christ within the Household Code is to one who precisely does *not* dominate, who loves the other not only 'as himself' but to the extent of giving his life for the liberation of the other, in this case spouse, offspring and slave? Is it unfaithful to the text to see it as an invitation to a Spirit-filled life in which all domestic relationships become the stage to act out the drama of liberation? Is it unfaithful to the text to place it in continuity with the deeply mysterious way in which chosen vulnerability serves the victory of the reign of God over violence?

Subordination to authorities – 'Romans 13'

We come now to one of the most notorious texts in the New Testament, Romans 13.1–7, often simply referred to as 'Romans 13'. Here 'we strike a reef that threatens to capsize every Christian liberative project'.[31] Everyone is to be subordinate to the authorities, who are there by God's will and serve as God's servants of wrath against those who do evil and as God's rewarders of those who do good. The recipients of this letter are to be 'non-resistant', discharging their civic duties of paying taxes and giving honour. Once again, subordination and violence appear in the same frame.

Readers will recall that in 1 Peter 2.13 the Household Code begins with, 'Be subordinate to every human creation'. 'Human creation' (*anthropinē ktisis*), often translated 'human institution', encompasses a whole range of authority structures, including 'the king as supreme' (*basileus hōs huperechōn*) and 'leading authorities' (*hēgemones*), who are said to be 'sent by God' to punish those who do wrong and praise those who do right. They are all to be shown 'honour' (*timaō*; v. 17).

The similarity to Romans 13.1–7 is obvious to even a casual reader. It can be rendered carefully as follows: every person is to be subordinate (*hypotassō*) to the supreme authorities (*exousiai huperechousiai*). All of them are there 'by God' who has 'ordered' (*tassō*) them all (v. 1). To resist them (*antitassō*; lit. 'to order oneself over against') is to resist

---

[31] Neil Elliott, *Liberating Paul: The Justice of God and the Politics of the Apostle* (Maryknoll, NY: Orbis, 1994), 217.

(*anthistēmi*)[32] God's order (*diatagē*, from *diatassō*). Those who do will be liable to judgement (v. 2). As in 1 Peter, rulers (*archontes*) bring fear to those who do bad and reward the good (v. 3). Again as in 1 Peter, where the *hēgemones* are 'sent' by God, the authority (*exousia*) is identified as God's servant (*diakonos*), both in rewarding good and in bearing the sword (*machaira*) as means of instilling fear. The authority is an 'avenger' (*ekdikos*) bringing 'wrath' (*orgē*) on those doing evil (v. 4). Subordination is not only motivated by fear of wrath, however, but also for reason of conscience (v. 5). That is why one pays taxes, since servants (*leitourgoi*)[33] are devoted to this very thing (v. 6). The pericope ends with a terse order to discharge all obligations (*opheilē*; lit. 'owings'), taxes (*phoros*, *telos*), fear (or respect; *phobos*) and honour (*timē*).

Given its sharp and concise focus and its presence in the greatest and most influential of Paul's letters, it is easy to see why this text has exerted enormous influence. It has no doubt served to create respect for the social and civil order, connecting 'secular' institutions to the lordship of God. It has also contributed to a Christian culture of obedience to state authorities. In the light of the long history of state-sponsored violence and warfare within the sphere of 'Christian' civilization, from the Holocaust to the readiness to incinerate the earth's population through nuclear weapons, to the present 'wars against terror', the role this text has played as a handmaiden of Christian support or at least acquiescence has made interpreters nervous, and in some cases intensely critical.

Studies of this text are plentiful.[34] I will do little more here than identify some of what should be kept in mind in assessing its relation to violence. In the process we will attend to the textual and historical context of this text, keeping in mind the focus on the relationship between subordination and violence.

---

[32] The same term is used in Matt. 5.39 (see discussion in Chapter 2).

[33] *Leitourgia*, *leitourgos*, are at the root of the English 'liturgy', where it is related to worship and priestly service. It is not originally a religious term, even if in the Jewish context, also in the New Testament, it often has sacral or cultic meaning (see, e.g., Rom. 15.16). Here it seems to have the very general meaning of administrative duties in raising taxes. See Hermann Strathmann, '*leitourgeō, ktl.*', *TDNT* 4.215–31.

[34] The scholarly literature is vast, both in terms of exegesis and ethics. Commentaries are excellent and plentiful. I can do no more in the chapter than dip into this vast pond. Books and articles cited contain copious pointers to further literature.

Textual context

This text as much as any in the New Testament has suffered from being isolated from its context within Paul's letter to the Romans. The reality that 'Romans 13' usually refers to the first seven verses only makes the point. Romans 13.1–7 is, however, one part of a larger *paraenesis* or 'exhortation'. The particular line of exhortation begins at Romans 12.1 and concludes with the end of chapter 13. The *paraenesis* continues into chapter 15. On the basis of the 'mercies of God', which he has rehearsed in the previous 11 chapters,[35] Paul urges his readers in 12.1–2 to respond to God's benefactions with grateful worship and radical nonconformity to the present age. Readers are to offer their bodies as living sacrifices (*thusia*)[36] and minds transformed, so as to be able to discern the good, the acceptable, and the holy. This is not the only time subordination and nonconformity are set alongside each other. Readers will recall that the Household Code in Ephesians is similarly preceded by an equally sharp summons to nonconformity (Eph. 5.3–21), followed, as in the case of Romans 13.11–14, by a call to arms (Eph. 6.10–20).

Paul's exhortations are by their very nature more pep talk than organized ethical discourse. So also here. Members of Christ's 'body' are to practise solidarity and service toward each other for the good of the whole (vv. 3–8, 13, 15–16). There is nothing tepid about such corporate existence: mercy is to be practised with 'hilarity' (v. 8); evil is not only to be avoided but also hated, and the good embraced with equal passion (v. 9); there is to be fierce competition for honour, but only in the sense of showing it toward others (v. 10); zeal is to be red hot, fanned by the wind (Spirit) of God (v. 11); the needs of fellow members of the community are to be responded to as if they were one's own (*koinōneō*; v. 13); hospitality is to be a matter of aggressive pursuit (*diōkō*) of strangers with love (*philoxenia*; v. 13).

In a group of instructions remarkably resonant with what we see in the Sermon on the Mount (see Chapter 2), Paul addresses response

---

[35] Recall the closing doxology with which Chapter 5 ended.
[36] Notice the use of sacrificial terminology for what is clearly not intended to imply any violence.

to harm.[37] Paul follows the call to aggressive hospitality with a call to bless persecutors (v. 14). Translators typically miss Paul's startling wordplay. The verb *diōkō*, poorly translated as 'extend' (NRSV) or 'practise' (e.g. NIV) in v. 13, is here correctly translated as 'persecute'. 'Pursue' with love and blessing those who are 'pursuing' you violently! Paul surely intended this clash of two radically different forms of aggression: persecution is to be aggressively pursued with love and blessing. Further, in a world of hostility and violence, the faithful are to be in solidarity both with those who have reason to rejoice and those who have reason to weep, sparing no effort to live peaceably, refusing to return evil for evil. Combating any hint of quietism, readers are urged to be victorious (*nikaō*) over evil with good (vv. 15–21). The quotation in verse 20 of Proverbs 25.21 regarding giving bread and water to a hungry and thirsty enemy gives colour to this remarkable picture. Romans 12 is Paul's Sermon on the Mount, with the same disposition of spirited non-violence and defiant vulnerability, of giving oneself aggressively and energetically to the well-being of others, whether insiders or enemies, as befits the members of the body of the self-giving Messiah.

Before addressing the matter of leaving vengeance to God (v. 19), I wish to point out that the emphases we have been observing in Romans 12 are present on the other side of 13.1–7. Whereas 13.7 concludes with an injunction to pay all 'owings' (*opheilē*), verse 8 insists that the faithful 'owe' (*opheilō*) nothing other than to love each other. Again reminiscent of the antitheses of Matthew 5, Paul sees this as the fulfilling of Torah, quoting the injunction to love the neighbour from Leviticus 19.18.[38] Matching the energy and passion of Romans 12, the exhortation comes to a climax with a summons to Messiah-like militancy. The eschatological ambience of Paul's exhortation is unmistakable: since the present moment (*kairos*) is pregnant with liberation (v. 11), believers are to 'put on the weapons

---

[37] See, e.g., Gordon Zerbe, 'Paul's Ethic of Nonretaliation and Peace', in *The Love of Enemy and Nonretaliation in the New Testament* (ed. Willard M. Swartley; Studies of Peace and Scripture, Institute of Mennonite Studies; Louisville, KY: Westminster/John Knox, 1992), 177–222.

[38] See Lev. 19.18 explicitly in Matt. 5.43 and implicitly in Matt. 18.15–20. We saw it present also just behind the curtain in the Household Code in Eph. 5.28.

of light' (v. 12).[39] In the parallel phrase in verse 14 they are to 'put on the Lord Jesus Messiah'. Echoing the call to nonconformity in 12.1, believers are to have nothing to do with the 'works of darkness' and leave no room for the 'flesh' (13.12–13). Evil is to be defeated (12.21). The instruments of victory are the 'weapons of light' (13.14).

Before tackling Romans 13.1–7, we return briefly to what is for many a deeply troubling aspect of Paul's exhortation. Romans 12.19 reads: 'Loved ones, never avenge (*ekdikeō*) yourselves, but leave room for wrath (*orgē*).' To bolster that exhortation, Paul quotes from the war hymn in Deuteronomy 32.35. 'Vengeance is mine, I will repay, says the Lord.' The non-violence and non-retaliation demanded of the faithful is placed within a framework in which vengeance (*naqam/ekdikēsis*) and payback (*antapodidōmi*)[40] are God's prerogative. Stated bluntly: the warrior looks out for the pacifist. The reference to 'vengeance' and 'payback' can represent reassurance that justice will ultimately be established by God.[41] But it might also be read as reassurance that the enemies will 'get it' in the final judgement, with an intensity the faithful could never match. As one of my teachers, Krister Stendahl, liked to characterize such eschatological *Schadenfreude*: 'Why walk around with a little shotgun when the atomic blast is imminent?'[42]

The quotation from Deuteronomy informs how the following quotation of Proverbs 25.22 regarding heaping coals of fire on the

---

[39] In Pauline circles the baptismal ritual included 'taking off' the old clothes representing the old way of life in conformity to this 'age' and 'putting on' the new clothes representing identification with the Messiah, here, as in Eph. 6.10–20, interpreted as arming for battle. The militancy could not have been missed by eschatologically excited Jews in Paul's readership. Recall the famous War Scroll from the Dead Sea, 'The War of the Sons of Light against the Sons of Darkness' (1QM).

[40] While in this context the word clearly carries the connotations of revenge or punitive payback, it is also used in a positive sense (e.g. Luke 14.14; 1 Thess. 3.9).

[41] *Ekdikēsis* in both noun and verb form can also, as the etymology of the word hints at, mean to wrest justice from injustice, as in the case of the parable of the stubborn widow who demands justice from the judge against the one who is denying it to her (e.g. Luke 18.3). One should thus be careful not to assume one can readily determine the degree to which violence is central to the way the term is being used. See George E. Mendenhall, *The Tenth Generation: The Origins of the Biblical Tradition* (Baltimore, MD: Johns Hopkins University Press, 1973).

[42] Krister Stendahl, 'Hate, Nonretaliation, and Love: Coals of Fire', Krister Stendahl, *Meanings: The Bible as Document and as Guide* (Philadelphia, PA: Fortress Press, 1984), 137–61 (139).

head of the enemy is interpreted. Scholars such as Stendahl interpret the coals on the head in relation to the anticipated vengeance of God. Blessing persecutors or treating enemies with kindness is non-violent or non-retaliatory only in the present moment but actually serves to intensify the judgement awaiting them.[43] What Paul prohibits is vigilante justice, taking the law into one's own hand. Vengeance, 'wrath', belongs to God and, given 13.1–7, to those God orders to carry it out even before the final judgement.

An alternate interpretation sees the coals on the head as an image of shaming the one doing harm into repentance. Rather than deferred gratification, it represents an attempt to 'save' the enemy from judgement, a variant of the efforts to 'win' an errant fellow member of the community in Matthew 18.15–20 (see Chapter 3), or an unbelieving husband in 1 Peter 3.1. William Klassen, going further, has interpreted the coals of fire on the head in the light of an Egyptian repentance ritual, in which it serves as an expression of a desire to end the strife, which would place it in continuity with the unexpected gestures in the mini-parables in Matthew 5.39–42 (see Chapter 2).[44]

Whatever one will make of this particular image, judgement or 'wrath' is inescapably part of the larger picture in which Paul's exhortation takes place.[45] That conviction sets Paul apart from no one in the New Testament, including Jesus. But it is just as true that God is a judge and 'warrior' whose mercy equals his majesty, as Ecclesiasticus 2.17 puts it unforgettably (cf. Wisd. 11.21—12.11), whose ways are past predicting (Rom. 11.32–36). This divine 'avenger' is one who loves people even while they are still enemies (Rom. 5.10). Paul can thus unequivocally lay responsibility for redress at God's feet

---

[43] Recall the assurances of covenanters at Qumran that while they promise not to repay evil with harm, they also promise to hate the evildoer with unremitting hatred (Chapter 2).

[44] William Klassen, 'Coals of Fire: Symbol of Repentance or Revenge?', *NTS* 9 (1963), 337–50; *Love of Enemies: The Way to Peace* (Overtures to Biblical Theology 15; Philadelphia, PA: Fortress Press, 1984), 34–7. Klassen bases his work on that of S. Morenz, 'Feurige Kohlen auf dem Haupt', *TLZ* 78 (1953), 187–92.

[45] Luise Schottroff, '"Give to Caesar What Belongs to Caesar and to God What Belongs to God": A Theological Response of the Early Christian Church to Its Social and Political Environment', in *The Love of Enemy and Nonretaliation in the New Testament* (ed. Willard M. Swartley; Studies of Peace and Scripture, Institute of Mennonite Studies; Louisville, KY: Westminster/John Knox, 1992), 223–57; Zerbe, 'Paul's Ethic'.

without in any way undercutting the loving and hospitable energy and creativity the faithful are to exercise toward siblings, guests and enemies alike. That is how they will be victorious over evil (12.21).[46]

Does Romans 13.1–7 fit Paul's exhortation?

At first glance there is significant distance between the energy-filled eschatologically oriented radicalism of the *paraenesis* enveloping 13.1–7 and its call to subordination to authorities. There indeed are a number of factors that contribute to the impression of being a distinct element within the flow of exhortation.

First, there is the strong similarity to 1 Peter 2.13–17, where the call to be subordinate to all 'human creations' introduces the Household Code. It may be that the author of 1 Peter borrowed from Romans. It is more likely that Romans 13.1–7, along with 1 Peter, represents a distinct tradition, perhaps at one time part of a larger body of 'subordination' injunctions, as 1 Peter suggests.

Second, the language and vocabulary strengthens the impression of a well-worn tradition that can easily stand on its own. We notice, first, the general nature of the language: every 'soul' (*psuchē*); all authorities; reward and punishment for unspecified doers of good and bad; taxes and honour to whomever they are due. The text seems much like a general answer to abstract questions. Why are there authorities? What are they for? How are they related to God's authority or sovereignty? The answers the text offers hardly fit what we know of governments or authorities in Paul's day. Actual imperial authorities and Jewish authorities do not match the benign description here. Nor does the description of 'authorities' and 'powers' conform to the apocalyptic view of the 'powers' we know of in Paul's writings.[47] The highly conflictual intersection of believers with their hostile surroundings hinted at in the references to persecution and the need for peaceableness does not register in any explicit way in 13.1–7. Remember too that at the very centre of Paul's *euangelion* was the death of Jesus at the hands of imperial authorities. Paul

---

[46] Willard M. Swartley, *Covenant of Peace: The Missing Peace in New Testament Theology and Ethics* (Grand Rapids, MI: Eerdmans, 2006), 239, n. 34.

[47] See, e.g., 1 Cor. 2; Col. 2.15; Eph. 6.12; see my essay on the 'Powers' in *Ephesians*, 353–9.

himself would die a martyr's death at the hands of these 'authorities' and *not* for doing evil. Surely neither he nor his readers were blind to their reality.

Romans 13.1–7 thus appears to be proverb-like wisdom about the place of authorities under God's sovereign ordering of the cosmos, akin to the roughly contemporaneous Wisdom of Solomon 6.1–11. Buttressing the impression of a well-formed bit of wisdom is that many of the Greek terms are related to the same root – *tassō* (see above, 108–9), suggesting that the text shows the marks of careful construction in a way that lends itself to proverbial use in a wide variety of settings.

Third, in contrast to the Household Code, no appeal is made to Jesus. Some do see in the injunction to pay taxes and give honour in verse 7 an echo of the tradition of Jesus' words regarding paying taxes to Caesar (Matt. 22.21//Mark 12.17//Luke 20.25),[48] but it is not at all clear that that association was intended by Paul or would have been picked up by the readers as an allusion to Jesus' teaching.

Given this standalone quality, what is it doing in this exhortation? We have several options. One is that Paul neither wrote the passage nor placed it into the present context. Romans 13.1–7 is an interpolation or insertion by a later author or editor.[49] We would indeed not miss these verses were they not present. We would simply move from how one deals with hostility from outsiders and enemies at the end of Romans 12 to mutual love within the community in 13.8–10. Just as the Household Code is seen to reflect the return to patriarchy, so also here the instructions to be subordinate to the authorities reflect the waning of nonconformity and resistance to growing support for structures of authority, including imperial authority. Paul's eschatologically motivated radicalism is, in effect, undone by the interpolator.

This proposal has the benefit of not laying at the feet of Paul a text that has so much blood on it. Since it is not 'authentically' Paul, in the eyes of many that also lessens its canonical force, reflecting

---

[48] E.g. William R. Herzog, II, 'Dissembling, a Weapon of the Weak: The Case of Christ and Caesar in Mark 12.13–17 and Romans 13.1–7', *Perspectives in Religious Studies* 21/4 (1994), 339–60.

[49] See, e.g., Munro, *Authority*; James Kallas, 'Romans XIII.1–7: An Interpolation', *NTS* 11 (1964–5), 365–74 (365–6).

instead the patriarchal and pro-imperial orientation that would come into full play once the Church became the imperial religion some centuries later.

While an interpolation is by no means impossible, the majority of scholars see it as genuine, even if they wrestle with its meaning within Paul's exhortation. Some sense of possible circumstances might shed some light on how Paul himself might have used this tradition.

Historical context

Various suggestions have been offered. Years ago Ernst Käsemann proposed that the context informing Paul's use of this text was his fight with 'enthusiasm', that is, the tendency to abandon the importance of human institutions this side of the return of Christ.[50] More recently scholars have sought for historical context in the realities of the Roman Empire, and the place of Jews in that world, specifically also in Rome. At the time of the writing of Romans, Nero was emperor. There is some evidence of tax revolts, which might explain some of the emphasis on paying of taxes. During the reign of Claudius a few years earlier, there were riots over someone named 'Chrestus', resulting in the expulsion of at least a good number of Jews. If this is a misspelling by Roman historians of 'Christus' then this might suggest turmoil within the large Jewish community over Jesus sufficient to draw imperial attention and action. Perhaps some believers in Jesus were tempted to vigilantism and retaliation, alluded to perhaps in the latter part of Romans 12 and the second half of 13. Paul would have written at a time when a good number of Jews believing in Jesus would have returned following expulsion to what was an increasingly Gentile *ekklēsia*, and to a whole set of conflicts and tensions, reflected in the rest of the exhortation in chapters 14 and 15.

There is no consensus as to the exact historical circumstances, other than that empire and relations within the Jewish community, and between Jews and non-Jews, probably all had significant impact on the *ekklēsiai* in Rome. Were the Roman believers tempted to participate in militancy? (The Judaean war with Rome was not far off the horizon.) Were they tempted to vigilantism vis-à-vis those

---

[50] Ernst Käsemann, *Commentary on Romans* (Grand Rapids, MI: Eerdmans, 1980), 356–8.

who had done them harm in the struggles over messianic claims made about Jesus? Was Paul trying to protect Jesus-believers from the growing hostility of Rome towards Jews? Was he wishing their behaviour would not endanger fellow Jews?

Some thus see Paul wishing to make sure Roman believers show deference and respect for the authorities, that they pay their taxes, and that they show proper honour. Mark Nanos has suggested that the 'authorities' addressed in 13.1–7 refer not to imperial authorities but to synagogue authorities, who carry the symbolic 'sword', that is, the authority to discipline as servants of God, who also have the responsibility to collect the temple tax. Paul is suggesting his readers, including Gentiles, subordinate themselves to these authorities.[51] I suspect, despite the evident value in broadening our imagination as to what the historical context might have been, that Nanos over-specifies who the authorities are.

In short, historians identify a number of factors that might present a context for 'Romans 13'. Given the evident difficulties in determining with any certainty what the circumstances were, we can nevertheless see these factors as helping us to establish a 'life context' (*Sitz im Leben*).[52]

What did Paul intend with Romans 13.1–7?

But can we make sense of what Paul is saying? Several proposals have been made that take seriously the imperial and religious context. One is that Paul is being highly ironic, even dissembling.[53] He knows as well as his readers do that the authorities are nothing like those described in our text. Given the evident dangers of public criticism of imperial authorities, Paul chooses rather to hide his true convictions behind false praise, or only allows the truth to poke out, for example, when referring to the authority as '*diakonos*' ('table waiter'; v. 4).[54] This is how folks who are completely powerless and vulnerable use 'hidden transcripts' to communicate safely. If read this way, the distance between 13.1–7 and the exhortation before and after

---

[51] Mark D. Nanos, *The Mystery of Romans: The Jewish Context of Paul's Letter* (Minneapolis, MN: Fortress Press, 1996), 289–336.

[52] Schottroff, '"Give to Caesar"', 224–30.

[53] Timothy L. Carter, 'The Irony of Romans 13', *Novum Testamentum* 46/3 (2004), 209–28; Herzog, 'Dissembling'.

[54] Herzog calls this a 'surgical strike' ('Dissembling', 356).

lessens immediately. Neither rebellion nor avenging injuries is permissible, not because there is good government but because of who the readers are and how they are called to live in the present moment on the cusp of liberation (13.11). Even though on the surface Paul is pro-empire, in actual fact he knows he can count on his readers to know better. If true, the irony has been missed by readers for two millennia, with enormous consequences.

With some difference, John Marshall has proposed that Paul is in some sense of two minds, as is typical of persons living under the lid of overwhelming colonial or imperial power. He suggests that Paul is accepting of imperial power structures, even as he at a more fundamental level resists their hold. He considers the subordination of Roman believers to authorities 'an acceptable price for their stability to support his radical mission'.[55] We should not expect 'purity' from those living in settings of extreme vulnerability, but rather the 'hybridity' we observe when we read 13.1–7 in its setting in Romans 12 and 13. This interpretation too does not read Paul as providing theological justification for state violence, nor for Christian participation in it. But it requires of the interpreter a very sophisticated understanding of the effect of imperial and colonial power on marginalized subjects.

These suggestions all take it that Paul more or less composed these seven verses. A third option sees Paul using a tradition he did not himself compose.[56] For reasons quite similar to those just stated, he utilizes a tradition in order to dissuade Roman believers in Jesus from taking the law or the sword into their own hands, leaving the ultimate right-setting to God ('wrath' and 'vengeance'). Paul employs a nugget of general Jewish wisdom to shore up the core of his exhortation in chapter 12, much the way a preacher might use an illustration to reinforce a point. The link between his exhortation and this tradition would be the 'wrath' (*orgē*) in 12.19 and the *orgē* the authorities

---

[55] John W. Marshall, 'Hybridity and Reading Romans 13', *JSNT* 31/2 (2008), 157–78 (172). For a different take on the vulnerability of the community, see James D. G. Dunn, 'Romans 13:1–7: A Charter for Political Quietism?', *Ex auditu* 2 (1986), 55–68.

[56] Käsemann refers to it as 'an independent block' (*Commentary*, 352). See also, e.g., Ernst Bammel, 'Romans 13', in *Jesus and the Politics of His Day* (ed. Ernst Bammel and C. F. D. Moule; Cambridge: Cambridge University Press, 1984), 365–83; Dieter Georgi, *Theocracy in Paul's Praxis and Theology* (trans. David E. Green; Minneapolis, MN: Fortress Press, 1991), 102.

exercise. Even the reference to the 'sword' (*machaira*) in 13.4 serves to provide a verbal link to the quotation of Deuteronomy 32 in 12.19.[57] This would explain why 13.1–7 seems to be so christologically and eschatologically distinct in content and vocabulary from the rest of the *paraenesis*.

If we take this approach, which I find most plausible, we should interpret 13.1–7 as a supportive illustration drawn from Jewish wisdom, intended to reinforce Paul's teaching *against* participation in violence and *for* aggressive overcoming of evil with good, with the 'weapons of light', with the 'Lord Jesus Christ' (13.12, 14).

Whether or not Paul 'composed' this famous text, to view it has having a subordinate relationship to the surrounding exhortation brings 'subordination' into the practice of deliberate and defiant vulnerability we have noted repeatedly in our study. Subordination becomes part of the 'arsenal' of aggressively pursuing the stranger with love and the persecutor with blessing.[58] With the emphasis on 'subordination' Paul may well wish to prevent being understood to have invited insurrection. After all, his messianic and eschatologically enthusiastic readers might otherwise misunderstand Paul's summons to 'defeat' evil (12.21) with 'weapons of light' (13.12). Such subordination will be mistaken by the powers as 'non-resistance' to their authority. But Paul knows that Jesus' slave-like behaviour and most especially Jesus' ignominious and scandalous death at the hands of the imperial forces was not defeat but an act of liberation looking to all the world like the ultimate in subjugation (e.g. 1 Cor. 2.8). How could it be different for the liberator's body (Rom. 12.5)?

We should thus be careful to respect the 'subordinate' status of Romans 13.1–7 to its larger context, and allow it to reinforce the ethos of Paul's exhortation rather than to undermine it, as has happened in the history of the Church. I half suspect that had Paul known what mischief this 'sermon illustration' would stir, he might have done without it. It is our responsibility not to let it drown out the sermon.

---

[57] The LXX of Deut. 32.41–42 refers to God's sword (*machaira*) as means of judgement. I think, given the nature of the tradition, that *machaira* thus is neither as a symbol of judicial authority (contra Yoder, *Politics*, 203) nor military authority (contra just about everyone else). See Nanos, *Mystery*, 310–14.

[58] Yoder calls subordination the 'Christian form of rebellion' (*Politics*, 200, n. 10).

That does not prevent us from acknowledging its value within that subordinate status. It has no doubt had positive effect in emphasizing a conviction Paul shared with fellow Jews, namely, that God is sovereign over all nations and their rulers, indeed over all authorities, and that they are all answerable to God, as Wisdom of Solomon 6 illustrates clearly. As such it holds up a mirror to ways the empire is *not* as God wishes the authorities to be. Oppressed groups have often held up these verses to governments who have become a terror to those doing good, rather than evil. It may well have encouraged the development of good government. But it has also been used to pull the teeth on the Church's witness, to undermine its nonconformity, and thus to compromise its mission as the body of the Messiah, and thereby to justify and even promote violence. If true to Paul, the text should not be allowed to serve as a kind of constitutional basis for the divine right of rulers and the divinely sanctioned subjugation of the Church to their orders and to uncritical obeisance in money and honour.

Whether we see Paul using deliberate irony, or employing a wisdom nugget for purposes of shoring up his exhortation in the rest of Romans 12 and 13, this leaves little room for the traditional reading, in which Paul simply and directly demands subordination to what-ever authorities there are, since God has put them there as God's servant. Such 'subordination' is too easily understood as 'subjection' and 'obedience'. The harrowing consequences can be seen in the Holocaust and equally in the support for weapons that can incinerate the world many times over. Nor does our reading support a tradition that uses the positive picture of government as a basis for armed revolution, as has also happened within Christendom.[59]

So is 'Romans 13' violent? Does it condone, even support violence? The answer is yes. And the answer is again also no. It depends who is reading or misreading it. Decisive, in my view, is what readers bring to the text. Are they in positions of power, or of marginalization, or

---

[59] Interestingly, these interpretations can run up against each other, as they did in South Africa, where the apartheid regime appealed to Rom. 13 in order to quell resistance, and the resistance appealed to it because the government was clearly not living up to its divine mandate to secure justice. E.g. Jan Botha, 'Creation of New Meaning: Rhetorical Situations and the Reception of Romans 13:1–7', *Journal of Theology for Southern Africa* 79 (1992), 24–37; James Moulder, 'Romans 13 and Conscientious Disobedience', *Journal of Theology for Southern Africa* 21 (1977), 13–23.

even oppression? Do they read 'Romans 13' as a timeless charter for government and the Church's call to subjection and obedience? Or do they read it from within the call to radical nonconformity to this age and its ruling powers? Who is the Christ readers bring to the reading? What is the *ekklēsia*, and its mission as the Messiah's body? The matter of violence will depend entirely on how those questions are answered or, better, how the text is lived.

Conclusion

There is deep mystery in the relationship between subordination and transformation, a mystery that pervades the New Testament and resides in the central figure of Jesus. The scandal of Jesus' life and death is that they can be seen both as the costly rejection of violence and domination and at the same time as acquiescence, as *non*-resistance to violence. Why should domestic relationships and public life be exempt from this ambiguity? To lift the Household Code or Romans 13 out of that larger scenario of reconciliation and new creation is to turn the ploughshare into a sword, to render subordination into a means of undoing what Jesus is remembered for.

This approach to the text may be too uncertain, even dangerous. But a stance of mutual subordination (Ephesians), or of patient suffering in the sure hope of transformation (1 Peter), or of subordination (not subjection or obedience) to the authorities, opens the door to a future of reconciliation and restoration, but always also to potential harm. Nothing in such a stance takes violence lightly, whether structural, cultural or physical. Nothing in this stance diminishes the rage one must share with Jesus at violence against the vulnerable (see Matt. 18). But there is also no way of getting around the scandal of 'subordination' in a fallen world, without also getting around the crucified slave/lord. A call to subordination is dangerous business in a world of violence and oppression. It forces the issue of the difference between patient suffering and acquiescence, between hopeful if vulnerable engagement with and collusion in violence. Voluntary subordination, which it is by virtue of being a summons, will always be the same kind of scandalous engagement with violence that marked that of the Jesus who went to the cross and thereby 'killed enmity'.

7

Divine warfare in the New Testament

In the popular view of the Bible, warfare is typically associated with the Old Testament. It is no stranger to writers of the New Testament, however, as we just saw in Romans 12.19. The arrival of the reign of God in the teaching and ministry of Jesus, for example, is nothing less than an invasion into the realm of evil, illustrated dramatically by Jesus' routing of the 'Legion' of demons by sending them to their watery death (Mark 5 and par.). A good deal of such imagery reflects an apocalyptic understanding of reality as a conflict between God and Satan, between angels and demons, and, at times, between the faithful and the godless, regardless of whether the 'theatre of war' is understood to be within earthly history or beyond.[1] As we saw intimated in Romans 13.11–14, this conflict is anticipated to intensify as the arrival of God's full reign draws nearer. As Romans 16.20 assures its readers: 'The God of peace will shortly crush Satan under your feet.' In short, the vocabulary and imagery of warfare is not a special province of the Hebrew Bible, but is woven no less into the very fabric of the New Testament.

Despite centuries of use made of Romans 13.1–7 to justify Christian participation in warfare, there is a rough scholarly consensus that engagement in human warfare was largely rejected in the first three centuries.[2] Warfare imagery in the New Testament is thus popularly viewed as symbolic or metaphorical, or as 'only' spiritual. While some of this imagery is indeed metaphorical, for New Testament writers there is never an 'only' attached to 'spiritual'. First-century Jews, and along with them Jesus, apostles, and evangelists alike, viewed

---

[1] 'Apocalyptic language was (among many other things, to be sure) an elaborate metaphor-system for investing historical events with theological significance' (N. T. Wright, *Jesus and the Victory of God* (Christian Origins and the Question of God, Vol. 2; Minneapolis, MN: Fortress Press, 1997), 96.

[2] That does not mean that New Testament texts, such as Rom. 13.1–7, Jesus' use of the whip in John 2.15 or his ordering his disciples to buy swords in Luke 22.36, have not been used in Christian history to justify participation in warfare.

life as battle, one in which God's reign will ultimately prevail, but which now is marked by the need for vigilance, discipline, resistance and suffering. This is most especially the case for those with an apocalyptic outlook, as was the case with Jesus and his followers.

We will again take some core samples. The most obvious place to drill is the Apocalypse of John, or the book of Revelation, often viewed as a violent anomaly within an otherwise peaceful and non-violent New Testament. A second probe will be the motif of the community in the divine armour, first in 1 Thessalonians 5.1–11, then in the closely related Ephesians 6.10–20.

The Lamb's war (The Apocalypse of John)

In his introduction to the New Testament, Luke Timothy Johnson sums up the thought of many readers of John's Apocalypse: 'Few writings in all of literature have been so obsessively read with such generally disastrous results as the Book of Revelation.'[3] He may be right, although the 'disastrous results' are today keeping many from reading this difficult text, least of all 'obsessively', in large measure because of the intense violence, while others are drawn to it for that very same violence, however 'spiritual'. We cannot avoid engaging this rich and mysterious document, even if we can do so here only in cursory fashion, restricting ourselves to the matter of violence.

The Apocalypse is commonly held to have been written late in the first century, probably during the reign of Domitian, by a seer or prophet named John,[4] exiled to the island of Patmos. A number of scholars have argued that the fit is better during the time period closer to the Jewish war against Rome (66–70 CE), during the last

---

[3] Luke Timothy Johnson, *The Writings of the New Testament: An Interpretation* (2nd edn; Minneapolis, MN: Fortress Press, 1999), 583. There are many excellent introductions and commentaries on John's Apocalypse with extensive bibliographies. The following pages provide no more than a sampling of the rich resources. One that addresses the question of violence throughout is Christopher C. Rowland, *The Book of Revelation: Introduction, Commentary, and Reflections* (The New Interpreter's Bible, Vol. XII; Nashville, TN: Abingdon, 1998), 503–743.

[4] It makes little difference whether or not this 'John' was the apostle John or another person named John. It would, however, need to have been one with sufficient standing in the cells of Jesus adherents for his writings to be received, preserved and eventually canonized.

years of Nero or shortly after his death.[5] Regardless of date or specific setting, few miss the ambience of intense hostility to Rome pervading the writing.

John sees himself as a mouthpiece of the risen and exalted Messiah, addressing communities of adherents. His intended readers are the *ekklēsiai* of Jesus-believers in Asia Minor. His visions are a volatile and intentionally incendiary mix of worship and prophetic engagement and address, infused with scriptural and apocalyptic metaphors of both violence suffered and committed. We cannot be sure of how representative his views are among those to whom they are directed. As in the case of the great writing prophets of the Hebrew Scriptures, we might well allow for an adversarial relationship with at least some of those to whom he directs his writing, as the oracles in chapters 2 and 3 hint. Quite possibly the Apocalypse is witness to a fierce dispute over how believers in Jesus should view 'Babylon', the Roman empire. John's Revelation may well be a prophetic exposé of the imperial system, as well as a prophetic warning to the followers of Jesus not to be swayed by what John perceives to be nothing less than idolatry. To do that the seer of Patmos employs the imagery of warfare with an intensity hardly matched anywhere else in the Bible.[6]

Violence and war in John's Revelation

We cannot do without at least a brief 'fly-over' of relevant terrain. We begin in Revelation 5 with the image of the 'lamb that was slain' (5.6).[7] Readers are to see in this image a reference to Jesus' death at the hands of imperial power. But they are to see much more. Casting Jesus' death as the slaughter of a lamb connects it implicitly with the

---

[5] See, e.g., John W. Marshall, *Parables of War: Reading John's Jewish Apocalypse* (ESCJ; Waterloo, ON: Wilfrid Laurier University Press, 2001); Marshall, 'Collateral Damage: Jesus and Jezebel in the Jewish War', in *Violence in the New Testament* (ed. Shelley Matthews and E. Leigh Gibson; New York/London: T&T Clark, 2005), 35–50 (37).

[6] Craig Koester, 'Revelation's Visionary Challenge to Ordinary Empire', *Interpretation* 63/1 (2009), 5–18, esp. 13.

[7] In doing so there is no intention to downplay the concerns others have regarding violence in John's Apocalypse that take issue with John's characterization of his rivals in chs 2 and 3 as rhetorically violent; e.g. Paul B. Duff, *Who Rides the Beast: Prophetic Rivalry and the Rhetoric of Crisis in the Churches of the Apocalypse* (Oxford: Oxford University Press, 2001), 83–133; John W. Marshall, 'Collateral Damage', 44–50; Tina Pippin, *Death and Desire: The Rhetoric of Gender in the Apocalypse of John* (Louisville, KY: Westminster/ John Knox, 1992). The focus here is on the motif of warfare and battle.

Passover and explicitly with 'buying' for God a kingdom and priests from every tribe and tongue (v. 9; see Chapter 5 above for discussion of *Christus Victor* (80–91)). This concentrated image combines victimization with messianic power and victory.[8]

In a scene set in the great throne room of heaven the question is asked who is worthy to open the scroll with seven seals (5.2). To the seer's deep consternation, there is no one, until his gaze is directed to the royal and military figure of 'the lion of the tribe of Judah' (v. 5). But when he turns to look he sees not a conquering lion but a lamb showing the signs of having been slaughtered. The now living lamb is alone 'worthy' to open the scroll and to break its seals (v. 6–7). We might ask: is the lion the lamb? Or is the lamb the lion? Victim or victor?

As the Lamb opens the seals on the scroll, recurring visions of escalating violence and warfare ensue in the serial form of seven seals, seven trumpets and seven bowls of 'wrath'. Amid unimaginable carnage unleashed by the notorious four horsemen of the Apocalypse, the souls of those killed on account of the *Logos* of God and their faithful witness (*marturia*) plead for God to avenge their blood (6.9–11). All of humanity, including its powerful rulers, frantically plead in turn for protection from the 'wrath of the lamb' (6.16–17). The cycle of violence begins anew with the angels blowing the seven trumpets (chs 8 and 9), with devastation so intense that people will vainly seek death (9.6). Like the ancient myths of the combat of the gods,[9] 'war in heaven' breaks out in chapter 12, in which Michael and his angels fight against the dragon (Satan), who intends to devour the child of the 'woman clothed with the sun' (v. 1) at the moment of its birth. It is difficult not to read this with the infancy narratives of Matthew and Luke on our minds. While 'our brothers' have 'conquered' the dragon by means of the blood of the lamb and their own witness to the point of death (v. 11), the dragon is able to continue to make war on the rest of the woman's offspring (v. 17).

As in Chapter 7, an interlude of worship interrupts the carnage. The worship of the dragon and the beast, a barely veiled allusion

---

[8] Richard Bauckham, *The Theology of the Book of Revelation* (Cambridge: Cambridge University Press, 1993), 70–3.

[9] Adela Yarbro Collins, *The Combat Myth in the Book of Revelation* (Missoula, MT: Scholars Press, 1976).

to the satanically empowered emperors of Rome and their imperial cult, is pitted against the worship of the Lamb. Everything is at stake in this 'worship war'. Those engaging in the emperor cult will end up drinking the wine of God's wrath, and will be tortured eternally in the presence of the Lamb and the angels (14.9–11).

Yet another cycle of violence is introduced with the imagery of judgement, harvest, sickle and winepress (14.14–20), followed by seven angels with the seven plagues pouring out the seven bowls of the 'wrath of God' (chs 15–16). The victory taunt 'Fallen, fallen, is Babylon the great!' is heard amid the cacophony of war (14.8; 18.2), along with a dirge lamenting the economic collapse of Rome (ch. 18). A particularly violent motif is Babylon/Rome depicted as the 'mother of whores' (17.5), drunk with the blood of the martyrs. God is said to 'put it into the hearts' of the kings who have enjoyed her services now to strip her naked and tear her apart, eating her flesh and burning her body (17.15–18). The grotesque scene of this 'one hour' of horrifying destruction culminates in the joyous 'hallelujahs' of the great multitude of the faithful looking on as Rome becomes a smouldering ruin 'forever' (19.1–4). God has kept his promise to the martyrs to avenge their blood (6.10–11).[10]

Chapter 19 presents the reader with what may be for readers an even more troubling image. Jesus appears now as a fearsome warrior, riding on a white horse at the head of the armies of heaven, clad in a robe drenched with blood. The winepress of God, a chilling metaphor of warfare and judgement (Isa. 63; see earlier Rev. 14.17–20) adds to the violence of this imagery. The rider is called Faithful, True and 'Word of God'. A great sword emerges from his mouth (recall 1.16), as he wields an iron rod with which to judge and rule the nations. In a rather gruesome juxtaposition, the invitation to the wedding banquet of the Lamb (19.9) is set next to the invitation to the birds of heaven to gather for the 'supper of God', to feast on the flesh of kings and their armies (vv. 17–21). Is this the lamb that was slain? Or has this Lamb been doing the slaying?

---

[10] While for many the Hallelujah chorus of Handel's Messiah will come to mind, Austrian composer Franz Schmidt's oratorio *Das Buch mit sieben Siegeln* (The Book with Seven Seals), composed in 1937, makes the links between the First and the Third Reich chillingly palpable.

Bringing the narration to its climax is the throwing of Satan and his forces into the 'lake of fire', to be tormented forever (ch. 20). What alleviates the overwhelmingly dark violence of this imagery is that Death itself will be thrown into that lake, ushering in a new heaven and a new earth (chs 21 and 22). The heavenly Jerusalem will descend onto the earth to provide God, the Lamb and the peoples of the earth with a home.

Even such a brief rehearsal weighs heavily on the imagination. John intends the images of violence to appal, even overwhelm. But how and why?

A number of issues need to be kept in mind before taking stock of the violence in John's Apocalypse. First, if it has been true for previous 'probes' that meaning and significance is shaped by who is reading and from where, then that is doubly so for John's Apocalypse. It makes a great difference whether this text is approached from within the security (however illusory) of the Global North, or whether the violence in Revelation is resonant with readers' own experience of oppression and brutality. Where one might turn away in revulsion, another drawn to it voyeuristically like a violent video game,[11] for yet another the Apocalypse is a mirror of life lived under the threat of violence and brutality, and a lifeline of the promise of liberation.[12] The brutality of the imagery may give voice to outrage and at the same to the intensity of hunger for justice.

Second, it is a frequently expressed caution not to impose too quickly on a first-century prophet the conventions of rhetoric employed in our own day. Much of the imagery is scriptural or from the scenery department of Apocalyptic, its symbolic significance more easily discernible for John's readers than for us.[13]

---

[11] Crossan's phrase 'pornography of violence' comes to mind (John Dominic Crossan, *God and Empire: Jesus Against Rome, Then and Now* (San Francisco, CA: HarperSanFrancisco, 2007), 217–35.

[12] E.g. Allan A. Boesak, *Comfort and Protest: The Apocalypse from a South African Perspective* (Philadelphia, PA: Westminster, 1987).

[13] See the excellent 'Reflection' on violent imagery in Revelation by M. Eugene Boring, *Revelation* (Interpretation: A Bible Commentary for Teaching and Preaching; Louisville, KY: John Knox, 1989), 112–19; also J. Nelson Kraybill, *Apocalypse and Allegiance: Worship, Politics, and Devotion in the Book of Revelation* (Grand Rapids, MI: Brazos, 2010), 133–7; Rowland, *Book of Revelation*, 615–17.

A third observation is that John's Revelation is read by scholars and non-scholars alike as prophecy. But what does 'prophecy' mean? An enormously popular approach leads in the modern era from the Dispensationalism of John Nelson Darby and the Scofield Reference Bible, via the writings of Hal Lindsay's *Late Great Planet Earth*,[14] to the wildly popular Left Behind series by Tim LaHaye and Jerry Jenkins.[15] In this case 'prophecy' means prediction, and the apocalyptic imagery is a set of coded indicators of an entirely predetermined scenario. John's Apocalypse becomes part of an elaborate map of a future that God has unalterably set in place. Many today thus look for signs in the geopolitical context, whether the State of Israel or natural disasters, to prove that the events decoded in Revelation are coming true, including the infamous battle at Armageddon (16.16). Prophecy is a matter of deciphering the code, and repentance a guarantee of escape from inexorable catastrophe.

Biblically, however, prophecy is less often about prediction than proclaiming the divine word of both hope and judgement into a world of violence and oppression. Prophecy is less about 'foretelling' the future than it is about 'forth-telling' the truth about the present, as the common wordplay has it, the divine word spoken into a dynamically unfolding story. Thus much of critical scholarship today sees John's Revelation as prophetic critique and assurance of hope, employing the imagery familiar in Apocalyptic literature.[16]

That does not settle the question of whether John's Apocalypse is violent. Biblical prophecy often depicts God as a judge 'warring' against those who commit violence and brutality against the vulnerable and the poor. The means by which such divine warfare takes place is, however, often the violence of the nations against each other. God is said to 'hand over' the nations to their own violence as judgement against them.[17] Thus one important question is whether

---

[14] Hal Lindsey, *The Late Great Planet Earth* (Grand Rapids, MI: Zondervan, 1970).

[15] Tim F. LaHaye and Jerry B. Jenkins's Left Behind series (Wheaton, IL: Tyndale House) has according to their website sold 80 million volumes.

[16] See the brief but excellent discussion in Michael J. Gorman, *Reading Revelation Responsibly: Uncivil Worship and Witness: Following the Lamb into the New Creation* (Eugene, OR: Cascade Books, 2011), 12–29. See also Richard Bauckham, *The Climax of Prophecy: Studies on the Book of Revelation* (Edinburgh: T&T Clark, 1993), 38–91.

[17] Joseph L. Mangina, *Revelation* (Brazos Theological Commentary on the Bible; Grand Rapids, MI: Brazos, 2010), 124.

the violence and carnage of warfare is God's war against Rome, or whether Rome's own warfare is exposed and painted against the canvass of the war between good and evil, God and Satan? Whose violence is described? Or might it mysteriously be both at the same time? The Apocalypse of John depicts God and the Lamb 'warring' against an arrogant and self-assured empire callously victimizing anyone in its path, most especially those giving witness with their lives to their allegiance to Jesus. Given the juxtaposition of biblical warfare imagery as metaphor for judgement and the association of the 'lamb' with vulnerability and sacrifice, we should not be surprised that John's Apocalypse is interpreted in ways diametrically opposed to each other.

A violent Apocalypse

Even among those who see John's Apocalypse as resistance literature, as an anti-imperial prophetic attack, there is great discomfort with its violence. While the dragon and the beast and their hordes are quite obviously violent, the solution to this violence appears to be the hyper-violence of God and the Lamb. David Barr captures such a reading well: 'The ultimate value in this story seems to be power, power exercised ruthlessly. One even has the sense that God is willing to engage in torture in an effort to induce humanity to repent.'[18]

It is not just that God and the Lamb are perceived to be fiercely violent, it is also that the book's imagery as a whole soaks the imagination in violence, potentially stoking hatred not just for Satan and his powers, even if understood as forces empowering imperial authorities, but for humanity under their sway. The stark polarities seem to leave little room for any empathy with victims of this violence other than with the martyrs following the Lamb.

Feminists, such as Tina Pippin, perceive a deep-seated misogyny in the characterization of evil-as-woman, nowhere more so than in the image of the great whore, Babylon (chs 17—19). Pippin states flatly: 'The Apocalypse means death to women.'[19] She rejects also the

---

[18] David L. Barr, 'The Lamb Who Looks like a Dragon? Characterizing Jesus in John's Apocalypse', in *The Reality of Apocalypse: Rhetoric and Politics in the Book of Revelation* (ed. David L. Barr; Atlanta, GA: Society of Biblical Literature, 2006), 205–20 (211).

[19] Pippin, *Death and Desire*, 86. See also a wide range of feminist studies edited by Amy-Jill Levine with Maria Mayo Robbins, *A Feminist Companion to the Apocalypse of John* (New York/London: T&T Clark, 2009).

martyrdom in Revelation as a form of 'patriarchal abuse'.[20] Violence and misogyny are still or especially in our day a lethal mixture, whether we have in mind the entertainment industry, pornography or rape as a weapon of war. Pippin perceives John's Apocalypse, and especially its readers, to be fully at home in that dehumanized view of women.

While John Dominic Crossan concedes that the Lamb in Revelation 5 has some affinity to the Jesus of the Gospels, he views Revelation 19's rider on the white horse as a counter-vision to the Lamb. The Jesus of the Second Coming is diametrically opposed to the Jesus of the First Coming. 'The Slaughtered becomes the Slaughterer.'[21]

The critique of Revelation as violent thus runs the gamut from what is taken to be warfare imagery, misogyny, vilification, violent judgement, to a dualism that takes no prisoners. Even when its anti-imperialism is acknowledged, it is perceived ironically to have fallen victim to the ideology of empire, making God and the Lamb into mega-versions of what they war against. Put simply, John's Revelation is deeply 'flawed'.[22] Like Crossan, many find it difficult if not impossible to mesh what we know about Jesus with the Lamb looking on the eternal torment of those bearing the mark of the beast (14.9–11). The Lion seems to have devoured the Lamb, to use the metaphor of Revelation 5.

Revelation as anti-violent

There is a host of scholars, however, who read John's Revelation very differently. They fully recognize the anti-imperial stance of the author. They acknowledge the element of rage that is clearly present, suggesting that John's Apocalypse be read in some measure like the imprecatory psalms (e.g. Pss. 35; 69; 109; 137), not as an invitation to vengeance, but as an unvarnished explosion of outrage and hurt.[23]

---

[20] Pippin, *Death and Desire*, 101–2.

[21] Crossan, *God and Empire*, 218.

[22] Adela Yarbro Collins, *Crisis and Catharsis: The Power of the Apocalypse* (Philadelphia, PA: Westminster, 1984), 172; so also Elisabeth Schüssler Fiorenza, *The Book of Revelation: Justice and Judgement* (Philadelphia, PA: Fortress Press, 1985).

[23] Boring, *Revelation*, 113–14; Kraybill, *Apocalypse*, 122–3; Kraybill, *Imperial Cult and Commerce in John's Apocalypse* (*JSNT* 132; Sheffield: Sheffield Academic Press, 1996), 205; Miroslav Volf, *Exclusion and Embrace: A Theological Exploration of Identity, Otherness, and Reconciliation* (Nashville, TN: Abingdon, 1996), 296–7. We remember Matthew's recollection of Jesus' rage at those who abuse the 'little ones' in Matt. 18 (see Chapter 3 above).

Decisive for their reading of the Apocalypse is the motif of the slain Lamb in Revelation 5, even if there are variations in the way they elaborate their understanding.[24] These interpreters find in that pivotal scene the key to reading Revelation against the grain of inherited interpretation. It is the Lamb that is worthy to break the seals on the scroll. It is not that the Lion is replaced by the Lamb, that the victim replaces the victor. Rather, the Lamb *is* the Lion, winning the victory over evil, but through *his own* death.[25] Likewise, the faithful witnesses 'conquer' through their endurance, their witness and *their own* blood, thereby participating in the Lamb's victory. Death will not have the last laugh, least of all death at the hands of the enemies of the Lamb and his followers. As Griffith puts it, resurrection is nothing less than 'the terror of God' against the reign of death (cf. 11.11).[26]

---

[24] E.g. Barr, 'Lamb Who Looks like a Dragon?', 209; Bauckham, *Theology*, 70–6; Mark Bredin, *Jesus, Revolutionary of Peace: A Nonviolent Christology in the Book of Revelation* (Milton Keynes/Waynesboro, GA: Paternoster, 2003), esp. 181–99; Greg Carey, 'The Book of Revelation as Counter-Imperial Script', in *In the Shadow of Empire: Reclaiming the Bible as a History of Faithful Resistance* (ed. Richard A. Horsley; Louisville, KY/London: Westminster John Knox, 2008), 157–76, esp. 169–70; Ronald R. Clark, Jr., 'Sent Ahead or Left Behind? War and Peace in the Apocalypse, Eschatology, and the Left Behind Series', in *A Cry Instead of Justice: The Bible and Cultures of Violence in Psychological Perspective* (ed. Dereck Daschke and Andrew Kille; New York/London: T&T Clark, 2010), 182–94; Gorman, *Reading Revelation*, 102–15; Lee Griffith, *The War on Terrorism and the Terror of God* (Grand Rapids, MI/Cambridge: Eerdmans, 2002), 203–18; Wes Howard-Brook and Anthony Gwyther, *Unveiling Empire: Reading Revelation Then and Now* (Maryknoll, NY: Orbis, 1999), 136–56; Loren L. Johns, *The Lamb Christology of the Apocalypse of John: An Investigation into Its Origins and Rhetorical Force* (WUNT 2/167; Tübingen: Mohr Siebeck, 2003), 150–205; Johns, 'Leaning toward Consummation: Mission and Peace in the Rhetoric of Revelation', in *Beautiful upon the Mountains: Biblical Essays on Mission, Peace, and the Reign of God* (ed. Mary H. Schertz and Ivan Friesen; Elkhart, IN: Institute of Mennonite Studies/Scottdale, PA/Waterloo, ON: Herald Press, 2003), 247–68; Kraybill, *Apocalypse*, 97–107; Patricia M. McDonald, *God and Violence: Biblical Resources for Living in a Small World* (Scottdale, PA/Waterloo, ON: Herald, 2004), 245–77; Mangina, *Revelation*, 84–94; Willard M. Swartley, *Covenant of Peace: The Missing Peace in New Testament Theology and Ethics* (Grand Rapids, MI: Eerdmans, 2006), 324–55; Rowland, *Book of Revelation*, 605–7; Rowland, *Revelation* (London: Epworth, 1993), 74–80; J. Denney Weaver, *The Nonviolent Atonement* (2nd edn; Grand Rapids, MI/Cambridge: Eerdmans, 2011), 20–35; John Howard Yoder, *The Politics of Jesus: Vicit Agnus Noster* (2nd edn; Grand Rapids, MI: Eerdmans/Carlisle: Paternoster, 1994), 228–47.

[25] See, e.g., Boring, *Revelation*, 108–12; also Volf, *Exclusion and Embrace*, 293.

[26] Griffith, *War on Terrorism*, 214.

Some interpreters go so far as to see all the violence against evil that takes place in the rest of Revelation as having already taken place in the moment of Jesus' own death.[27] In other words, God's 'violence' against Babylon took place on the cross, and was borne by the Lamb himself. The judgement has taken place already.

The mystery of human violence and divine overcoming of it we explored regarding atonement in Chapter 5 is again present in this reading of the Apocalypse. These interpreters point out that there is never any actual combat engaged in by God. The 'sword' wielded by the Messiah/Lamb is one coming out of his mouth (1.16; 2.12; 19.15; cf. Eph. 6.17; Heb. 4.12).[28] The kings of the earth, who have presumably gone down with the beast in chapter 19, are there again in the New Jerusalem, bringing the glory of the nations into the city as tribute to God (21.24). To be sure, such an interpretation requires that one read Revelation not in a linear fashion but rather as vignettes describing the violence of empire and God's strange judgement on it. Evil and the powers of evil have already been vanquished, much as in Colossians 2.14–15.

An oft-stressed aspect of this reading is the characterization of the Lamb as the Lion of Judah, appearing in chapter 19 as the warrior whose garments are drenched *in his own* blood. Likewise, his followers 'conquer' through their own 'endurance' (*hupomonē*) or, as Schüssler Fiorenza interprets the term, through their 'consistent resistance',[29] their fearless witness (*marturia*) and their blood, which is nothing less than participation in the ironic victory of the Lamb. There is nothing passive in the suffering of the Lamb; he is after all the Lion of Judah, the rider on the white horse. Just so, there

---

[27] E.g. Jacques Ellul, *Apocalypse* (New York: Seabury, 1977), 123.

[28] But David Frankfurter reminds us of the power of words in the mind both of John and his readers; words are acts, lethal swords coming out of mouths: 'The Legacy of Sectarian Rage: Vengeance Fantasies in the New Testament', in *Religion and Violence: The Biblical Heritage* (ed. David A. Bernat and Jonathan Klawans; Sheffield: Sheffield Phoenix, 2007), 114–28, esp. 123. See also Rowland, *Book of Revelation*, 701, and the penetrating analysis of Paul's language of warfare in 2 Corinthians by Calvin J. Roetzel, 'The Language of War (2 Cor. 10:1–6) and the Language of Weakness (2 Cor. 11:21b—13:10)', *Biblical Interpretation* 17 (2009), 77–99. His observations are relevant to the rhetoric of Revelation.

[29] Fiorenza, *Book of Revelation*, 4, 182.

is nothing passive in the conception of discipleship in John's Apocalypse.[30]

Is John's Apocalypse violent?

Even a glance as brief as this shows the enormous diversity of interpretations John's visions have occasioned, also with respect to violence. As resolutely as some scholars see John's Apocalypse as violent, just as resolutely many others see it not only as non-violent but as anti-violent.

To read the Apocalypse as forecasting the dénouement of the world as one of cosmic violence raises disquieting questions as to what kind of a God is implied, and what kind of a piety it generates.

To read Revelation, second, as resistance literature attacking a violent and arrogant empire may explain the fierce hostility in the imagery and language, but still leaves the question open as to whether or not liberation will come via the violence of warfare, even if the faithful do not themselves take up arms.

To read the Apocalypse, third, as employing the metaphor of divine warfare as deeply ironic or, relatedly, to signal that the ultimate war *has been* waged and won in and through the suffering of the slain Lamb clearly renders it *anti*-violent. But such a reading requires of readers a nimble facility to read against the grain of inherited interpretation and against the surface meaning of the text. Is that too tall an order? We might wonder whether at times such an anti-violent theological and ethical take is less an inference drawn from the reading of Revelation than the theological, ethical or ideological lens through which it is read. While that is an ever present danger for all interpreters, it is indeed quite possible that the irony expressed in the 'Lamb's war' was appreciated by the writer of the Apocalypse in much the same way we have already observed it in soundings taken elsewhere in the New Testament. As the Sermon on the Mount, Paul's exhortation and the atonement insist, deliberate and defiant vulnerability is the way evil is conquered. In short, to view such an interpretation as expecting too much of readers might witness less to what John of Patmos could demand of his readers than how much

---

[30] See David E. Aune, 'Following the Lamb: Discipleship in the Apocalypse', in *Patterns of Discipleship in the New Testament* (ed. Richard N. Longenecker; Grand Rapids, MI/ Cambridge: Eerdmans, 1996), 269–84.

contemporary Christians have lost sight of the 'surprise' inherent in the gospel.

This element of surprise is inseparable, as we have also seen repeatedly, from the conviction that God remains sovereign and the ultimate guarantor of the outcome of history. That is, after all, the premise of hope. As much as I am convinced that the slain Lamb is alone worthy to open our reading of John's Apocalypse, I am not persuaded that that motif exhausts the meaning of the book, or that John intends all of the images of violence to be collapsed into that image without remainder. Every probe we have taken in our investigation presupposes that God remains the sovereign judge before whom all, including the greatest empires and the powers behind them, are answerable.[31] At the same time, every one of our soundings has also shown that there is a great mystery to the intrusion of God into the affairs of humanity, also in judgement, a mystery residing in the love of a Creator of his creation, in both the persistent and ingenious drive to reconcile, and the equally baffling patience to give it time. No system can accommodate such dynamic sovereignty. To collapse judgement into Revelation 5 runs the risk of not taking a future of violence seriously, one that includes in our own time the Holocaust, Hiroshima and Nagasaki, and the still present threat of nuclear annihilation, all perpetrated by empires claiming the Christian heritage. The blindness of Christians to their own complicity in the violence of imperial power is not, I would argue, because Revelation is read as John intended but because it is not.

There are two ways those can betray John's Apocalypse who read it from within the (illusory) safety of 'Rome'. One is to turn away from it in judgement of its violence, refusing to ponder the central motif of the 'lamb that was slain' and of the divine rage at violence and imperial callousness and arrogance. The other is to domesticate its (intentionally) nightmarish quality into a self-serving scenario in which 'imperial' Christians do not see themselves in the crosshairs of this vision, as it were, but as its beneficiaries, even as they cheer on the violence of their own empires.

I take the Apocalypse as the prophet from Patmos' attempt to disrupt the worship of the *ekklēsiai* of Asia Minor with his own

---

[31] Howard-Brook and Gwyther, *Unveiling Empire*, 155; Volf, *Exclusion*, 295–301.

songs and visions, speaking the disturbing, angry but also intensely hopeful word of judgement and salvation, summoning the community of the Lamb's followers to defiant and vulnerable witness in imitation of and in participation with the Lamb. While the prophet John did not wear a yoke like Jeremiah (Jer. 27), walk about naked like Isaiah (Isa. 20), or eat his food prepared on a piles of dry excrement like Ezekiel (Ezek. 4), he did intend to shake up a community tempted by empire, to shock believers into an awareness of its demonic nature, and to remind them of their mission.[32] John intrudes rudely into our own orderly and polite worship no less, intending to disturb our cosy relationship with empire. Like Jesus in the temple, when he leaves we are left with his nightmarish tirade ringing in our ears. Is this a way the Word becomes flesh and takes on voice where flesh is so easily enticed by power and violence?

Even so, CAVEAT LECTOR (reader beware!) should be stamped all over the Apocalypse. Johns calls it 'arguably the most dangerous book in the history of Christendom'.[33] It eludes an ideologically or theologically clean reading. The images slip out of control too easily.[34] Moreover, their meaning and thus their relationship to violence cannot be ascertained apart from who is reading the document, with what set of inherited metaphors and images, with what kind of Christology, with what intensity of hunger for justice, with what courage to suffer in the process of offering resistant witness and with what confidence in a God whose mysterious sovereignty will snatch victory from the jaws of the beast.

The divine warrior in disguise (1 Thessalonians 5.1–11)

We will now drill a second bore hole, this time from what is probably the very earliest of the writings we have in the New Testament. Much like John's Apocalypse, 1 Thessalonians 5.1–11 brings the Roman imperial context, in particular the *pax Romana*, into clear

---

[32] Johns, 'Leaning', 265.

[33] Johns, *Lamb Christology*, 186.

[34] Barr, 'Lamb Who Looks like a Dragon?', 208; Mangina (*Revelation*, 179) refers to the Apocalypse's 'bifocal vision', in which the same metaphor can mean diametrically opposed things at the very same time.

view, unmasking it as a violent and oppressive system ripe for divine judgement.[35]

The setting of this text is more easily discernible than John's Apocalypse. The Thessalonians were a community of Jewish and non-Jewish believers (Acts 17.1–9; 1 Thess. 1.9).[36] They were evidently drawn to the community by the promise of the imminent arrival of the liberator or saviour, Messiah Jesus (see 1 Thess. 4.13–18), with varying degrees of understanding of what that might mean. Their adherence to a 'lord' with a criminal record and as one who would soon appear to liberate them evidently put them in the crosshairs of their pro-Roman fellow citizens, in particular the authorities. As Acts 17.7 recalls, Thessalonian believers were accused of suggesting that there was 'another king besides Caesar'. It may be that hostility erupted into violence against the community, as the references to persecution suggest (1 Thess. 1.6; 2.14–16; 3.3). The death (by persecution?) of adherents raised questions among believers about how long it would take for the Anointed liberator to appear. Paul probably wrote this letter to this *ekklēsia* in mid-century.

In responding to the Thessalonians' immediate eschatological anxieties, Paul and his co-authors Silvanus and Timothy intend to bolster their confidence and allay their fears. As is typical of Paul, his pastoral interventions are a gold mine of theology and ethics. He first assures them that the 'dead in Christ' will not be left out of the welcoming party going out to meet Christ (4.13–18). He then addresses specifically the arrival of the 'day of the Lord' in 5.1–11.[37]

The day of the Lord and the *pax Romana*

'The day of the Lord' is an old scriptural allusion to the day of judgement and/or vindication.[38] By the time Paul comes to employ the

---

[35] I have discussed this text more fully in Thomas R. Yoder Neufeld, '*Put on the Armour of God*': *The Divine Warrior from Isaiah to Ephesians* (Sheffield: Sheffield Academic Press, 1997), 73–93.

[36] Jacob W. Elias, *1 & 2 Thessalonians* (BCBC; Scottdale, PA/Waterloo, ON: Herald, 1995), 26–8; Robert Jewett, *The Thessalonian Correspondence: Pauline Rhetoric and Millenarian Piety* (Philadelphia, PA: Fortress Press, 1986).

[37] The fact that the eschatological concern seems to have been addressed in 1 Thess. 4.13–18 has led to the suggestion, much as in the case of Rom. 13.1–7, that 1 Thess. 5.1–11 is an interpolation. Even if there were agreement on that, which there is not, the matter has little bearing on our investigation.

[38] E.g. Amos 5.18; 8.9; Ezek. 30.2, 3; Joel 1.15; 2.1, 2; Zeph. 1.10–18.

phrase it has strong eschatological overtones, reflecting the intense expectation of Paul and his fellow believers that this 'old age' will soon give way to the 'new age' or 'new creation'. The 'day of the Lord' represents that pivotal moment. Whereas Paul typically uses 'Lord' as a synonym for Jesus as Messiah, 'the day of the Lord' retains its traditional reference to the day of God's intervention in judgement and salvation.

Paul sketches the coming of the 'day of the Lord' with colours and images familiar from traditions of judgement. The 'day' dawns suddenly on an unsuspecting world steeped in darkness, night, sleep and drunkenness, code within both prophetic and wisdom literature for life lived in alienation from and in rebellion to God.[39] It comes as 'sudden destruction', like a thief who sneaks in at night, like the pains of labour invariably catch a woman by surprise (5.2–3).[40] Those who dwell in such darkness are typically not aware of it. Like those who pass the night in a drunken stupor, they live in a dream world of delusions of plenty and power, of 'peace and security' (v. 3). We hear echoes here of Jeremiah 6.14; 8.11; Ezekiel 13.10, 16; and Micah 3.5 where the slogan 'Peace! Peace!' provides cover for violence and oppression.[41] Here it is not the covenant community but Roman imperial delusions of peace and security that are in view. 'Peace and Security' (*eirēnē kai asphaleia* or Latin *pax et securitas*) captures perfectly the cultural and military prowess and confidence of Rome.[42]

While many Thessalonians no doubt benefited from the close association the city had with Rome, many did not, including those

---

[39] E.g. Amos 6.4–6; Isa. 24.17–20; 28.1–4, 7–8; 59.9–10; Wisd. 17; and 18. Recall Rom. 13.11–14 and the discussion in Chapter 6 above (111–12, 119).

[40] We are reminded of the thief-like coming of the Son of Man as eschatological judge in Matt. 24.42–44//Luke 12.35–40.

[41] Elias, *1 & 2 Thessalonians*, 193–4.

[42] Klaus Wengst, *Pax Romana and the Peace of Jesus Christ* (trans. John Bowden; Philadelphia, PA: Fortress Press, 1987), 87, considers the slogan to capture the essence of what imperial Rome could offer. See also Ernst Bammel, 'Romans 13', in *Jesus and the Politics of His Day* (ed. Ernst Bammel and C. F. D. Moule; Cambridge: Cambridge University Press, 1984), 365–83; W. H. C. Frend, *Martyrdom and Persecution in the Early Church: A Study of a Conflict from the Maccabees to Donatus* (Oxford: Blackwell, 1965), 96; Dieter Georgi, *Theocracy in Paul's Praxis and Theology* (trans. David E. Green; Minneapolis, MN: Fortress Press, 1991), 25–31. This is a translation of the German 'Gott auf den Kopf stellen' (turning God upside down) in Jacob Taubes, ed., *Theokratie* (Paderborn: Ferdinand Schöningh, 1987).

drawn to Paul's liberationist gospel.[43] By so obviously pitting 'the day of Lord' against the empire, we might thus suspect Paul of stoking strong feelings of vindictiveness. Perhaps there were those within the circle of believers who would take pleasure in the violent end of those at whose hands they suffered. The disputed passage in 1 Thessalonians 2.14–16 is, for example, often read as an example of precisely such *Schadenfreude*, albeit directed at Judaea.[44] We are already familiar with this phenomenon from our study of John's Revelation. As typical and understandable it is for those who suffer at the hands of the violent to wish to see the empire and its minions go down, Paul does not permit such an attitude.

Here is where we now encounter a surprising twist. We expect Paul's assurance that the dark night of judgement and destruction will not affect the Thessalonian believers. That is intimated in 1.9. But Paul rejects the 'fortunate bystander' and 'satisfied onlooker' option. In verse 5 Paul refers to them as 'sons of light and sons of day',[45] thereby implicating them in the invasion of that fearsome day. The specific phrase 'sons of light' appears only here in the Pauline writings. But we recall that in Romans 13.11–12 readers are to 'put on the weapons of light'. We get a sense of the militancy of this language from the name of the famous War Scroll of Qumran, 'The War of the Sons of Light against the Sons of Darkness' (1QM). The covenanters at the Dead Sea understood that to refer to the war between the forces of God and their Roman enemies, one in which, given their 'collaborative eschatology',[46] they would join.

Paul adds to 'sons of light' the apparently redundant 'sons of day'. On the one hand, this reflects typical apocalyptic dualism, pitting 'day' against 'night', 'light' against 'darkness', 'sobriety' against 'drunkenness', and 'wakefulness' against 'sleep' (vv. 5–8; cf. Rom. 13.11–14).

---

[43] Jewett, *Thessalonian Correspondence*, 89–132, esp. 123–5.

[44] For that reason it is often taken to be an interpolation, unbefitting Paul. 2 Thessalonians, for which Pauline authorship has also been questioned, assures the faithful of God's paying back their tormentors (e.g. 1.6). Elias, *1 & 2 Thessalonians*, 84–92; Jewett, *Thessalonian Correspondence*, 37–8.

[45] 'Sons' is not to be taken as exclusive, as in the case of earlier chapters in this book. I use it here because of its associations, as will be come clear. 'Sons and daughters' would be better than 'children', as the NRSV has it. 'Sons' communicates not dependency so much as status and authority, precisely the implication in its present use (see also Chapter 2).

[46] Crossan, *God and Empire*, 235.

But we still have ringing in our ear the 'day of the Lord' from verse 2. Are we meant to connect 'sons of day' with that 'day'? Could it be that Paul is drawing this rather bewildered and fearful collection of new 'recruits' into the 'day' of the invasion of the divine warrior/judge?

The armour of God

Paul springs yet another surprise on his readers. Where Romans 13.11 spoke of 'weapons of light', the daughters and sons of light and day are now invited to put on breastplate and helmet (v. 8). No doubt some of Paul's readers would simply have taken this as a military metaphor for which there would have been multiple daily referents. But for those with ears attuned to the prophetic Scriptures, they would have noticed that Paul is reaching back to the iconic text of God as warrior in Isaiah 59.17: 'He put on righteousness like a breastplate, and a helmet of salvation on his head.'

Isaiah 59 is a poetic evocation of a world of brutality, in which the powerful victimize the weak, in which there is no safety for the vulnerable, no honesty in court, and violence for those wishing to live in keeping with God's will.[47] God takes note of the absence of anyone to establish true justice, peace and security for the vulnerable (59.15b–16). As a result, God arms himself for battle by putting on a breastplate of justice, a helmet of liberation, and a cloak of vengeance (v. 17). The metaphor of God in armour serves to highlight God's agency in bringing justice to a corrupt and brutal world.[48]

Isaiah 59 stresses divine agency very strongly, to the point where some interpret it as asserting God's sole prerogative for judgement ('Vengeance is mine!').[49] This only heightens the surprise. Paul summons the anxious and bewildered Thessalonians (1 Thess. 4.13–18)

---

[47] Yoder Neufeld, *'Put on the Armour'*, 15–47.

[48] I have explored Isa. 59 and its relationship to 1 Thess. 5 and Eph. 6 in *'Put on the Armour'*, and in relation to Ephesians also in Thomas R. Yoder Neufeld, *Ephesians* (BCBC; Scottdale, PA/Waterloo, ON: Herald, 2002), 308–10. The extent to which the ultimate agency of God as divine warrior came to be understood as sole agency, to that extent the radicality of the reinterpretation Paul offers of the divine warrior in 1 Thess. 5.1–11 takes on greater relief. See also Elias, *1 & 2 Thessalonians*, 206–9.

[49] E.g. Millard C. Lind, *Yahweh Is a Warrior: The Theology of Warfare in Ancient Israel* (Scottdale, PA/Kitchener, ON: Herald, 1980); Ben C. Ollenburger, *Zion, the City of the Great King: A Theological Symbol of the Jerusalem Cult* (JSOTSup 41; Sheffield: JSOT Press, 1987), esp. 'Yahweh's Exclusive Prerogative', 81–144.

to put on *God*'s armour. Paul tells them, in effect, that for them to be 'sons of the day' and 'sons of light' is not reassurance that they will be safe when the 'wrath' comes, but that they will be participants, wearing God's own armour.

It is difficult to appreciate the full extent of Paul's creativity in using Scripture. It appears that in the act of 'repopulating' the divine armour he informs the Thessalonians that they are no longer simply the beneficiaries of God's grace who await the intervention of the divine warrior on their behalf. They are being summoned, rather, as 'sons of the day' to put on God's own armour, in effect to act as divine warrior. In Dieter Georgi's words, 'God joins the people.'[50] As surprising as was Amos' announcement that the 'day of the Lord' is not salvation but judgement, is not day but night (Amos 5.18), so also is Paul's reconceiving of the divine warrior as the community of the faithful, drawn from among those once worshipping idols (1 Thess. 1.9).

Were this to be the full extent of the surprise, we should be alarmed. Participation in divine warfare, along with the assurance of divine empowerment to bring destruction upon an evil world, is playing with fire, as would become real in Judaea a decade or so after this letter was written, and as our own age knows too well – we call it 'terrorism'. Were Paul to have stopped here we might suspect him of summoning the 'saints' to participate, however misguidedly and delusionally, in the punitive judgement of their enemies.

Renaming the armour

But Paul does not stop there. He takes Isaiah 59's two elements of armour-breastplate and helmet, and renames them with his favourite triad – faith, love and hope.[51] Given that he has two items of armour and three virtues, the exercise is a bit clumsy. But that only increases our awareness that Paul is working with a scriptural precedent, and invites us to reflect on the moves he is making.

First, by renaming the breastplate of *dikaiosunē* (righteousness, justice) as the breastplate of *pistis* (trust, faith, faithfulness) and *agapē* (love), Paul establishes an intimate connection between divine justice and faithful love. That is, of course, a thoroughly Pauline

---

[50] Georgi, *Theocracy*, 25–31; see also Yoder Neufeld, '*Put on the Armour*', 86.
[51] Cf. 1 Thess. 1.3; also Rom. 5.1–5; Gal. 5.5, 6; Col. 1.4, 5; and esp. 1 Cor. 13.13.

understanding of the shocking nature of God's justice. In Romans 3.21–26 the 'faith of Jesus Christ' manifests God's justice *as* right-making or justifying grace.[52] Here, in 1 Thessalonians 5, the divine warrior's justice is expressed in the practice of the community's faith(fulness) and love. In asking them to put on God's breastplate, Paul is inviting the Thessalonians to participate in the 'terror' of God against evil through love and faithfulness. Just as in Isaiah 59 God's breastplate and helmet are a form of engagement in the affairs of a violent world, so too this breastplate signifies that fidelity and love are directed not in this instance toward God but toward the human community. The divine warrior invades the violent realm of 'peace and security' in the 'sons of the day' decked out in his breastplate of justice, exercising fidelity and love.

Further, in Paul's deft handling of the metaphor, Isaiah's 'helmet of salvation/liberation' has become the helmet of the 'hope (*elpis*) of salvation'. Perhaps this is no more than a way Paul is able to work 'hope' into his version of the divine armour. But there may be a deeper intention at work. Given the protective nature of 'armour' such as breastplate and helmet, we might initially take this as reassuring the Thessalonians that they can be confident in their own salvation from the coming 'wrath' (1.10), one they do not yet see but one that rests secure 'in hope'. That would certainly fit with the assurances given in 4.13–18. As important as hope is in this letter (e.g. 1.9, 10), to read it in this way misses the point that Paul is placing the 'hope of liberation' onto the armour of *God*. In Isaiah 59 the armour signifies the *activity* of God as divine warrior, and not God's *protection*. God doesn't need saving. Liberation is, rather, the point of God's armour; it is what God *does*.

When read in that light, the community's exercise of faith, love and hope of liberation suggests not the promise of God *to* believers so much as God's intervention *through* the 'sons of day' *for the sake of* a world stumbling about in a drunken stupor of false security and peace. When in 1 Thessalonians 5.9 Paul says that God has appointed us not for wrath but to obtain salvation, the inherent force of the motif of the faithful community in the armour of the divine

---

[52] See, e.g., Richard B. Hays, *The Faith of Jesus Christ: An Investigation into the Narrative Substructure of Galatians 3:1—4:11* (2nd edn; Grand Rapids, MI: Eerdmans, 2002); John E. Toews, *Romans* (BCBC; Scottdale, PA/Waterloo, ON: Herald, 2004), 108–11.

warrior suggests that the believers have been appointed for the task of obtaining liberation. The phrase 'through Jesus Christ our Lord' becomes then more than an identification of the source of 'our' salvation, which it surely also is. 'In Christ' – in and through God's Anointed – saints participate in the obtaining of salvation.[53]

Paul certainly conceives of his own apostolate as participation in salvation. In 2 Corinthians 6.1–10 Paul describes himself as a warrior wielding the 'weapons of justice' (*hopla dikaiosunēs*; v. 7),[54] working together with God (*synergountes*) on the present day of liberation or salvation (*nun hēmera sōotērias*; vv. 1, 2).[55] By clothing the Thessalonian believers with the divine armour, Paul is making much the same claim about the whole community of believers.

Dieter Georgi catches the wondrous and comical absurdity of Paul's recasting of Scripture: 'the fools take the field and make fools of the would-be mighty'.[56] We can hear Paul muster the troops:

> [26] Consider your own call, brothers and sisters: not many of you were wise by human standards, not many were powerful, not many were of noble birth. [27] But God chose what is foolish in the world to shame the wise; God chose what is weak in the world to shame the strong; [28] God chose what is low and despised in the world, things that are not, to reduce to nothing things that are. (1 Cor. 1.26–28)

Does the violence in the warfare imagery Paul employs in this exhortation valorize violence, or does it by being fused with the exercise of faithfulness, love and hope – virtues that have their most intense demonstration in the ministry, death and resurrection of Jesus – subvert, redefine and finally undo the violence of war? Is it enmity that kills or enmity that is killed? In my view the answer is the latter. The metaphors of warfare, invasion and destruction create a highly

---

[53] Cf. 2 Cor. 5.17—6.10, where the ministry of reconciliation is exercised on behalf of Christ (5.20) by 'co–workers' of God (6.1), announcing the presence of salvation (6.2).

[54] Romans 6.1–14 illustrates that Paul understands baptism to be, first, identification with Christ in both his death and his resurrection (vv. 1–11) and, second, as a rite of enlistment, where the believers' 'members' are presented to God as 'weapons of justice' (*hopla dikaiosunēs*; v. 13).

[55] Should we read Rom. 13.11–14 as 'armed' participation in the 'day of salvation?' Colossians 1.24 speaks of Paul 'completing what is still lacking in the sufferings of Christ'.

[56] Georgi, *Theocracy*, 27.

ironic image of a community of 'sons and daughters of light and day', caught up in the costly, confrontational, anti-imperial stealth invasion of the empire through their exercise of deliberate, defiant, and hopeful vulnerability.

Ephesians 6.10–20: 'Put on the whole armour of God!'

Ephesians again takes up the motif of the community in the armour of God.[57] The breastplate and helmet are again listed, only now exactly like in Isaiah 59 as justice and liberation (or righteousness and salvation) rather than as faith, love and hope. What sets it apart from both Isaiah and 1 Thessalonians is that the number of items of armour is greatly expanded, fully utilizing the metaphorical suggestiveness of the motif, much as happens in Wisdom of Solomon's adaptation of Isaiah 59.[58] Added to the breastplate of justice and the helmet of liberation is the belt of truth (v. 14), the footwear of readiness to announce peace (v. 15), the shield of faith (or faithfulness; v. 16) and the sword of the Spirit, the word of God (v. 17).[59] Unlike in Isaiah or in Wisdom of Solomon, and as in 1 Thessalonians, it is the 'holy ones' who are to put on God's armour.

More than probably this call to 'put on' would have been taken as an allusion to the baptismal drama of 'putting on' Christ (see also Romans 13.14). As in 1 Thessalonians the motif appears as part of the *paraenesis*, serving in Ephesians to bring the exhortation to a resounding climax. The *paraenesis* begins in Ephesians 4.1 with a call to unity, to radical and transformative nonconformity (5.3–21), and

---

[57] I have explored this in *Ephesians*, 290–316, and in *'Put on the Armour'*, 94–153. See also Ched Myers and Elaine Enns, *Ambassadors of Reconciliation; Vol. 1, New Testament Reflections on Restorative Justice and Peacemaking* (Maryknoll, NY: Orbis Books, 2009), 111–16. For full discussion and relevant literature, see: Clinton E. Arnold, *Ephesians* (ZECNT; Grand Rapids, MI: Zondervan, 2010), 435–75; Ernest Best, *Ephesians* (ICC; Edinburgh: T&T Clark, 1998), 584–611; Harold W. Hoehner, *Ephesians: An Exegetical Commentary* (Grand Rapids, MI: Baker Academic, 2002), 817–66; Andrew T. Lincoln, *Ephesians* (WBC 42; Dallas, TX: Word Books, 1990), 429–60; Frank Thielman, *Ephesians* (BECNT; Grand Rapids, MI: Baker Academic, 2010), 411–37.

[58] In Wisd. 5.17–20 God arms himself for battle on behalf of the righteous in a war of vindication against those who have done them harm. For full discussion see Yoder Neufeld, *'Put on the Armour'*, 48–72.

[59] For two quite different discussions of the items of armour, see, on the one hand, Arnold, *Ephesians*, 450–68; and, on the other, Yoder Neufeld, *Ephesians*, 298–307; Myers and Enns, *Ambassadors*, 114–15.

to mutual subordination within the economy (*oikonomia*) of the household (5.21—6.9; see Chapter 6). We recall from our discussion of Romans 13.1–7 that that subordination text too was wedged between a radical call to nonconformity (ch. 12) and a summons to put on the 'weapons of light' because the *kairos* of salvation is just around the corner (13.11–14). Again, as in 1 Thessalonians 5, the faithful are not bystanders to the messianic struggle for liberation, but full participants.

The *ekklēsia* and the powers

There are some distinct aspects to Ephesians' treatment of the motif of the divine armour. First, some of the intensity of eschatological expectancy has apparently given way to a wider, more expansive temporal horizon. This is accompanied by an increased stress on the *ekklēsia* as the body of the Messiah.[60] Believers are *together* the recipients of God's grace, in that they have been raised *together* with the Messiah and seated *together* with him in the 'heavenlies', as 2.4–6 stresses. We should notice both the perfect tense with respect to resurrection and exaltation and also the breathtaking status bestowed on the faithful. Put bluntly, the *ekklēsia* is the active 'embodied' presence of the Messiah engaged in God's gathering up all things (1.10). That is the larger context in which the saints are caught up in the war against the powers resisting that 'gathering up'.

Second, in Ephesians we encounter not the *pax et securitas* of Rome, as in 1 Thessalonians, but the myriad 'spiritual' powers that reside behind and within that system and all others keeping the world in thrall (6.13; cf. 2.1–3). Traditionally these powers have been interpreted 'spiritually' as Satanic or demonic. 'Spiritual warfare' is prominent in many parts of Christianity as a way to conceive of the Church's engagement with the world. While Clinton Arnold can say, 'Spiritual warfare is the solution to human warfare',[61] the concerns

---

[60] Many scholars, myself included, conclude for a variety of reasons that Ephesians was probably written after Paul's death in his name. For arguments and literature, see Yoder Neufeld, *Ephesians*, 24–8, 359–62. Among such reasons are the change in eschatology and the stress on ecclesiology. For recent arguments in favour of Paul's authorship, see Arnold, *Ephesians*, 46–50; Hoehner, *Ephesians*, 2–61; Thielman, *Ephesians*, 1–5.

[61] Arnold, *Ephesians*, 455.

of social and political violence and oppression, let alone of 'empire', tend not to be central to such a reading of Ephesians 6.[62]

Others, however, tie these 'powers' to the oppressive structures and institutions of 'empire' in its various guises. The work of Walter Wink is particularly well known,[63] but this line of interpretation emerged earlier in the work of the Dutch scholar Hendrik Berkhof, followed by John Howard Yoder and numerous others.[64] Yoder refers to the 'powers' as

> religious structures (especially the religious undergirdings of stable ancient and primitive societies), intellectual structures (-ologies and –isms), moral structures (codes and customs), political structures (the tyrant, the market, the school, the courts, race, and nation). The totality is overwhelmingly broad.[65]

Walter Wink famously characterizes the 'Domination System' as powers that are

> both visible *and* invisible, earthly *and* heavenly, spiritual *and* institutional. The Powers possess an outer, physical manifestation (buildings, portfolios, personnel, trucks, fax machines) and an inner spirituality, or corporate culture, or collective personality.[66]

Wink is reaching for what New Testament writers all would have taken as a given, namely that an either/or between spiritual and material, social and political is inconceivable. We must today try to put together what they could not have conceived of as coming apart.

---

[62] For fuller discussion of various scholarly approaches to the powers, see Yoder Neufeld, *Ephesians*, 290–316, and my essay on 'Powers' in *Ephesians*, 353–9; see also Arnold, *Ephesians*, 470–75; Arnold, *Ephesians: Power and Magic: The Concept of Power in Ephesians in Light of Its Historical Setting* (SNTSMS 63; Cambridge/New York: Cambridge University Press, 1989); Arnold, *3 Crucial Questions about Spiritual Warfare* (Grand Rapids, MI: Baker Books, 1997). See also the so-called 'Third Wave' movement; e.g. C. Peter Wagner, ed., *Engaging the Enemy: How to Fight and Defeat Territorial Spirits* (Ventura, CA: Regal Books, 1991).

[63] See Wink's three volumes, *Naming the Powers: The Language of Power in the New Testament* (1984); *Unmasking the Powers: The Invisible Forces That Determine Human Existence* (1986); and *Engaging the Powers: Discernment and Resistance in a World of Domination* (1992) (all by Minneapolis, MN: Fortress Press).

[64] Hendrik Berkhof, *Christ and the Powers* (trans. John Howard Yoder; Scottdale, PA/ Kitchener, ON: Herald, 1977); Marva J. Dawn, *Powers, Weakness, and the Tabernacling of God* (Grand Rapids, MI: Eerdmans, 2001); John Howard Yoder, *Politics*, 134–61.

[65] John Howard Yoder, *Politics*, 142–3.

[66] Wink, *Engaging the Powers*, 3. See also Volf, *Exclusion*, 87.

The powers and violence

What are the implications for the question of violence? A 'spiritual' understanding of the powers might seem to avoid the issue of violence. Traditional interpretation individualizes the text and sees the armour as providing protection in face of the strategies of the devil (Eph. 6.11). Personal temptations and struggles with faith are the arena for such struggle. This approach runs the risk of leaving the violence (social, political, military) beyond the horizon of concern.

In recent years 'spiritual warfare' has in some circles been taken out of the individual and personal sphere into a kind of 'power encounter' between divine and Satanic forces, a culture war in which the kingdom of God clashes with the cultures of the 'world' and in which God's people take part. With little awareness of the deep irony, such 'spiritual warfare' is often fused with conservative social and political agendas. Once again, as in the case of John's Apocalypse, the imagery and metaphors are vulnerable to aiding and abetting the violence of contemporary 'empires'.

Those who see in the powers a kind of spirituality that pervades the structures, institutions and ideologies of the world, not least those identified as 'imperial', would understand the work of these 'spiritual' powers to include violence – poverty, militarism, sexism and all other forms of 'domination'. Ephesians 6 is then read in light of what is often another kind of clash of cultures, where 'truth', 'justice', 'peace' and so on are 'wielded' in a way akin to social and political activism.

The question of violence is thus exceedingly complex. One might avoid physical violence in seeing the fight and the arms as 'only' spiritual. To do so would mask the extent to which such a view of reality can create or participate in non-physical forms of 'violence', where a sense of rock solid certainty and messianic identity, what Crossan calls 'collaborative eschatology and divine violence',[67] can lead to demonization of those who are different and, when access to power is available, to lethal violence. Equally, the 'messianic' certainty of being morally and ethically both right and superior with respect to politics and social justice too is vulnerable to arrogance and moral smugness.

---

[67] Crossan, *God and Empire*, 235.

The body of Christ in the armour of God

To be called upon to engage as the body of God's 'Anointed one' in the struggle against the forces and powers of this present 'darkness' is most definitely a 'spiritual' one, but for that no less relevant to the social, cultural and political sphere. What is unambiguously clear in 1 Thessalonians and Ephesians is that to be the 'body' of God's Anointed is to be drawn into divine agency to set things right. There is no room for passivity. 'Ephesians' catechism gets the "troops" dressed for battle.'[68] If in Isaiah 59 God puts on the armour because 'there is no one' (Isa. 59.16), here the Messiah has a 'body' with which to continue the messianic mission. That makes it absolutely crucial (with pun fully intended) that it is always remembered that this is the 'body' of the one who went to the cross precisely for those who put him there, whose 'victory' was achieved through giving his own life for his enemies (Rom. 5.6, 8, 10). The 'weapons' are thus 'only' ever faith, hope, love, truth, justice, the good news of peace, salvation and the word of God. If putting on this armour means 'war', if this is 'terror', it is never ever *against* 'blood and flesh' (6.12) but *for* blood and flesh. This warrior is not *non*-violent, but *anti*-violent, engaged in a campaign to 'kill enmity' (Eph. 2.16).

Neither 1 Thessalonians 5 nor Ephesians 6 lend themselves to prohibition or command so much as to exhortation and the summons to be and do the work of the Messiah's body. At the same time, they do invite a certain kind of casuistry, namely, an inventive and creative strategizing from within an imagination informed by being the body of the reconciler, exploiting every opportunity to effect liberation and reconciliation with God. The contextually specific Roman imperial slogan 'Peace and Security!' in 1 Thessalonians 5.3 is a crucial reminder not to escape into generalization and thus avoidance of real violence. The intentionally comprehensive list of 'powers' in Ephesians 6.12 is an equally crucial reminder not to reduce the messianic calling to either a 'spiritualized' agenda or to a socio-political 'peace and justice' agenda. 'In Christ' God is, after all, gathering up *all things*, 'things' in heaven and 'things' on earth (Eph. 1.10). No 'thing' – however spiritual or material – is left out.

---

[68] Myers and Enns, *Ambassadors*, 113.

Despite its vulnerability to being 'wielded' by the violent, to jettison the image of God as warrior from our operative canon would exact a price too great. We would lose a sense of the preposterousness and 'sneakiness' of the kind of divine warrior we find in 1 Thessalonians 5 and Ephesians 6, indeed in the figure of Jesus and his great apostle Paul. We would forgo the challenge in contemplating how the practice of truth, love, hope and faith are the judgement of God at work, however mysteriously. We would lose a sense of the way the motif in the New Testament witnesses to the confrontative and costly nature of the struggle for justice in a violent world. And we might lose a sense that God is both judge and saviour, as we have seen in each of our soundings. By having the divine warrior appear in the guise of a community of believers wearing the strangely renamed armour also instils in us a deep reluctance to determine the nature of divine judgement. Surprise has become an essential element of the good 'news'.

As always in our study of texts throughout this book, it matters who is reading, and from where. I give the last word to James Nayler, an early Quaker leader. Experiencing repeated imprisonment and torture at the hands of authorities in a 'Christian' land, he published 'The Lamb's War' in 1658. He integrates seamlessly the texts we have considered in this chapter. His grasp of their import is peerless.

> As [the followers of the Lamb] war not against men's persons, so their weapons are not carnal nor hurtful to any of the creation; for the Lamb comes not to destroy men's lives nor the work of God, and therefore at his appearance in his subjects he puts spiritual weapons into their hearts and hands; their armor is the light, their sword the Spirit of the Father and the Son, their shield is faith and patience, their paths are prepared with the gospel of peace and good-will towards all the creation of God; their breastplate is righteousness and holiness to God, their minds are girded with godliness, and they are covered with salvation, and they are taught with truth. And thus the Lamb in them, and they in him, go out in judgment and righteousness to make war with his enemies, conquering and to conquer. Not as the prince of this world in his subjects, with whips and prisons, tortures and torments on the bodies of creatures, to kill and to destroy men's lives, who are deceived, and so become his enemies; but he goes forth in the power of the Spirit with the Word of Truth to pass judgment upon the head of the Serpent which does deceive and bewitch the world . . . And having kindled the fire and awakened the creature, and broken

148

their peace and rest in sin, [the Lamb] waits in patience to prevail to recover the creature and stay the enmity by suffering all the rage, and envy, and evil entreatings that the evil spirit that rules in the creature can cast upon him, and he receives it with meekness and pity to the creature, returning love for hatred, wrestling with God against the enmity with prayers and tears night and day, with fasting, mourning and lamentation, in patience, in faithfulness, in truth, in love unfeigned, in long suffering, and in all the fruits of the spirit, that if by any means he may overcome evil with good.[69]

---

[69] James Nayler, 'The Lamb's War Against the Man of Sin (1658)', in *Early Quaker Writings 1650–1700* (ed. Hugh Barbour and Arthur O. Roberts; Grand Rapids, MI: Eerdmans, 1973), 106–7. Nayler's title has become a catchword for Quakers, Mennonites and others for costly, suffering engagement for peace. E.g. John Howard Yoder's chosen title for his posthumously published collection of essays, *The War of the Lamb: The Ethics of Nonviolence and Peacemaking* (Grand Rapids, MI: Brazos, 2009).

Conclusion

The ironic and potentially subversive 'killing enmity' identified in the epigraph and the Preface has encountered us throughout each of our textual probes. In each instance we were forced to ask: is this violence legitimized or nurtured, or is this violence subverted and overcome? Is this an enmity that kills or is enmity itself killed?

No attempt has been made in this investigation to do a balanced or full reading of the New Testament. After all, as stated in the first chapter, by making 'violence' rather than 'peace' or 'gospel' our focus of study we came in through the back door. Even so, we have gathered a great deal of evidence, some of it mysterious and enigmatic, some of it surprising, and all of it occasioning considerable debate among interpreters. Present in each of the texts we have probed is the central figure of Jesus – sovereign yet vulnerable, a lord who lived and died as a slave, the lion who turned out to be the lamb, a divine master who demands the same of his all-too-human followers. We have seen – not always unambiguously, to be sure – that his presence as teacher and model, as prophet and dying and rising messiah, leads to the subversion of violence, not its legitimatization, let alone valorization. In various ways and in a variety of contexts the writers of the New Testament insist that the ministry, teaching, death and resurrection of Jesus, and the deliberate, defiant and creative vulnerability of his followers, are the victory *over* and not *of* violence.

We will not often find violence-free rhetoric in the New Testament with which to express this wondrous mystery, most especially when 'violence' is conceived of in broad terms (see Chapter 1). Might that be because grace is encountered, received and enacted within a world marked by violence? The words of Scripture participate in the incarnation, an enfleshment that takes place in this violent world. The Word always speaks to us in the Scriptures from within this world. Our wrestling with the issue of violence happens in a world in which violence resides not only in our social and political relationships but also in our minds and imaginations. Might that be why suffering, vulnerability and sacrifice are always both evidence of the reality of violence and, in the light of the cross, the scandalous

150

means by which the violence that produces them is subverted and finally overcome?

In the end it is the ingenuity of God's love, the compassion at the heart of grace and the persistent drive towards reconciliation and restoration that the writers of the New Testament wish to narrate. They do so with the consciousness that both they and their readers are participants in that story as it is still unfolding. And they do so with words and images that are at hand. It would be tragic to be preoccupied with and dismissive of their means and to miss the story they are telling, the news they are announcing. With all its twists and turns and surprises, that story is always much bigger and more mysterious than any ethical, theological or ideological distillations. It is in the nature of 'gospel' – 'news' – that all such distillations are at their very best transitory. Scripture will, thankfully, always slip out of even our firmest grasp.

In his posthumously published *To Hear the Word*,[1] John Howard Yoder insisted that we don't need the Bible for what we already know or what we hold to be self-evidently true. More, we should be wary of placing hermeneutics before a kind of listening that is open to surprise, lest we hear only the echo of our own voices. What we do need is to learn to listen for the Word amid the words, with humility about our own perch from which we look, with respect for other listeners, both within and outside the household of faith. That means that in the end all such listening is itself an act of deliberately and defiantly vulnerable faith.[2]

I have found myself tested on such faith throughout this study, not only because of the texts and the challenges they present but also because of the often noisy and conflictive nature of the 'hermeneutical community'. More than once Jacob's wrestling in the night came to mind (Gen. 32). He wrestled fiercely with a 'man' all night long, fierce enough to leave him limping at dawn. Yet in the morning Jacob named the place 'Peniel', 'for I have seen God face to face' (v. 30). Most especially when struggling with the question of

---

[1] John Howard Yoder, *To Hear the Word* (2nd edn; Eugene, OR: Cascade Books, 2010), 155–77.

[2] Richard B. Hays, 'Salvation by Trust? Reading the Bible Faithfully', *Christian Century* 114 (1997), 218–23.

violence in the New Testament we wrestle with the full humanity present in the pages of the New Testament, and the full humanity of the community of listeners and wrestlers. But in the morning, even if limping badly, we call the place 'Peniel'.

Bibliography

Anselm, St, *Basic Writings: Proslogium, Monologium, Gaunilon's On Behalf of a Fool, Cur Deus Homo* (trans. S. W. Deane; 2nd edn; La Salle, IL: Open Court, 1962)

Arnold, Clinton E., *Ephesians* (ZECNT; Grand Rapids, MI: Zondervan, 2010)

Arnold, Clinton E., *Ephesians: Power and Magic: The Concept of Power in Ephesians in Light of Its Historical Setting* (SNTSMS 63; Cambridge/New York: Cambridge University Press, 1989)

Arnold, Clinton E., *3 Crucial Questions about Spiritual Warfare* (Grand Rapids, MI: Baker Books, 1997)

Aulén, Gustav, *Christus Victor: An Historical Study of the Three Main Types of the Idea of the Atonement* (Eugene, OR: Wipf & Stock, [1931] 2003)

Aune, David E., 'Following the Lamb: Discipleship in the Apocalypse', in *Patterns of Discipleship in the New Testament* (ed. Richard N. Longenecker; Grand Rapids, MI/Cambridge: Eerdmans, 1996), 269–84

Avalos, Hector, *Fighting Words: The Origins of Religious Violence* (Amherst, NY: Prometheus Books, 2005)

Balch, David J., 'Household Code', *ABD* 3.318–20

Balch, David J., *Let Wives be Submissive: The Domestic Code in 1 Peter* (Chico, CA: Scholars Press, 1981)

Bammel, Ernst, 'Romans 13', in *Jesus and the Politics of His Day* (ed. Ernst Bammel and C. F. D. Moule; Cambridge: Cambridge University Press, 1984), 365–83

Bammel, Ernst, and C. F. D. Moule, eds, *Jesus and the Politics of His Day* (Cambridge: Cambridge University Press, 1984)

Barbour, Hugh, and Arthur O. Roberts, eds, *Early Quaker Writings 1650–1700* (Grand Rapids, MI: Eerdmans, 1973)

Barr, David L., 'The Lamb Who Looks like a Dragon? Characterizing Jesus in John's Apocalypse', in *The Reality of Apocalypse: Rhetoric and Politics in the Book of Revelation* (ed. David L. Barr; Atlanta, GA: Society of Biblical Literature, 2006), 205–20

Barr, David L., ed., *The Reality of Apocalypse: Rhetoric and Politics in the Book of Revelation* (Atlanta, GA: Society of Biblical Literature, 2006)

Bauckham, Richard, *The Climax of Prophecy: Studies on the Book of Revelation* (Edinburgh: T&T Clark, 1993)

Bauckham, Richard, *The Theology of the Book of Revelation* (Cambridge: Cambridge University Press, 1993)

Beilby, James, and Paul R. Eddy, eds, *The Nature of the Atonement: Four Views* (Downers Grove, IL: InterVarsity, 2006)

Berkhof, Hendrik, *Christ and the Powers* (trans. John Howard Yoder; Scottdale, PA/Kitchener, ON: Herald, 1977)

Bernat, David A., and Jonathan Klawans, eds, *Religion and Violence: The Biblical Heritage* (Sheffield: Sheffield Phoenix, 2007)

Best, Ernest, *Ephesians* (ICC; Edinburgh: T&T Clark, 1998)

Best, Ernest, *Ephesians* (New Testament Guides; Sheffield: JSOT Press, 1993)

Betz, Hans Dieter, *The Sermon on the Mount* (Hermeneia; Minneapolis, MN: Fortress Press, 1995)

Boersma, Hans, *Violence, Hospitality, and the Cross: Reappropriating the Atonement Tradition* (Grand Rapids, MI: Baker Academic, 2004)

Boesak, Allan A., *Comfort and Protest: The Apocalypse from a South African Perspective* (Philadelphia, PA: Westminster, 1987)

Borg, Markus J., *Conflict, Holiness and Politics in the Teachings of Jesus* (Studies in the Bible and Early Christianity, Vol. 5; New York/Toronto: Edwin Mellen, 1984)

Boring, M. Eugene, *Revelation* (Interpretation: A Bible Commentary for Teaching and Preaching; Louisville, KY: John Knox, 1989)

Botha, Jan, 'Creation of New Meaning: Rhetorical Situations and the Reception of Romans 13:1–7', *Journal of Theology for Southern Africa* 79 (1992), 24–37

Boustan, Ra'anan S., Alex Jassen and Calvin J. Roetzel, eds, *Violence, Scripture, and Textual Practices in Early Judaism and Christianity*, Biblical Interpretation XVII/1–2 (2009)

Brandon, S. G. F., *Jesus and the Zealots: A Study of the Political Factor in Primitive Christianity* (New York: Charles Scribner's Sons/Manchester: Manchester University Press, 1967)

Bredin, Mark R., *Jesus, Revolutionary of Peace: A Nonviolent Christology in the Book of Revelation* (Milton Keynes/Waynesboro, GA: Paternoster, 2003)

Bredin, Mark R., 'John's Account of Jesus' Demonstration in the Temple: Violent or Nonviolent?', *BTB* 33/44 (2003), 44–50

Brown, Joanne Carlson, and Rebecca Parker, 'For God so Loved the World?', in Joanne Carlson Brown and Carole R. Bohn, eds, *Christianity, Patriarchy, and Abuse: A Feminist Critique* (New York: Pilgrim, 1989), 1–30

Brown, Raymond E., *The Death of the Messiah* (2 vols; New York: Doubleday, 1999)

Brown, Robert MacAfee, *Religion and Violence* (2nd edn; Philadelphia, PA: Westminster, [1973] 1987)

Capps, Donald, *Jesus: A Psychological Biography* (St. Louis, MI: Chalice, 2000)

Carey, Greg, 'The Book of Revelation as Counter-Imperial Script', in *In the Shadow of Empire: Reclaiming the Bible as a History of Faithful Resistance* (ed. Richard A. Horsley; Louisville, KY/London: Westminster John Knox, 2008), 157–76

Carter, Timothy L., 'The Irony of Romans 13', *Novum Testamentum* 46/3 (2004), 209–28

Carter, Warren, 'Constructions of Violence and Identities in Matthew's Gospel', in *Violence in the New Testament* (ed. Shelley Matthews and E. Leigh Gibson; New York/London: T&T Clark, 2005), 81–108

Clark, Ronald R., Jr., 'Sent Ahead or Left Behind? War and Peace in the Apocalypse, Eschatology, and the Left Behind Series', in *A Cry Instead of Justice: The Bible and Cultures of Violence in Psychological Perspective* (ed. Dereck Daschke and Andrew Kille; New York/London: T&T Clark, 2010), 182–94

Clark, Ronald R., Jr., 'Submit or Else! Intimate Partner Violence, Aggression, Abusers, and the Bible', in *A Cry Instead of Justice: The Bible and Cultures of Violence in Psychological Perspective* (ed. Dereck Daschke and Andrew Kille; New York/London: T&T Clark, 2010), 87–106

Collins, Adela Yarbro, *The Combat Myth in the Book of Revelation* (Missoula, MT: Scholars Press, 1976)

Collins, Adela Yarbro, *Crisis and Catharsis: The Power of the Apocalypse* (Philadelphia, PA: Westminster, 1984)

Collins, John J., 'The Zeal of Phinehas, the Bible, and the Legitimation of Violence', in *The Destructive Power of Religion: Violence in Judaism, Christianity, and Islam*; Vol. 1, *Sacred Scriptures, Ideology, and Violence* (ed. J. Harold Ellens; Westport, CT/London: Praeger, 2004), 11–33; reprinted from *JBL* 122 (2003), 3–21; published as *Does the Bible Justify Violence?* (Facets; Augsburg: Fortress Press, 2004)

Crossan, John Dominic, *God and Empire: Jesus against Rome, Then and Now* (San Francisco, CA: HarperSanFrancisco, 2007)

Crossan, John Dominic, *The Historical Jesus: The Life of a Mediterranean Jewish Peasant* (San Francisco, CA: HarperSanFrancisco, 1991)

Crossan, John Dominic, *In Parables: The Challenge of the Historical Jesus* (New York/London: Harper & Row, 1973)

Crossan, John Dominic, *Jesus: A Revolutionary Biography* (San Francisco, CA: HarperSanFrancisco, 1994)

Crouch, James E., *The Origin and Intention of the Colossian Haustafel* (Göttingen: Vandenhoeck & Ruprecht, 1971)

Dawn, Marva J., *Powers, Weakness, and the Tabernacling of God* (Grand Rapids, MI: Eerdmans, 2001)

Desjardins, Michel, *Peace, Violence, and the New Testament* (Sheffield: Sheffield Academic Press, 1997)

Donaldson, Terence L., *Jews and Anti-Judaism in the New Testament: Decision Points and Divergent Interpretations* (Waco, TX: Baylor University Press; London: SPCK, 2010)

Driver, John C., *Understanding the Atonement for the Mission of the Church* (Scottdale, PA/Kitchener, ON: Herald Press, 1986)

Duff, Paul B., *Who Rides the Beast: Prophetic Rivalry and the Rhetoric of Crisis in the Churches of the Apocalypse* (Oxford: Oxford University Press, 2001)

Dunn, James D. G., *Jesus Remembered* (Christianity in the Making, Vol. 1; Grand Rapids, MI/Cambridge: Eerdmans, 2003)

Dunn, James D. G., 'Romans 13:1–7: A Charter for Political Quietism?', *Ex auditu* 2 (1986), 55–68

Edwards, George R., *Jesus and the Politics of Violence* (New York and London: Harper & Row, 1972)

Elias, Jacob W., *1 & 2 Thessalonians* (BCBC; Scottdale, PA/Waterloo, ON: Herald, 1995)

Ellens, J. Harold, 'Religious Metaphors Can Kill', in *The Destructive Power of Religion: Violence in Judaism, Christianity, and Islam*; Vol. 1, *Sacred Scriptures, Ideology, and Violence* (ed. J. Harold Ellens; Westport, CT/ London: Praeger, 2004), 255–72

Ellens, J. Harold, 'The Violent Jesus', in *The Destructive Power of Religion: Violence in Judaism, Christianity, and Islam*; Vol. 3, *Models and Cases of Violence in Religion* (ed. J. Harold Ellens; Westport, CT/London: Praeger, 2004), 15–37

Ellens, J. Harold, ed., *The Destructive Power of Religion: Violence in Judaism, Christianity, and Islam* (Westport, CT/London: Praeger, 2004): Vol. 1, *Sacred Scriptures, Ideology, and Violence*; Vol. 2, *Religion, Psychology, and Violence*; Vol. 3, *Models and Cases of Violence in Religion*; Vol. 4, *Contemporary Views on Spirituality and Violence*

Elliott, John H., *A Home for the Homeless: A Sociological Exegesis of 1 Peter, Its Situation and Strategy* (Philadelphia, PA: Fortress Press, 1981)

Elliott, Neil, *Liberating Paul: The Justice of God and the Politics of the Apostle* (Maryknoll, NY: Orbis, 1994)

Ellul, Jacques, *Apocalypse* (New York: Seabury, 1977)

Ellul, Jacques, *Violence: Reflections from a Christian Perspective* (trans. Cecelia Gaul Kings; New York: Seabury, 1969)

Finlan, Stephen, *Options on Atonement in Christian Thought* (Collegeville, MN: Liturgical Press, 2007)

Finlan, Stephen, *Problems with Atonement: The Origins of, and Controversy about, the Atonement Doctrine* (Collegeville, MN: Liturgical Press, 2005)

Fiorenza, Elisabeth Schüssler, *The Book of Revelation: Justice and Judgement* (Philadelphia, PA: Fortress Press, 1985)

Fiorenza, Elisabeth Schüssler, *In Memory of Her: A Feminist Theological Reconstruction of Christian Origins* (New York: Crossroad, 1983)

Fiorenza, Elisabeth Schüssler, ed., *Searching the Scriptures; Vol. 2, A Feminist Commentary* (New York: Crossroad, 1994)

Flusser, David, with R. Steven Notley, *Jesus* (Jerusalem: Hebrew University Magnes Press, 1997)

Ford, David F., and Graham Stanton, eds, *Reading Texts, Seeking Wisdom: Scripture and Theology* (Grand Rapids, MI/Cambridge: Eerdmans, 2003)

Frankfurter, David, 'The Legacy of Sectarian Rage: Vengeance Fantasies in the New Testament', in *Religion and Violence: The Biblical Heritage* (ed. David A. Bernat and Jonathan Klawans; Sheffield: Sheffield Phoenix, 2007), 114–28

Fredriksen, Paula, *Jesus of Nazareth, King of the Jews: A Jewish Life and the Emergence of Christianity* (New York: Vintage, 1999)

Frend, W. H. C., *Martyrdom and Persecution in the Early Church: A Study of a Conflict from the Maccabees to Donatus* (Oxford: Blackwell, 1965)

Fuller, Reginald H., ed., *Essays on the Love Commandment* (Philadelphia, PA: Fortress Press, 1978)

Galtung, Johan, 'Cultural Violence', *Journal of Peace Research* 27/3 (1990), 291–305

Galtung, Johan, 'Violence, Peace and Peace Research', *Journal of Peace Research* 6/3 (1969), 167–91

Georgi, Dieter, *Theocracy in Paul's Praxis and Theology* (trans. David E. Green; Minneapolis, MN: Fortress Press, 1991)

Girard, René, *The Scapegoat* (trans. Yvonne Freccero; Baltimore: Johns Hopkins University Press, 1986)

Girard, René, *Things Hidden since the Foundation of the World* (trans. Stephen Bann and Michael Metteer; Stanford, CA: Stanford University Press, 1987)

Girard, René, *Violence and the Sacred* (trans. Patrick Gregory; Baltimore, MD: Johns Hopkins University Press, 1977)

Glancy, Jennifer A., 'Violence as Sign in the Fourth Gospel', *Biblical Interpretation* 17 (2009), 100–17

Gorman, Michael J., *Reading Revelation Responsibly: Uncivil Worship and Witness: Following the Lamb into the New Creation* (Eugene, OR: Cascade Books, 2011)

Green, Joel B., 'Kaleidoscopic View', in *The Nature of the Atonement: Four Views* (ed. James Beilby and Paul R. Eddy; Downers Grove, IL: InterVarsity Press, 2006), 157–85

Green, Joel B., and Mark D. Baker, *Recovering the Scandal of the Cross: Atonement in New Testament and Contemporary Contexts* (Downers Grove, IL: InterVarsity, 2000)

Griffith, Lee, *The War on Terrorism and the Terror of God* (Grand Rapids, MI/Cambridge: Eerdmans, 2002)

Grimsrud, Ted, and Loren L. Johns, eds, *Peace and Justice Shall Embrace: Power and Theopolitics in the Bible* (Millard Lind Festschrift; Telford, PA: Pandora Press US, 1999)

Gundry, Robert H., *Matthew: A Commentary on His Literary and Theological Art* (Grand Rapids, MI: Eerdmans, 1982)

Hays, Richard B., *The Faith of Jesus Christ: An Investigation into the Narrative Substructure of Galatians 3.1—4.11* (2nd edn; Grand Rapids, MI: Eerdmans, 2002)

Hays, Richard B., *The Moral Vision of the New Testament: A Contemporary Introduction to New Testament Ethics* (San Francisco, CA: HarperSanFrancisco, 1996)

Hays, Richard B., 'Salvation by Trust? Reading the Bible Faithfully', *Christian Century* 114 (1997), 218–23

Henderson, Suzanne Watts, 'Taking Liberties with the Text: The Colossians Household Code as Hermeneutical Paradigm', *Interpretation* 60/4 (2006), 420–32

Hengel, Martin, *Crucifixion in the Ancient World and the Folly of the Message of the Cross* (Philadelphia, PA: Fortress Press/London: SCM Press, 1977)

Hering, James P., *The Colossian and Ephesians* Haustafeln *in Theological Context: An Analysis of Their Origins, Relationship, and Message* (New York/Frankfurt am Main: Peter Lang, 2007)

Herzog, William R., II, 'Dissembling, a Weapon of the Weak: The Case of Christ and Caesar in Mark 12:13–17 and Romans 13:1–7', *Perspectives in Religious Studies* 21/4 (1994), 339–60

Herzog, William R., II, *Jesus, Justice, and the Reign of God: A Ministry of Liberation* (Louisville, KY: Westminster/John Knox, 2000)

Herzog, William R., II, *Parables as Subversive Speech: Jesus as Pedagogue of the Oppressed* (Louisville, KY: John Knox, 1994)

Hoehner, Harold W., *Ephesians: An Exegetical Commentary* (Grand Rapids, MI: Baker Academic, 2002)

Horsley, Richard A., '"By the Finger of God": Jesus and Imperial Violence', in *Violence in the New Testament* (ed. Shelley Matthews and E. Leigh Gibson; New York/London: T&T Clark, 2005), 51–80

Horsley, Richard A., 'Ethics and Exegesis: "Love Your enemies" and the Doctrine of Non-violence', *JAAR* LIV/1 (1986), 3–32

Horsley, Richard A., *In the Shadow of Empire: Reclaiming the Bible as a History of Faithful Resistance* (Louisville, KY/London: Westminster John Knox, 2008)

Horsley, Richard A., *Jesus and Empire: The Kingdom of God and the New World Order* (Minneapolis, MN: Fortress Press, 2003)

Horsley, Richard A., *Jesus and the Spiral of Violence: Popular Jewish Resistance in Roman Palestine* (San Francisco: Harper & Row, 1987)

Horsley, Richard A., and John S. Hanson, *Bandits, Prophets, and Messiahs: Popular Movements at the Time of Jesus* (San Francisco, CA: Harper & Row, 1985)

Howard-Brook, Wes, and Anthony Gwyther, *Unveiling Empire: Reading Revelation Then and Now* (Maryknoll, NY: Orbis, 1999)

Hultgren, Arland J., *The Parables of Jesus: A Commentary* (Grand Rapids, MI/Cambridge: Eerdmans, 2000)

Jersak, Brad, and Michael Hardin, eds, *Stricken by God? Nonviolent Identification and the Victory of Christ* (Grand Rapids, MI/Cambridge: Eerdmans, 2007)

Jewett, Robert, *The Thessalonian Correspondence: Pauline Rhetoric and Millenarian Piety* (Philadelphia, PA: Fortress Press, 1986)

Johns, Loren L., *The Lamb Christology of the Apocalypse of John: An Investigation into Its Origins and Rhetorical Force* (WUNT 2/167; Tübingen: Mohr Siebeck, 2003)

Johns, Loren L., 'Leaning toward Consummation: Mission and Peace in the Rhetoric of Revelation', in *Beautiful upon the Mountains: Biblical Essays on Mission, Peace, and the Reign of God* (ed. Mary H. Schertz and Ivan Friesen; Elkhart, IN: Institute of Mennonite Studies/Scottdale, PA/Waterloo, ON: Herald Press, 2003), 247–68

Johnson, Luke Timothy, *The Writings of the New Testament: An Interpretation* (2nd edn; Minneapolis, MN: Fortress Press, 1999)

Jordan, Clarence, *The Substance of Faith and Other Cotton Patch Sermons* (New York: Association Press, 1972)

Kallas, James, 'Romans XIII.1–7: An Interpolation', *NTS* 11 (1964–5), 365–74

Käsemann, Ernst, *Commentary on Romans* (Grand Rapids, MI: Eerdmans, 1980)

Keener, Craig S., *A Commentary on the Gospel of Matthew* (Grand Rapids, MI/Cambridge: Eerdmans, 1999)

Keener, Craig S., *The Gospel of John: A Commentary* (Peabody, MA: Hendrickson, 2003)

Keesmaat, Sylvia C., 'Strange Neighbors and Risky Care (Matt. 18:21–35; Luke 14:7–14; Luke 10:25–37)', in *The Challenge of Jesus' Parables* (ed. Richard N. Longenecker; Grand Rapids, MI/Cambridge: Eerdmans, 2000), 263–85

Klassen, William, 'Coals of Fire: Symbol of Repentance or Revenge?', *NTS* 9 (1963), 337–50

Klassen, William, 'Jesus and Phineas: A Rejected Role Model', *Society of Biblical Literature Seminar Papers* 25 (1986), 490–500

Klassen, William, *Love of Enemies: The Way to Peace* (Overtures to Biblical Theology 15; Philadelphia, PA: Fortress Press, 1984)

Klawans, Jonathan, 'Introduction: Religion, Violence, and the Bible', in *Religion and Violence: The Biblical Heritage* (ed. David A. Bernat and Jonathan Klawans; Sheffield: Sheffield Phoenix, 2007), 1–15

Koester, Craig, 'Revelation's Visionary Challenge to Ordinary Empire', *Interpretation* 63/1 (2009), 5–18

Kraybill, Donald B., Steven M. Nolt and David Weaver-Zercher, *Amish Grace: How Forgiveness Transcended Tragedy* (San Francisco, CA: Jossey-Bass, 2007)

Kraybill, J. Nelson, *Apocalypse and Allegiance: Worship, Politics, and Devotion in the Book of Revelation* (Grand Rapids, MI: Brazos, 2010)

Kraybill, J. Nelson, *Imperial Cult and Commerce in John's Apocalypse* (*JSNT* 132; Sheffield: Sheffield Academic Press, 1996)

Kroeger, Catherine Clark, and James R. Beck, eds, *Women, Abuse, and the Bible: How Scripture Can Be Used to Hurt or to Heal* (Grand Rapids, MI: Baker Books, 1996)

Lapide, Pinchas, *Sermon on the Mount* (Maryknoll, NY: Orbis, 1986)

Lassere, Jean, 'A Tenacious Misinterpretation', in *Occasional Papers of the Council of Mennonite Seminaries and Institute of Mennonite Studies*, 1 (ed. Willard M. Swartley; Elkhart, IN, 1981), 35–47

Levine, Amy-Jill, with Maria Mayo Robbins, eds, *A Feminist Companion to the Apocalypse of John* (New York/London: T&T Clark, 2009)

Lincoln, Andrew T., *Ephesians* (WBC 42; Dallas, TX: Word Books, 1990)

Lincoln, Andrew T., 'The Household Code and Wisdom Mode of Colossians', *JSNT* 74 (1999), 93–112

Lind, Millard C., *Yahweh Is a Warrior: The Theology of Warfare in Ancient Israel* (Scottdale, PA/Kitchener, ON: Herald, 1980)

Lindsey, Hal, *The Late Great Planet Earth* (Grand Rapids, MI: Zondervan, 1970)

Longenecker, Richard N., *Patterns of Discipleship in the New Testament* (Grand Rapids, MI/Cambridge: Eerdmans, 1996)

Longenecker, Richard N., ed., *The Challenge of Jesus' Parables* (Grand Rapids, MI/Cambridge: Eerdmans, 2000)

Love, Gregory Anderson, *Love, Violence, and the Cross: How the Nonviolent God Saves Us through the Cross of Christ* (Eugene, OR: Cascade Books, 2010)

McDonald, Patricia M., *God and Violence: Biblical Resources for Living in a Small World* (Scottdale, PA/Waterloo, ON: Herald, 2004)

McNight, Scot, *A Community Called Atonement* (Nashville, TN: Abingdon, 2007)

McNight, Scot, *Jesus and His Death: Historiography, the Historical Jesus, and Atonement Theory* (Waco, TX: Baylor University Press, 2005)

Mangina, Joseph L., *Revelation* (Brazos Theological Commentary on the Bible; Grand Rapids, MI: Brazos, 2010)

Marshall, Christopher D., 'Atonement, Violence and the Will of God: A Sympathetic Response to J. Denny Weaver's The Nonviolent Atonement', *MQR* 77 (2003), 69–92

Marshall, Christopher D., *Beyond Retribution: A New Testament Vision for Justice, Crime, and Punishment* (Grand Rapids, MI: Eerdmans, 2001)

Marshall, John W., 'Collateral Damage: Jesus and Jezebel in the Jewish War', in *Violence in the New Testament* (ed. Shelley Matthews and E. Leigh Gibson; New York/London: T&T Clark, 2005), 35–50

Marshall, John W., 'Hybridity and Reading Romans 13', *JSNT* 31/2 (2008), 157–78

Marshall, John W., *Parables of War: Reading John's Jewish Apocalypse* (ESCJ; Waterloo, ON: Wilfrid Laurier University Press, 2001)

Martin, Ernest D., *Colossians* (BCBC; Scottdale, PA/Waterloo, ON: Herald, 1993)

Matthews, Shelley, and E. Leigh Gibson, eds, *Violence in the New Testament* (New York/London: T&T Clark, 2005)

Meier, John P., *A Marginal Jew: Rethinking the Historical Jesus: Vol. 4, Law and Love* (New Haven/London: Yale University Press, 2009)

Mendenhall, George E., *The Tenth Generation: The Origins of the Biblical Tradition* (Baltimore, MD: Johns Hopkins University Press, 1973)

Miller, John W., *Jesus at Thirty: A Psychological and Historical Portrait* (Minneapolis, MN: Fortress Press, 1997)

Moberly, Walter, 'Jonah, God's Objectionable Mercy, and the Way of Wisdom', in *Reading Texts, Seeking Wisdom: Scripture and Theology* (ed. David F. Ford and Graham Stanton; Grand Rapids, MI/Cambridge: Eerdmans, 2003), 154–68

Morenz, S., 'Feurige Kohlen auf dem Haupt', *TLZ* 78 (1953), 187–92

Moulder, James, 'Romans 13 and Conscientious Disobedience', *Journal of Theology for Southern Africa* 21 (1977), 13–23

Munro, Winsome, *Authority in Paul and Peter: The Identification of a Pastoral Stratum in the Pauline Corpus and 1 Peter* (Cambridge: Cambridge University Press, 1983)

Murphy, Nancey, Brad J. Kallenberg and Mark Thiessen Nation, eds, *Virtues and Practices in the Christian Tradition: Christian Ethics after MacIntyre* (Harrisburg, PA: Trinity Press International, 1997)

Myers, Ched, *Binding the Strong Man: A Political Reading of Mark's Story of Jesus* (2nd edn; Maryknoll, NY: Orbis Books, 2008)

Myers, Ched, and Elaine Enns, *Ambassadors of Reconciliation; Vol. 1, New Testament Reflections on Restorative Justice and Peacemaking* (Maryknoll, NY: Orbis Books, 2009)

Nanos, Mark D., *The Mystery of Romans: The Jewish Context of Paul's Letter* (Minneapolis, MN: Fortress Press, 1996)

Nayler, James, 'The Lamb's War Against the Man of Sin (1658)', in *Early Quaker Writings 1650–1700* (ed. Hugh Barbour and Arthur O. Roberts; Grand Rapids, MI: Eerdmans, 1973), 106–7

Neville, David J., 'Toward a Teleology of Peace: Contesting Matthew's Violent Eschatology', *JSNT* 30/2 (2007), 131–61

O'Brien, Julia M., and Chris Franke, eds, *The Aesthetics of Violence in the Prophets* (New York/London: T&T Clark, 2010)

Ollenburger, Ben C., *Zion, the City of the Great King: A Theological Symbol of the Jerusalem Cult* (JSOTSup 41; Sheffield: JSOT Press, 1987)

Perkins, Pheme, *Love Commands in the New Testament* (New York: Paulist, 1982)

Pippin, Tina, *Death and Desire: The Rhetoric of Gender in the Apocalypse of John* (Louisville, KY: Westminster/John Knox, 1992)

Powell, Marvin A., 'Weights and Measures', *ABD* 6.907–8

Purvis, Sally B., *The Power of the Cross: Foundations for a Christian Feminist Ethic of Community* (Nashville, TN: Abingdon, 1993)

Reesor-Taylor, Rachel, 'Anselm's Cur Deus Homo for a Peace Theology: On the Compatibility of Non-violence and Sacrificial Atonement' (PhD; Montreal: McGill University, 2007)

Reid, Barbara E., OP, 'Violent Endings in Matthew's Parables and Christian Nonviolence', *CBQ* 66 (2004), 237–55

Reimer, A. James, *Christians and War: A Brief History of the Church's Teaching and Practices* (Minneapolis, MN: Fortress Press, 2010)

Reiser, Marius, *Jesus and Judgment: The Eschatological Proclamation in Its Jewish Context* (trans. Linda M. Maloney; Minneapolis, MN: Fortress Press, 1997)

Roetzel, Calvin J., 'The Language of War (2 Cor. 10:1–6) and the Language of Weakness (2 Cor. 11:21b—13:10)', *Biblical Interpretation* 17 (2009), 77–99

Rowland, Christopher C., *The Book of Revelation: Introduction, Commentary, and Reflections* (The New Interpreter's Bible, Vol. XII; Nashville, TN: Abingdon, 1998)

Rowland, Christopher C., *Revelation* (London: Epworth, 1993)

Russell, Letty M., 'Authority and the Challenge of Feminist Interpretation', in *Feminist Interpretation of the Bible* (ed. Letty M. Russell; Philadelphia, PA: Westminster, 1985), 137–46

Russell, Letty M., *Imitators of God: A Study Book on Ephesians* (New York: Mission Education and Cultivation Program Department, General Board of Global Ministries, 1984)

Russell Letty M., ed., *Feminist Interpretation of the Bible* (Philadelphia, PA: Westminster, 1985)

Sanders, E. P., *The Historical Figure of Jesus* (New York/London: Penguin, 1993)

Sanders, E. P., *Jesus and Judaism* (Philadelphia, PA: Fortress Press, 1985)

Schertz, Mary H., 'Nonretaliation and the Haustafeln in 1 Peter', in *The Love of Enemy and Nonretaliation in the New Testament* (ed. Willard M. Swartley; Studies of Peace and Scripture, Institute of Mennonite Studies; Louisville, KY: Westminster/John Knox, 1992), 258–86

Schertz, Mary H., and Ivan Friesen, eds, *Beautiful upon the Mountains: Biblical Essays on Mission, Peace, and the Reign of God* (Elkhart, IN: Institute of Mennonite Studies/Scottdale, PA/Waterloo, ON: Herald Press, 2003)

Schlabach, Gerald W., ed., *Just Policing, Not War: An Alternative Response to World Violence* (Collegeville, MN: Liturgical Press, 2007)

Schlabach, Theron F., and Richard T. Hughes, *Proclaim Peace: Christian Pacifism from Unexpected Quarters* (Urbana, IL: University of Illinois, 1997)

Schmiechen, Peter, *Saving Power: Theories of Atonement and Forms of the Church* (Grand Rapids, MI/Cambridge: Eerdmans, 2005)

Schottroff, Luise, '"Give to Caesar What Belongs to Caesar and to God What Belongs to God": A Theological Response of the Early Christian Church to Its Social and Political Environment', in *The Love of Enemy and Nonretaliation in the New Testament* (ed. Willard M. Swartley; Studies of Peace and Scripture, Institute of Mennonite Studies; Louisville, KY: Westminster/John Knox, 1992), 223–57

Schottroff, Luise, 'Nonviolence and the Love of One's Enemies', in *Essays on the Love Commandment* (ed. Reginald H. Fuller; Philadelphia, PA: Fortress Press, 1978), 9–39

Schrenk, Gottlob, 'δίκη, κτλ.', *TDNT* 2.182–91

Schroeder, David, 'Die Haustafeln des Neuen Testaments: Ihre Herkunft und ihr theologischer Sinn' (DTheol dissertation; University of Hamburg, 1959)

Schroeder, David, 'Lists, Ethical', *IDBSup.*, 546–7

Schweitzer, Albert, *The Quest of the Historical Jesus: A Critical Study of Its Progress from Reimarus to Wrede* (trans. W. Montgomery; London: A. & C. Black, 1910)

Sherwood, Yvonne, and Jonneke Bekkenkamp, 'Introduction: The Thin Blade of Difference between Real Swords and Words about "Sharp-Edged Iron Things" – Reflections on How People Use the Word', in *Sanctified Aggression: Legacies of Biblical and Post Biblical Vocabularies of Violence* (ed. Yvonne Sherwood and Jonneke Bekkenkamp; London/New York: T&T Clark, 2003), 1–9

Sherwood, Yvonne, and Jonneke Bekkenkamp, eds, *Sanctified Aggression: Legacies of Biblical and Post-Biblical Vocabularies of Violence* (London/New York: T&T Clark, 2003)

Sloyan, Gerard Stephen, *The Crucifixion of Jesus: History, Myth, Faith* (Minneapolis, MN: Fortress Press, 1995)

Snodgrass, Klyne R., *Stories with Intent: A Comprehensive Guide to the Parables of Jesus* (Grand Rapids, MI/Cambridge: Eerdmans, 2008)

Standhartinger, Angela, 'The Origin and Intention of the Household Code in the Letter to the Colossians', *JSNT* 79 (2000), 117–30

Stassen, Glen H., *Just Peacemaking: Transforming Initiatives for Justice and Peace* (Louisville, KY: Westminster/John Knox, 1992)

Stassen, Glen H., *Living the Sermon on the Mount: A Practical Hope for Grace and Deliverance* (San Francisco, CA: Jossey-Bass, 2006)

Stassen, Glen H., with Michael Westmoreland White, 'Defining Violence and Nonviolence', in *Teaching Peace: Nonviolence and the Liberal Arts* (ed. J. Denny Weaver and Gerald Biesecker-Mast; Lanham, ML: Rowman and Littlefield, 2003), 17–37

Stendahl, Krister, 'Hate, Nonretaliation, and Love: Coals of Fire', in Krister Stendahl, *Meanings: The Bible as Document and as Guide* (Philadelphia, PA: Fortress Press, 1984), 137–61

Strathmann, Hermann, 'λειτουργέω, κτλ.', *TDNT* 4.215–31

Swartley, Willard M., *Covenant of Peace: The Missing Peace in New Testament Theology and Ethics* (Grand Rapids, MI: Eerdmans, 2006)

Swartley, Willard M., 'War and Peace in the New Testament', *Aufstieg und Niedergang der Römischen Welt*, 2.26.3: 2298–408

Swartley, Willard M., ed., *The Love of Enemy and Nonretaliation in the New Testament* (Studies of Peace and Scripture, Institute of Mennonite Studies; Louisville, KY: Westminster/John Knox, 1992)

Swartley, Willard M., ed., *Occasional Papers of the Council of Mennonite Seminaries and Institute of Mennonite Studies*, No. 1 (Elkhart, IN, 1981)

Swartley, Willard M., ed., *Violence Renounced: René Girard, Biblical Studies, and Peacemaking* (Telford, PA: Pandora Press; Scottdale, PA: Herald Press, 2000)

Tannehill, Robert C., 'The "Focal Instance" as a Form of New Testament Speech: A Study of Matthew 5.39–42', *JR* 50 (1970), 372–85

Tanzer, Sarah J., 'Ephesians', in *Searching the Scriptures, Vol. 2, A Feminist Commentary* (ed. Elisabeth Schüssler Fiorenza; New York: Crossroad, 1994), 325–48

Taubes, Jacob, ed., *Theokratie* (Paderborn: Ferdinand Schöningh, 1987)

Thielman, Frank, *Ephesians* (BECNT; Grand Rapids, MI: Baker Academic, 2010)

Tite, Philip L., *Conceiving Peace and Violence: A New Testament Legacy* (Dallas, TX/New York/Oxford: University Press of America, 2004)

Toews, John E., *Romans* (BCBC; Scottdale, PA/Waterloo, ON: Herald, 2004)

Travis, Stephen H., *Christ and the Judgement of God: The Limits of Divine Retribution in New Testament Thought* (Peabody, MA: Hendrickson/Milton Keynes: Paternoster, 2008)

Verhey, Allen, *Remembering Jesus: Christian Community, Scripture, and the Moral Life* (Grand Rapids, MI/Cambridge: Eerdmans, 2002)

Volf, Miroslav, *Exclusion and Embrace: A Theological Exploration of Identity, Otherness, and Reconciliation* (Nashville, TN: Abingdon, 1996)

Wagner, C. Peter, ed., *Engaging the Enemy: How to Fight and Defeat Territorial Spirits* (Ventura, CA: Regal Books, 1991)

Walsh, Brian J., and Sylvia C. Keesmaat, *Colossians Remixed: Subverting the Empire* (Downers Grove, IL: InterVarsity, 2004)

Weaver, Dorothy Jean, 'Transforming Nonresistance: From *Lex Talionis* to "Do Not Resist the Evil One"', in *The Love of Enemy and Nonretaliation in the New Testament* (ed. Willard M. Swartley; Studies of Peace and Scripture, Institute of Mennonite Studies; Louisville, KY: Westminster/ John Knox, 1992), 38–47

Weaver, J. Denny, *The Nonviolent Atonement* (2nd edn; Grand Rapids, MI/ Cambridge: Eerdmans, 2011)

Weaver, J. Denny, 'The Nonviolent Atonement: Human Violence, Discipleship and God', in *Stricken by God? Nonviolent Identification and the Victory of Christ* (ed. Brad Jersak and Michael Hardin; Grand Rapids, MI/Cambridge: Eerdmans, 2007), 316–55

Weaver, J. Denny, and Gerald Biesecker-Mast, *Teaching Peace: Nonviolence and the Liberal Arts* (Lanham, ML: Rowman and Littlefield, 2003)

Wengst, Klaus, *Pax Romana and the Peace of Jesus Christ* (trans. John Bowden; Philadelphia, PA: Fortress Press, 1987)

Wink, Walter, *Engaging the Powers: Discernment and Resistance in a World of Domination* (Minneapolis, MN: Fortress Press, 1992)

Wink, Walter, *Naming the Powers: The Language of Power in the New Testament* (Minneapolis, MN: Fortress Press, 1984)

Wink, Walter, 'Neither Passivity nor Violence: Jesus' Third Way (Matt. 5.38–42 par.)', in *The Love of Enemy and Nonretaliation in the New Testament* (ed. Willard M. Swartley; Studies of Peace and Scripture, Institute of Mennonite Studies; Louisville, KY: Westminster/John Knox, 1992), 102–25

Wink, Walter, *Unmasking the Powers: The Invisible Forces That Determine Human Existence* (Minneapolis, MN: Fortress Press, 1986)

Wright, N. T., *Jesus and the Victory of God* (Christian Origins and the Question of God, Vol. 2; Minneapolis, MN: Fortress Press, 1997)

Yoder, Elizabeth G., ed., *Peace Theology and Violence against Women* (Occasional Papers 16; Elkhart, IN: Institute of Mennonite Studies, 1992)

Yoder, John Howard, *The Politics of Jesus: Vicit Agnus Noster* (2nd edn; Grand Rapids, MI: Eerdmans/Carlisle: Paternoster, 1994)

Yoder, John Howard, 'Practicing the Rule of Christ', in *Virtues and Practices in the Christian Tradition: Christian Ethics after MacIntyre* (ed. Nancey Murphy, Brad J. Kallenberg and Mark Thiessen Nation; Harrisburg, PA: Trinity Press International, 1997), 132–60

Yoder, John Howard, 'A Theological Critique of Violence', in *The War of the Lamb: The Ethics of Nonviolence and Peacemaking* (ed. Glen Stassen, Mark Thiessen Nation and Matt Hamsher; Grand Rapids, MI: Brazos, 2009), 27–41

Yoder, John Howard, *To Hear the Word* (2nd edn; Eugene, OR: Cascade Books, 2010)

Yoder, Perry, *Shalom: The Bible's Word for Salvation, Justice, and Peace* (Newton, KS: Faith and Life, 1987)

Yoder Neufeld, Thomas R., *Ephesians* (BCBC; Scottdale, PA/Waterloo, ON: Herald, 2002)

Yoder Neufeld, Thomas R., '"For he is our peace": Ephesians 2:11–22', in *Beautiful upon the Mountains: Biblical Essays on Mission, Peace, and the Reign of God* (ed. Mary H. Schertz and Ivan Friesen; Elkhart, IN: Institute of Mennonite Studies/Scottdale, PA/Waterloo, ON: Herald Press, 2003), 215–33

Yoder Neufeld, Thomas R., 'Paul, Women, and Ministry in the Church', *Conrad Grebel Review* 8 (1990), 289–99

Yoder Neufeld, Thomas R., 'Power, Love, and Creation: The Mercy of the Divine Warrior in the Wisdom of Solomon', in *Peace and Justice Shall Embrace: Power and Theopolitics in the Bible* (ed. Ted Grimsrud and Loren L. Johns; Millard Lind Festschrift; Telford, PA: Pandora US, 1999), 174–91

Yoder Neufeld, Thomas R., *'Put on the Armour of God': The Divine Warrior from Isaiah to Ephesians* (Sheffield: Sheffield Academic Press, 1997)

Yoder Neufeld, Thomas R., *Recovering Jesus: The Witness of the New Testament* (Grand Rapids, MI: Brazos; London: SPCK, 2007)

Yoder Neufeld, Thomas R., 'Resistance and Nonresistance: The Two Legs of a Biblical Peace Stance', *Conrad Grebel Review* 21 (2003), 56–81

Zerbe, Gordon, 'Paul's Ethic of Nonretaliation and Peace', in *The Love of Enemy and Nonretaliation in the New Testament* (ed. Willard M. Swartley; Studies of Peace and Scripture, Institute of Mennonite Studies; Louisville, KY: Westminster/John Knox, 1992), 177–222

Index of biblical references

Index of biblical references

Index of authors

Index of authors

Index of subjects

Thomas R. Yoder Neufeld is Professor of Religious Studies (New Testament) at Conrad Grebel University College at the University of Waterloo in Waterloo, Ontario, Canada. Prior to beginning his teaching career in 1983 he served as a hospital and prison chaplain, as well as a congregational pastor in the Mennonite Church. Yoder Neufeld received both a Master of Divinity (1973) and a Doctor of Theology (1989) at Harvard Divinity School.

In addition to numerous articles, both scholarly and popular, Tom has published several books, among them *'Put on the Armour of God':* *The Divine Warrior from Isaiah to Ephesians* (Sheffield Academic Press, 1997), *Ephesians* (BCBC; Herald Press, 2002), and *Recovering Jesus:* *The Witness of the New Testament* (Brazos and SPCK, 2007).